Language, Literacy & Communication
in the Early Years

A Critical Foundation

CAROL HAYES

First published in 2016 by Critical Publishing Ltd

British Library Cataloguing in Publication Data
A CIP record for this book is available from the British Library

ISBN: 978-1-910391-54-9

This book is also available in the following e-book formats:

MOBI ISBN: 978-1-910391-55-6
EPUB ISBN: 978-1-910391-56-3
Adobe e-book ISBN: 978-1-910391-57-0

Text design by Greensplash Limited
Cover design by Out of House Limited
Project Management by Out of House Publishing
Printed and bound in Great Britain by TJ International

Critical Publishing
152 Chester Road
Northwich
CW8 4AL
www.criticalpublishing.com

MIX
Paper from
responsible sources
FSC
www.fsc.org   FSC® C013056

Contents

Meet the author

Carol Hayes has worked in early years for the past 40 years as a teacher and tutor. She worked at Staffordshire University for six years as a principal lecturer and academic group leader, where she helped to develop a thriving early childhood studies department with programmes from foundation degrees to Masters in early childhood. Her specialist areas are cognitive development, language, literacy and communication, and her main research interests are dyslexia, communication difficulties and the role of graduate teaching assistants in the workforce.

Acknowledgements

I am indebted to Lewis Hayes, the illustrator of this book.

I wish to thank Barry for his technical support, the staff and children from Staffordshire University nursery and my patient and long-suffering husband for his encouragement and understanding.

Foreword

It is vital that young children develop good language skills as they lay the foundations for interactions with others and are fundamental to communicating their needs, views, feelings and ideas. I worked closely with Carol Hayes for several years at Staffordshire University and share her passion for early childhood and the professionalisation of the early years workforce. Carol has always had a professional interest in language and I know she has undertaken a considerable amount of research in the production of this book, which will certainly equip those of you who are working in the early years sector with valuable knowledge on language and the skills young children need to become competent users of all aspects of communication, language and literacy.

At regular intervals throughout the book, Carol invites you to reflect critically on what you have read and relate it to your previous knowledge and understanding and your experiences as early years practitioners. It is through critical reflection on practice that you will continue to gain professional understanding of the children in your care. It involves examining your own underlying principles and beliefs and reassessing them in the light of new knowledge and thinking, and I urge you to take the opportunities presented as you read each chapter. Once you become accomplished at reflecting critically, you will find yourself unable to stop! My own reflections relate back to my earlier experiences as a nursery nurse and mother, and to more recent ones as a lecturer and grandmother.

I know that many practitioners and leaders have reported a lack of confidence or competence within early years teams supporting children's communication and language skills, particularly as they are now working more frequently with children entering nursery or Reception year without having reached the expected stage of development in this area. Last year, one of my BA student practitioners conducted research on the impact of Every Child a Talker (ECAT) across local settings and her findings suggested the most significant benefit of this government initiative was that it appeared to have increased the practitioners' confidence in their skills to support children's emerging language and to recognise potential difficulties in their development. An evaluation of the latest DfE initiative, the Early Language Development Programme (ELDP), similarly found that it has positively impacted on practitioners' knowledge and confidence, as well as improving their practice in supporting speech, language and communication development (OPM, 2015).

It is certainly heartening to read that such programmes appear to be improving the quality of early years provision; however, it is evident that the levels of some children's communication and language development remain a concern. In particular, we need to continue in our efforts to support those children living in the poorest areas of the country, who still appear significantly less likely than their peers to reach the expected levels at the end of the Early Years Foundation Stage (EYFS), despite all these targeted initiatives. The latest EYFS profile data (DfE, 2014) show that across England, 23 per cent of children at the end of the EYFS were assessed as not having reached the expected level of communication and language development, a figure far too high, given the importance of these skills to their future reading and writing abilities, as well as other aspects of their learning, personal, social and emotional development and well-being.

So why do some early years practitioners lack confidence in their knowledge and understanding of aspects of communication, language and literacy development? One reason may be that it is widely accepted that specific teaching strategies are not required for children to learn their native language in the early years (as discussed in Chapter 2). It is clear, however, that they *do* need knowledgeable practitioners around them, who understand *how* they acquire language and can work in partnership with parents to provide environments that will support this important area of their development.

The view that children develop language naturally through exposure to it in their social environment may have led to an insufficient emphasis on language development in initial training courses for early years practitioners, another possible reason for their lack of confidence in this area. During my own initial learning about early child development on an NNEB course, although many years ago now, language was not even acknowledged as an area of development in its own right; development was divided into four areas: physical, intellectual (and language), emotional and social (PIES). I realise that compartmentalising a child's development using any criteria is artificial and purely academic, which at best only serves to facilitate a focus on important aspects contributing to an individual child's unique and holistic development. I do think, however, that the complex nature of communication, language and literacy development is worthy of study in its own right, even though its interdependence on, and interrelationships with, all other aspects of development also need to be fully understood and acknowledged. Carol successfully brings together all aspects of development in the concluding chapter of this book (Chapter 10) and considers the holistic child within the context of their individual culture and where language is central to their unique development as a person.

I have always considered myself knowledgeable about the skills children need to become literate and competent in using strategies to support their emergent reading and writing skills, providing playful auditory and visual discrimination and mark making activities, for example. However, I admit feeling ill-prepared to use formal methods to teach reading and writing as an NNEB. This is something we probably share in our profession, as teaching these formal skills has generally been considered more within the remit of our colleagues with qualified teacher status, although many of you will have undergone specific training and been guided well within professional teams to successfully deliver reading and writing programmes within early years departments in schools. In the current climate, however, where there is an ever-increasing expectation for children to be grounded in phonemic awareness before they start school, most early years practitioners are required to be sufficiently knowledgeable and to provide developmentally appropriate experiences for this to happen across all types of pre-school provision. In Chapter 4, Carol wittily refers to the 'magical powers' of teaching literacy skills mysteriously acquired by teachers during their training, before proceeding to comprehensively de-mystify some of them for the benefit of us all. Carol also presents compelling reasons why adults need to be able to read. Statistics on literacy levels in England and their links to child poverty serve to remind us why it is so important to 'get it right' when supporting young children's literacy skills.

As Carol points out in Chapter 3, risk taking is just as important to developing language skills as it is to developing physical ones. I must confess to being rather reticent in the use of my limited French vocabulary when travelling abroad for fear of getting it wrong; but without taking such risks, my abilities are unlikely to improve. We all need to remember that children need to be given the time and attention to be listened to respectfully, as they develop the confidence to try out their language skills without fear of ridicule. Adults who are prepared to take risks themselves to continue learning language create excellent role models for children, so have the confidence to introduce some of the new vocabulary and ideas you come across in this book in professional discussions with colleagues and parents.

In Chapter 6, Carol shares up-to-date knowledge about specific learning difficulties, including dyslexia, a disorder accurately defined and recognised only in England during my career, despite many clearly needing support to overcome its associated difficulties. Working with early years practitioners returning to academic learning, I have come across many whose self-esteem has been seriously damaged because such difficulties have not been identified and whose personal and professional development has often been limited as a result. Gaining a thorough understanding of this and similar disorders will enable you to spot children displaying potential differences early and give them sufficient support to prevent them experiencing similar issues with their self-esteem.

Neuroscience seems to show that there are discernible physiological differences in boys' and girls' brains. However, I am concerned about some current trends in practice aimed to address the apparent gender gap in attainment: focusing too much on perceived differences in boys' and girls' learning styles may perpetuate gender stereotypes that could expand rather than close it. Some of the myths surrounding genderised learning are explored clearly and without emotion in Chapter 7, as well as some pedagogical suggestions to improve the language skills of all children.

The value of stories and storytelling is discussed in Chapter 9, reminding me of the introduction of the daily 'Literacy Hour' in primary classrooms, as part of the National Literacy Strategy (DfEE, 1998). Sadly, this appeared to herald the end of the comfortable ritual of reading a story to infant school children each day, as many teachers either struggled to justify the time, or considered that the clinical dissection of story texts that became part of this daily routine was sufficient to replace the literacy experience of sharing a book for pleasure. The powerful quotation from Wolf (2008), used to conclude the final chapter, reinforces how understanding of language is increased by hearing stories. So even if you do nothing else after reading this book, please take any available opportunity to share a story with children.

The influence of national and international government policies on children's lives and early years practice cannot be underestimated and should be considered as an integral part of your critical reflection. I admire Carol for devoting part of Chapter 10 to much-needed expla-nations of political processes and examples of relevant 'political manoeuvring', especially as many writers shy away from discussing politics in any detail.

Carol ends with a thought-provoking list of priorities for future research, which I hope you will find inspiring. However, it is her final suggestion to consider the language skills we want future generations to acquire that will continue to agitate my mind. Thank you, Carol, it is an honour to be associated with this book.

Ann Whitehouse

References

DfE (2014) *Early Years Foundation Stage Profile Results: 2013 to 2014.* www.gov.uk/government/statistics/early-years-foundation-stage-profile-results-2013-to-2014 (accessed 10.08.15).

Department for Education and Employment (DfEE) (1998) *The National Literacy Strategy: Framework for Teaching.* London: DfEE.

Office for Public Management (OPM) (2015) *Evaluation of the Early Language Development Programme.* www.talkingpoint.org.uk/sites/talkingpoint.org.uk/files/ELDP/ELDP%20Report%20Summary_Jan2015.pdf (accessed 10.08.15).

1 Origins of language

So Baloo, the Teacher of the Law, taught him the Wood and Water Laws: how to tell a rotten branch from a sound one; how to speak politely to the wild bees when he came upon a hive of them fifty feet above ground; what to say to Mang the Bat when he disturbed him in the branches at midday; and how to warn the water-snakes in the pools before he splashed down among them. None of the Jungle People like being disturbed, and all are very ready to fly at an intruder. Then, too, Mowgli was taught the Strangers' Hunting Call, which must be repeated aloud till it is answered, whenever one of the Jungle-People hunts outside his own grounds. It means, translated, 'Give me leave to hunt here because I am hungry'. And the answer is, 'Hunt then for food, but not for pleasure'.

(Rudyard Kipling, *The Jungle Book*, chapter 3, Kaa's Hunting)

Introduction

As you read this book you need to understand that there are contained within it very few *facts* and fewer *truths*. That is not so say that I have set out to write a book full of lies and untruths, but rather you need to understand the difference between a fact and a theory. Most textbooks are based on theory and conjecture rather than fact. Critically any text discussing such a complex and multifaceted topic such as language development is going to be based more on inference, and the so-called experts' 'best guess' of the process, and you need to start reading this knowing what we do *not* know. There has been a great deal of research into the field of language acquisition, which you will notice if you type 'language development' into Google, but in reality this research only serves to create more questions and very few answers. All of us are capable of thinking critically and we do so every day of our lives: how often have you put on a new outfit and considered whether it suits you, whether it suits the occasion, what others will think of you if you wear it and what sort of message you are creating by wearing it? Yet somehow we find it hard to apply the same principles to academic reading and writing, often because we are afraid, or even embarrassed, to question the unquestionable. The whole premise of this book is to help you to do just that, and as you read on you need to keep this in mind, read between the lines, weigh up the arguments, reflect on the issues and remain sceptical. Only then can you reach analytical conclusions and take a reasoned stance within the debate.

Some questions that you might like to keep in your mind as you read through the chapters in this book could be:

1.   What is the writer trying to say?

2.   What are the key points and ideas?

3.   Has the writer offered a range of points of view?

4.   Can you see an alternative explanation for what you have read?

5.   Has the writer offered well-founded evidence for the conclusions drawn?

What is language?

What appears to be such a simple question is perhaps not so easy to explain. We are all skilled and proficient in our mother tongue, but what does this really mean? Language is clearly made up of symbols, but these symbols have no meaning in themselves. You could use a nonsense word such as 'drun' and depending upon your tone and attitude it can mean anything that you want it to. On its own 'drun' means nothing, but if you put it into context you can begin to narrow down the variables:

> I want to eat drun on my toast for my breakfast.

Now it has limitations to its meaning and becomes more than just a noise but involves representation and understanding. You can then combine these noises and symbols into strings of sound, but they mean something only if individually and societally we have all agreed their meaning. Of course language is changing and expanding all the time, as society and culture demand. You only have to look at the following words to see how they have changed even in the period of your lifetime: *gay*; *cool*; *wicked*; *fantastic.* But you need more than just symbols to make a language; you need systems of organising the symbols, so that means creating a system of rules and order, and you also need underlying mental representations for those words, if they are to mean anything to anyone.

Is language used exclusively by humans?

Language appears on the surface to be a uniquely human means of communication and can be spoken, listened to, read or written. But above all it is the ability to understand language that makes it such a powerful medium for human communication, setting us apart from all other species. I would suggest that this is one reason why the human species has succeeded, in an evolutionary sense, over all other animals. Language could literally be a matter of life and death; as humans we are born totally helpless and depend on our ability to communicate to get the attention of those around us for our survival. Think of the baby giraffe which has to be up on its feet and running within minutes of birth or the dolphin which has to swim from the moment of birth. Compared to other mammals at delivery, our brains are very underdeveloped, and some estimates suggest that to have a comparable neurological development to a newborn chimpanzee, a human foetus would have to gestate for 18–21 months, compared to the usual 9 months. Not something most of you would want to contemplate! Despite this it is important to realise how comparatively little we really know about the origins of language. The genus for our own species, Homo sapiens (translated as the 'wise man'), appeared approximately 1.9 million years ago, and although impossible to confirm, it is unlikely that any language that you would recognise today was around then. Archaeologists have, however, found ancient cave drawings, dating back to around 35,000 years ago which some researchers have proposed are the precursors to written symbolism, which suggests that an oral tradition was prevalent prior to this. Archaeological evidence (Lieberman, 1998) would indicate that Homo sapiens originated in Africa, and it took a considerable period of time before they spread to other areas of the globe, as noted in Table 1.1.

Table 1.1 *The spread of Homo sapiens, adapted from Lieberman (1998).*

Estimated date	Suggested event
250,000 years BP	Neanderthals in Europe could have had a very limited language/sound based form of communication
130,000 years BP	Homo sapiens emerged
120,000 years BP	Humans now appear to have the anatomical features needed for language to be developed
60,000–40,000 years BP	Behaviourally modern humans appear
50,000 years BP	Homo sapiens appear in Australia
47,000 years BP	Modern humans appear in West Asia
45,000 years BP	Modern humans appear in New Guinea
40,000 years BP	Modern humans appear in Europe
39,000 years BP	Modern humans appear in East Asia
30,000 years BP	Modern humans appear in Western parts of Oceania
14,500 years BP	Modern humans appear in the Americas
3000 years BP	Modern humans appear in Eastern parts of Oceania

Note: BP means 'Before Present' and is used by archaeologists to refer to dates usually obtained through radiocarbon dating methods.

Clearly the sophisticated systems of communication that you are familiar with today have not always been there. Looking at the drawings of the cave men you can see the possible beginnings of a symbolic system of communication, which today you might regard as primitive and confusing. The existence of language also depends upon the anatomical evidence of suitable structures in the articulatory organs, which are the mouth, tongue, throat (pharynx) and larynx, of a certain shape and size, alongside a minimum brain size and capacity. This would place the emergence of language not earlier than 120,000–100,000 years ago. Clearly language could have emerged in different parts of the world independently of each other and at different times (polygenesis), or this could have happened only once (monogenesis), implying that all the languages of the world have a common ancestor and origin. In any case we have no hard evidence for any of this.

Animal communication

There is no doubt that animals communicate with one another, from the dance of the bees, informing the rest of the hive where the best nectar can be found, to wolves howling to inform other wolves of their presence in the area, or monkeys using body language and facial movement to express pleasure, anger, fear etc. However, it is only humans who appear to have a *need* to engage in complex levels of communication. The smallest baby will delight in you making facial gestures, and pre-linguistic infants understand and use gesture to communicate, for example pointing, waving bye-bye etc. When understanding a particular language is difficult, even adults are able to communicate in gesture, as I found to my relief in France when my school level French failed to live up to my expectations. Watch any two people talking together; you will notice them waving their arms around, nodding and making facial expressions to augment the language. It is interesting that even on the telephone, when the parties engaged in the conversation cannot see each other, humans feel compelled to gesticulate. The problem with gesture alone is that it is very basic and cannot convey the nuances of expression that you use every day, often without thinking too much about it.

No other animal appears to have this capability, Tomasello (2008) calls human language a *'fundamentally co-operative enterprise'* (p 6) whereby humans are able to inform each other of things, request things, express emotions and feelings and engage in joint vision, goals and intentions, with mutually shared beliefs. This enables us as a society to engage in mutual understandings of representational and abstract concepts such as money, politics and government. Money, for example, has no value in itself; it is only human co-operation of purpose which ensures that we are all complicit in accepting it as a concrete example of a representational reality. Tomasello (2008) postulates that as part of the evolutionary process and the isolation of groups, humans produced cultural conventions, and words were organised into complex grammatical bonds, to enable expression of complex, and often abstract, frequently occurring situations. Bickerton (1984) suggested that a single gene mutation could have been responsible for human language capacity, similar to a Big Bang theory. This linked with previously understood traits of language, but ten years later Pinker (1994) reports a slower, more evolutionary process, over long periods of time. Neither of these theories can be proven with our current levels of research.

Societal communication

The other difference between humans and animals appears to be that humans have to learn the communication systems of their community: what we frequently call our 'mother tongue'. There are probably over 6900 different spoken languages in the world which can be grouped into more than 90 language families, that is, languages with a common origin. There are also possibly 4000–5000 signed languages. Yet it takes a child only 3–5 years to learn the tens of thousands of words and cultural linguistic grammar to make them understood in their home language. It is a different case with animals. A dog separated from other dogs at birth will still growl, bare teeth, woof and wag its tail to communicate with other dogs, and these gestures and sounds will be universally understood in the 'doggie' world, whether a Chihuahua or a Great Dane. It was suggested by Bickerton (1984) that what you are seeing in these 'talking animals' is what he calls proto-language, rather than true language. He explains this as a primitive combination of signals representing objects and actions. Such proto-language may also be seen in dolphins and sea lions. If these animals are able to do this without contact with their own kind, it is clear that this is not a socially learned communication system, but is in some way innate, unlike human linguistic symbols. For centuries people have wondered what would happen if a child was raised in an environment completely devoid of language stimulation, but clearly this is a very difficult area of research. To deliberately deprive a child of language would be highly unethical and would be considered abusive, so all the research in the field has had to be conducted on the few naturally occurring cases of this happening. Most of you will have heard of the story of Romulus and Remus, abandoned by their parents only to be raised by a pack of wolves and go on to found Rome. Most of you will have watched in awe the 1967 Disney film *The Jungle Book*, based on the book by Rudyard Kipling. The child Mowgli was supposedly raised by the jungle creatures. To my knowledge these are fictional characters, but there are some even more strange, real life cases, such as that of Victor.

CASE STUDY

The wild boy of Aveyon

In a well-documented case in 1797, a male child (later called Victor), was found wandering in the woods in France near a village called Lacaun. He was dirty, his body was scarred, he grunted like an animal and he appeared to have been fending for himself. The child, who was estimated to be 12 years old at the time, was taken by the villagers, and displayed in a cage in the centre of the village, as a freak and a savage. After a number of escapes and recaptures, he was finally taken to a young researcher and medical student called Jean-Marc Gaspard Itard. Itard realised the significance of this find, and attempted to teach him to speak, and to 'normalise' his behaviour. Itard was disappointed that Victor was able to learn only a very primitive form of communication, and only two recognisable words, *lait* and *dieu*. Victor finally died, at the age of 31, in 1828, never realising Itard's dream of 'normalisation'. This is a sad story that raises many questions.

1. While on the surface it would appear that Victor was not using language because of his depleted language background, can you think of any other reason why Victor was not able to learn language?

2. Do you think Itard was right to try to forcibly civilise Victor to a life of convention and restriction? There is no evidence that Victor was dissatisfied with his life in the woods or wanted to be experimented upon.

Primate research

Researchers Prüfer and Pääbo (2012) sequenced the bonobo and chimpanzee genomes, showing that they share as much as 99 per cent of their DNA with humans, making them our closest living relatives. For this reason much of the research into human behaviour starts with research into primate behaviour. Tomasello (2003), discusses some of this research into primates and concludes that despite their close genetic structure there are still fundamental differences in their ability to communicate.

> nonhuman primates do not use communicative signals to convey meaning or to convey information or to refer to things or to direct the attention of others, but rather use them to affect the behaviour or motivational states of others directly. If this interpretation is correct, then the deep evolutionary roots of human language lie in the attempts of primate individuals to influence the behaviour, not the mental states of conspecifics. To find the most direct precursors of human linguistic symbols as tools for directing attention, therefore, we can only look at the history of the human species since it began its own unique evolutionary trajectory. (p 11)

Another evolutionary happening that possibly affected our ancestors' ability to communicate in a sophisticated manner was the advent of bipedalism, the moment that we stood on two legs (approximately 5–6 million years ago). This significant evolutionary moment freed up our hands and arms, and potentially allowed more effective gesturing. Momentous as this was, it is unlikely that this extended the proto-language to grammatical communication, which possibly occurred approximately only 2 million years ago, when the genus Homo emerged.

Despite Tomasello's (2003) beliefs about language being uniquely human, research into the links between human and primate communication has been extensive and numerous experiments have been made to expose primates to a human environment and upbringing, to assess the impact of the environment over our innate abilities. The film *Project Nim*, released in 2011 and directed by James Marsh, charts the language progress of a chimpanzee called Nim when raised from birth by a human family. This film powerfully demonstrates that primates are able to learn sign language for individual objects or actions relatively easily, with Nim learning a well-documented 125 signs with American Sign Language. Teaching apes spoken language is not an option, as they do not have the anatomical muscular flexibility of structures of the lips, tongue, pharynx and larynx, to enable spoken words to be uttered. However, they do have sophisticated control over their arms and hands to gesture with, alongside a highly complex visual system. It is possible that even the Neanderthals, 250,000 years ago, had not really mastered the co-ordination of the lips, tongue, larynx and breathing that is necessary for full articulation. Ten years before the experiment with Nim, it is said that a chimp named Washoe was able to learn 350 signs, although this case is not as well documented as Nim's.

Creativity of language

Learning individual words as Nim did may not in itself be language, and what the primates do not appear to do is to use these signs to be creative with language in the way that even very young humans can, to create new meaning with the words. Almost every sentence that is spoken is a unique combination of words, therefore cannot be learned by imitation alone. Children develop rapidly, without formal instruction, to interpret and respond to these novel utterances. For example, a young three year-old child might use the following words, but is unlikely to have heard them before: *mouses, sheeps, goed.*

However, as they develop their linguistic skills, they begin to understand that adding an 's' to a word *usually* makes it plural and 'ed' *usually* creates past tense, and they become creative with their language. Such 'mistakes' or 'overgeneralisations' could indicate the child's increasing understanding of grammaticalisation. From a relatively small number of words understood, the child can create entirely new meanings and invent sentences that they have not heard before, demonstrating an open and dynamic aspect to language learning. Clearly you do need to be exposed to your mother tongue if you are to become proficient in it, but as you can see in the example earlier, simple mimicking cannot be the whole story. Children are frequently not exposed to syntactically correct language, as Wells (1986) showed in his research, that when adults talk to children they interrupt themselves, make errors, use contracted language etc. So if this exposure to ungrammatical language is to be mimicked by the child, it is unlikely that s/he will learn the complex, formalised structures of language which they need to become skilful language users.

Critical questions

» *Is it important for practitioners to know the origins of language? Explain your answer.*

» *How can this understanding of the roots of language development influence you as a practitioner when you are interacting with the children in your care?*

Referential and abstractive nature of language

The primates do satisfy one of the requirements of language; and that is that it is referential, in other words they refer to specific objects. For example, they are known to have different calls, to indicate the presence of a snake, a hawk, a leopard or some other impending danger. The interesting difference between this and human language is that the calls are made only when the object of the call is present in a concrete sense. Humans, on the contrary, use words when the concrete experience is not present; so you might discuss an outfit that you saw in a shop two days ago, or even something that never was concrete, so something that no one has ever seen, such as a Martian. This distinctive feature of human understanding is called 'recursion', that is, 'seeing that we are being seen' or 'I see, that he sees, that I see him'. This allows us as humans to escape the here and now and to even escape reality, transporting ourselves, in our minds, to another location, or another time frame or even another person's point of view. It is unlikely that other animals or even primates have this capacity. In brain scan mapping exercises, Corballis (2002) observed mirror neurons in *both* monkeys and humans. So the monkey brain responds in a similar way when it makes a gesture *and* when it observes a similar gesture from another monkey, suggesting that perhaps they do share a level of understanding between each other. This might even suppose a common ancestor between the humans and the monkeys.

The motivation and intentionality for language

Pinker (1994), in his iconic book *The Language Instinct,* describes language not as a cultural artefact but as a biological element within the brain:

> *A distinct piece of the biological make up of our brains. Language is a complex, specialised skill, which develops in the child spontaneously, without conscious effort or formal instruction, it is deployed without awareness of its underlying logic, is qualitatively the same in every individual, and is distinct from general abilities to process information or behave intelligently.*

> (Pinker, 1994, p 18)

In this quote Pinker refers to our capacity to process language as an instinct and biological birthright, the same way as spiders *know* how to spin webs; they do not have to be taught by another more able spider. Across the globe every Homo sapien appears to have some form of language; not even the most remote tribes have been discovered with no language or means of communication.

Tomasello (2008) talks of three motivational forces for human language:

1.   to request...

This, according to Tomasello, is the simplest of the motivational forces, usually involving a limited audience, and no great complexity of language structure, simple syntax and limited grammar.

2.   to inform...

When you try to inform others of your intentions and understandings, this starts to involve grammatical structures such as tense and location, which require communicative and cultural conventions to express. As has been seen earlier, language also needs a specific context of usage.

3.   to share...

You need to have a normative mode to deal with sharing, as this is an attempt to express views and realities of different social settings. This can be described as the grammaticalisation of communication.

It is interesting to note that in controlled research on primates who use sign language, 98 per cent of the signs were requests (Project Nim, 2011), which Tomasello (2008) regarded as the most basic level of language.

Gestures employed by very young children, such as pointing and hand waving, emerge and develop without formal teaching, as does an apparent *need* for shared intentionality; in other words children feel the need to communicate their requests and feelings to others and to share their thoughts. This 'shared intentionality', as Tomasello (2008) refers to it, is quickly enhanced by vocalisations, and for the most part the gestures are eventually displaced by those vocalisations. Tomasello (2008) also proposes that this human need to be co-operative and work in communication with each other is an evolutionary adaptation, which emerged phylogenetically and gave *Homo sapiens* the survival advantage over other species, which ensured their evolutionary success.

> *The grammatical dimension of human linguistic communication and cultural transmission of linguistic constructions...based on general cognitive skills as well as skills of shared intentionality and imitation...in order to meet the functional demands of the three basic communicative motives, leading to a grammar of requesting, a grammar of informing and a grammar of sharing and narrative.*
>
> (Tomasello, 2008, p 326)

You can see from this that perhaps the one thing that does distinguish our language from other non-human species is its generativity and creativity.

Environmentism versus innatism

Despite confusion and uncertainty one thing does appear to be certain: that human language symbols are socially learned. Children denied access to language do not learn the subtleties of a system of communication that a particular language can offer. Way back in 1957 B F Skinner, the behaviourist, became famous for his work on conditioning, with his experiments on rats. He further suggested that children learned language in the same manner:

Stimulus   ——————————→   Response

The child is exposed to a stimulus and is rewarded for using language, the response, by a parent smiling and giving them their request, for example:

> *Two year-old Rasheed sees the juice carton and says 'Ju Ju'. His mother smiles and pours him a cup of juice.*

The sight of the juice carton becomes the stimulus and his mother offering him the juice becomes the response and the reward, which encourages him to repeat the process and apply the principle to other situations.

For Skinner (1957) and other researchers who have followed, such as Bates and MacWhinney (1982), the acquisition of language is an environmental experience. Of course you have to take account of the fact that most of Skinner's work was conducted on animals, and it is highly possible that such research is not transferable to humans with their unique brain development. However, if language acquisition is an environmental experience, this implies that it is your interaction with the world around you that enables you to learn the signs and symbols that we call language, in particular, social interaction. This falls in line with the Vygotskian approach (1935) and Lev Vygotsky's concept of the Zone of Proximal Development (ZPD). Vygotsky believed that adults and more knowledgeable peers provide support and extension to the child's existing knowledge and language, and the ZPD is the difference between the learning that the child can achieve on their own, and the learning that they can achieve with support. This theory was unlike Piaget's (1923, translation 2007), who was also a cognitive, developmental theorist, but who placed the emphasis upon children learning for themselves and becoming problem solvers, rather than the environment and social interaction shaping the child. Piaget talked of actively manipulating the environment to create problem solving opportunities and experiences. In the case of Piaget, he believed that because the environments that most children encountered were similar, it is logical to consider that their thinking will develop along similar lines, in similar well-defined stages.

Skinner (1957) further suggested that adults shape children's language by rewarding the 'correct' word or accepted sequence, with praise, or by allowing the child's request, thereby reinforcing the appropriate use of the mother tongue. However, Noam Chomsky (1959), one of the leading intellectual figures of modern times, spoke out against this rather simplistic view of language acquisition, suggesting that while the language of request may well be reinforced in this manner, it is unlikely that the more complex forms of language and grammatical construction could possibly be achieved by simple reinforcement. He argued that the language that young children are exposed to in their environment is very simplistic. This does not expose them to the complex and abstract word and sentence constructions which are necessary to reinforce the compound language structures they are going to need. Consider for a moment the language that children are surrounded by in the home and the nursery, often single words, mostly nouns. Wells (1986) in his extensive research into language acquisition on children and families in Bristol demonstrated that adults modify their language to children, as they believe that it will enable better understanding. This is so prevalent that in many incidents we would not recognise it as a complex structure, as it is so 'watered down'. Clearly in that case the imitation of the language does not help language development, for example in the following exchange between a mother and child about a clock:

CHILD: *Whadat?*

ADULT: *Ticky tocky?*

CHILD: *Tic tic.*

ADULT: *You want ticky tocky?*

CHILD: *Tic tic.*

In Wells' (1986) iconic observations on language development, he suggested that children whose environment was rich in language enjoyed almost ten times as much exposure to words and sentences than those children whose environment was poor in language. However, the children in the poor language environments still continued to progress with their development albeit at a slower pace.

Innatism

Chomsky (1964) famously argued that language was not a learned process in this way, and that the only way that we can explain why we can talk but animals cannot is to consider that we have some inbuilt device (or at least some organising disposition), within the human brain, which allows an innate knowledge of the basic principles of language, a pre-disposition or readiness for language, initially called our Universal Grammar. In 1970 David McNeill renamed this as a Language Acquisition Device (LAD). This was not intended to be language specific but something hardwired within the brain to process certain universal elements of any language. Chomsky (1964) and later Pinker (1994) are the key proponents of the innatist theory of language development where the environment, far from 'shaping' language, merely provides the fuel for the language learner. Chomsky's (1964) theories differentiated between competence and performance, in other words he believed that what people *know* about a language, its correct syntax and grammar (if there is such a thing), is not necessarily what they verbalise.

Social interactionist

While Bruner (1960) agreed with much of Chomsky's hypotheses, and in particular the idea of a Language Acquisition Device (LAD), he felt that the child could not develop language without a network of support from the home learning environment. This led Bruner (1960) to suggest a social interactionist view, that there also needed to be a Language Acquisition Support System (LASS) in place, if the child was to learn their mother tongue. He described this as a network of people and opportunities to scaffold and support the child in their learning. Scaffolding on a construction site is there to support the construction workers to build in places, and at heights, that they would be unable to do without the scaffolding. The scaffolding is a temporary structure and once the building has been achieved it is removed, and the building stands alone, independent of the support. In the same way, the supported child eventually becomes autonomous and self-determining. Chomsky, on the contrary, was an advocate of the self-sufficient learner, believing that the child would learn language with minimal support.

Emergentism

A further theoretical stance can be seen in emergentism or guided distributed learning, which really attempts to bring together the extremes of innatism versus environmentism, accepting that both theories have merit and that language acquisition probably relies on an epigenesis of the two: the interaction between the environment and the innate structure of the brain (Karmiloff-Smith, 1992). Karmiloff-Smith (1992) suggested that the environment could act as a trigger to the innate brain structures to learning language, or could possibly shape the brain structures to support language acquisition. The emergentism theory suggests that language develops through the network of the brain, the interaction between pre-defined collections of brain tissue called 'nodes' and the connectors called edges.

> A node represents input (i.e. information established by the language learner). Each node has a link to output (i.e. expressive production or auditory comprehension).

The more frequent occurrence of a particular feature of spoken language results in greater strength of a node and the association among nodes.

(Levey and Polirstock, 2011, p 30)

Table 1.2 *Summary of major theoretical perspectives of language acquisition.*

Theoretical perspective	Sometimes referred to as	Related theorists	Theoretical content
Environmental theory	Pragmatic theory	Skinner (1957) Bates and MacWhinney (1982) Vygotsky (1935) Piaget (1954)	This is a two way interaction with the environment including social interaction. This relies on contact with a varied and challenging environment with opportunities for problem solving
Nativist theory	Innateness theory or Psycholinguistic theory	Chomsky (1964) Pinker (1994)	We are born with inbuilt mechanisms to enable us to attain language. There is an understanding of the syntax of language that is uniquely human.
Emergentism	Guided distributed learning theory	Karmiloff-Smith (1992)	There is an interaction between the environment and the genetic make-up of the child. This relies upon the maturational emergence of cognition, social development, attentional capacity and the ability to distinguish sounds, rhythm and intonation. This could result in the environment stimulating the innate mechanisms.

Critical questions

» Do the divergent theories, in Table 1.2, overlook the possibility of the child as an active participant in their learning, or do they see him/her as a passive recipient of language?

» What similarities can you see between these theories?

Universal Grammar

Chomsky talked about the Principles and Parameters Theory. These are the super rules (Principles) of language, and Chomsky (1959) claimed that these were innate, so that when children are learning a particular language they do not need to learn a long list of rules, but they are *born* knowing the super rules. For example, all they have to do is to learn whether their particular language has the parameter first, as in English, or last, as in Welsh (see the final line of this section). The child notices this by listening to his/her parents or carers talking, and applying this throughout, thereby understanding large elements of grammar which can be applied in all situations. In this way they are not learning lots of rules, but just a few overarching rules, thereby enabling the explosion of language that you see in children over such a short period of time.

Grammar

It is important to understand that grammar in this context does not relate to your school English grammar lessons, but to a set of unconscious rules that are responsible for governing all human speech. This does not necessarily involve meaning or even understanding. According to Smith (2004), in 1957 Chomsky devised a sentence which he claimed no one had heard before, and made no conceivable sense, but was nevertheless apparently grammatically correct:

Colourless green ideas sleep furiously.

Corballis (2002) suggests that one feasible explanation for this is that a sentence needs 'function words'. You can see this in Lewis Carroll's poem the 'Jabberwocky' from *Through the Looking Glass and What Alice Found There* (2013, originally published 1871).

T'was brillig and the slithy toves

Did gyre and gimble in the wabe

All mimsy were the borogoves

And the mome raths outgrabe.

(pp 64–65)

Although this has no apparent meaning it does appear to have some grammatical structure. Corballis (2002) then substitutes nonsense words for the function words.

G'wib brillig pog dup slithy toves

Kom gyre pog gimble ak dup wabe

Utt mimsy toke dup borogoves

Pog dup mome raths outgrabe.

You then have no idea whether it is grammatical or not, demonstrating the vital role that such function words play in language. Of course, different languages have different structures, and the order of words is vital to changes in understanding, so that in English we would say:

The man opened the door (ie subject --- verb --- object)

But in Welsh it would be:

agorodd y dyn y drws (ie verb --- subject --- object)

The critical period

The term 'critical period' in language acquisition relates to whether there is some genetically determined period of susceptibility to learning language, in other words a window of opportunity. It is possible that there is a 'critical period' for learning language, or at least an optimum time when the brain is sensitive to acquiring certain skills. This may apply to other learning skills as well as language.

Lenneberg (1967) promoted the idea of a critical period for language development. His research suggested that if you are to learn a language, you have to be exposed to it in your earliest years, and before approximately 12 years of age. If this window is passed, Lenneberg suggests, it becomes almost impossible to learn. After puberty, Lenneberg (1967) claimed that the brain loses some of its plasticity, and is unable to absorb language structures in a fully functional manner. This theory is certainly not unique, and in the animal world the famous experiments from Konrad Lorenz (1935) described by Lenneberg (1967), on imprinting in goslings, showed that it was an evolutionary imperative for the young geese to imprint on their mother in the first few days of birth, but after those initial days this imprinting mechanism appears to close down, to ensure that the goslings follow their mother but no other moving things, in other words a Critical Period of recognition.

Innatism theory

The innatist theorists point to the consistency of patterns of language development, where at about 8–12 months children appear to have a need to communicate. Schlesinger and Meadow (1972) worked with deaf children whose parents were also both deaf; their research showed that these children do as well with their sign language development as the speech of hearing children with hearing parents. Schlesinger and Meadow (1972) suggest that this is because they are exposed to sign language constantly, in the same way as hearing children are exposed to spoken language in their environment. However, the findings of this research also showed that non-hearing children with hearing parents had much more difficulty, possibly because the parents were communicating between themselves in spoken language and used sign language only to communicate with the child, thereby lacking the level of immersion within the language medium that the deaf parents with deaf children might have. This difference also extended to their later reading and writing language skills.

This would suggest that there is a window of opportunity, which implies that language can be learned only within that window, and beyond that the plasticity of the brain is insufficient to allow the development of appropriate neural connections, related to language. The question could then be posed as to whether there are other aspects of learning that have such a window of opportunity, and at what point that window will close. Clearly this idea is highly controversial and difficult to confirm or deny, leading to suggestions of 'hopeless cases', saving money on compensatory and supportive education because that window is now closed, and no amount of teaching, support or financial input will enable the child to learn what s/he has missed in the early years. This becomes a huge ethical and moral debate, which is too great to investigate here, but we will come back to it later in the text.

Avians

Corballis (2002) reminds us that there is one group of animals that do have the anatomical requirements to produce a complex range of sounds with variety and flexibility, that is, the avians or the birds. The sounds that they make, as with humans, are controlled by the left-hand side of the brain. Birds can and do develop speech-like sounds and even dialects, but to do this they need to hear the sounds very early on in their development (even before they are capable of making the sounds). This would appear to indicate a critical period for sound development much as Chomsky (1965) suggested in human language production. However, this is where the similarity ends, although birds have the ability to mimic sounds, often very articulately, this is not conversation or even two way communication, as birds have no idea what they are mimicking, nor are they doing it to shape another's mind, behaviour or thinking.

> Those seductive parallels between characteristics we fondly imagine to be unique to ourselves and their taunting counterparts in birds are most likely the results of what is known as convergent evolution – independent adaptations to common environmental challenges – rather than features that were handed down from that 250 million year old common ancestor. But if there is any one characteristic which distinguishes us from the birds and probably any other non-human creature, it is indeed that extraordinary accomplishment that we call language.
>
> (Corballis, 2002, p 3)

CASE STUDY

Genie

In 1970 a child was discovered in Los Angeles by an off-duty policeman. The child was living in appalling circumstances with a partially sighted mother and a psychotic father, who beat her regularly. Genie was incarcerated and either strapped to a potty chair or kept in a cage. What is important in this story is that Genie was almost never spoken to, and although when found she had a few individual words, such as *rattle, bunny* and *red*, she had no syntax at all. Despite having almost no language she *appeared* to be cognitively more capable than her language development would suggest, as she would respond to gestures.

For psychologists this was one of the rare opportunities for them to investigate Chomsky's Critical Period theory in an ethical manner, and Genie was subjected to intensive language teaching and exposure. What this case showed was that although Genie's vocabulary grew extensively her syntax *never* developed and when she did use language she was unable to arrange the words in a grammatical way:

> What red blue is in?

The researchers took this as evidence to suggest that the language input had come too late, outside the language learning window, and believed this to be an indicator of the presence of a Critical Period, in the way that Chomsky predicted.

Critical questions

Use the internet to research further the case study described; then consider the following questions.

» *Do you think that the case of Genie did show the possibility of a Critical Period for language development? Explain why.*

» *Could there be alternative explanations for why Genie did not learn creative and generative language? If so, what might these be? Use your critical thinking skills to consider some of the alternatives, do not be afraid of rejecting the received explanations, but try to explain your lines of thought.*

Comment

Some alternative suggestions to stimulate your critical thinking can be found here.

1. Consider whether this failure to learn language can be explained by the sensory deprivation and emotional scars which were left following the extreme abuse and mishandling of Genie's young life, and therefore it has no relevance to a Critical Period theory. This could perhaps be a 'smoke screen' to the theory.

2. It was not possible to assess Genie's cognitive competence prior to the abuse being conducted. It could be that she was born with a cognitive impairment, which would have prevented her learning language, even in a well-stimulated and loving home environment, and this was in part the reason for her abusive background and rejection by her parents.

3. The lack of balanced nutrition in her formative years could be a cause of her failure to develop language in a normative fashion.

Language propensity

It is important to understand that what Chomsky was *not* saying was that you are born already knowing a particular language, rather that you have a propensity and facility for acquiring language, and that all languages share common principles...nouns, verbs, tenses etc. Pinker (1994) urges us to consider not that there *is* a Critical Period but *why*. He suggests that while something is useful to us it will be retained, so your arms and legs remain useful throughout life and are used as much when you are 60 years old as when you were 6 years old, therefore they are unlikely to stop working or drop off; however, when it comes to learning language this is more temporary. It is important in your early years to have the ability to learn a language, but once this is achieved it is no longer of use; although you continue to learn new words and expand your vocabulary, the circuitry in the brain required to learn the structures of language is no longer needed, and can be switched off as it is now redundant. It is possible that this then allows other metabolic changes to occur, which are more useful at a later stage in life. To update Pinker's (1994) analogy, it is like borrowing a CD to load onto a computer, or borrowing a turntable to copy a treasured collection of old LPs, and once these jobs are done there is no need for the mechanisms and they can be returned or dismantled.

Lenneberg (1969) undertook research into children with aphasia; he concluded that those who were struck down by the condition prior to puberty, and received appropriate support for their language development, had a good chance of recovering normal language. However, children and adults who were affected after puberty seldom recovered their language in full, despite extensive and wide-ranging support programmes put in place. The same window appears to affect gesture language. Ploog (1984) investigated children learning American Sign Language and concluded that seven years of age may be the start of a downward turn in the language learning curve.

Clearly 'proof' of the presence of a Critical Period is hard to obtain, due to the ethical limitations on experimentation, and because of this very little formal research has been conducted into its existence. Singleton (1989), however, argues against the concept, stating that in his research there *was* evidence of language learning after puberty. Nevertheless, all his evidence does appear to be taken in a period not long after puberty and relates to aspects of vocabulary and pragmatic skills, rather than competence of the structural core of language. This may suggest that rather than a distinct and sudden cut off, this is a more gradual process, and perhaps the term Critical Period could be more helpfully referred to as a Sensitive Period or Continuum of Sensitivity. This is perhaps a more flexible concept and can vary between individuals in a graduated manner.

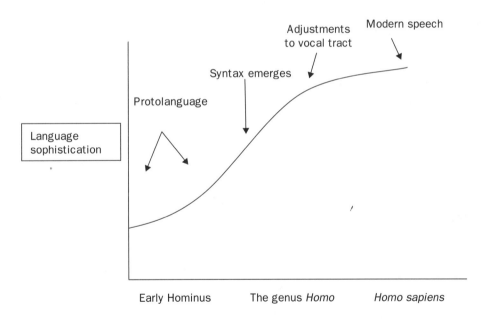

Figure 1.1 Schematic representation of the development of language in the course of hominid evolution, adapted from Corballis (2002, p 218).

Theory of mind

It is likely that the concept of 'theory of mind' is crucial to the holistic development of the child. Metacognition or theory of mind is really 'knowing about knowing'; it is a cognitive and intellectual process of development, but one which will affect children's ability to socialise, understand and rationalise emotional feelings and thought. A number of researchers, for example Baron-Cohen, Leslie, and Frith (1985), have linked a deficit of theory of mind to autism and autistic spectrum disorders in children. Potentially the development of theory of mind could also affect the physical development of the child by restricting their opportunities to socialise and engage in physical activities with peers. Theory of mind is your ability as a human being to relate to another person's mental states; this is when you are able to explain your own behaviour, needs and desires, in the light of what you are feeling in relation to your ability to interpret similar thoughts, needs and desires in other people around you. Theory of mind is also a growing understanding that other people may experience the world in different ways, so the child begins to understand that what we think is a representation of reality, not reality itself, and this in turn relates to any resultant actions. The child now knows that someone may believe something to be true, and may act on that belief even if it is a false belief.

CASE STUDY

Theory of mind

Tommy, who is four years old, puts his sweets in the blue jar in the kitchen and goes out to play in the garden. While he is out his mother moves them from the blue jar to the red jar. When Tommy returns from play he opens the blue jar and looks for his sweets; he believes that this is where they are even though this is a false belief. He then looks into the red jar and finds his sweets. This implies that at this age Tommy can represent reality in his mind, and that he knows that that representation is not reality itself, but belief still influences behaviour.

This leap of understanding is very important for the development of language, but is also made possible by the development of language, which enables the child to reflect upon their thoughts. This is further enhanced by their developing cognitive abilities, their social interaction and increased use of fantasy and make-believe play, enabling them to simultaneously hold different beliefs and representations in their mind.

Homo sapiens have survived through the ages with rather ill-equipped bodies compared to other species that may have big teeth, long claws and rhino-type hides. As a consequence it was essential that we worked together in groups or packs to forage, hunt and beat off our enemies. Being able to interpret other pack members' motives and intentions was essential to this hunting process, and the very existence of the pack. Despite this, Piaget (1923, translation 2007) famously claimed that very young children were unable to differentiate between themselves and others; they were unable to see the world through someone else's eyes and believed that whatever they were thinking or feeling, others were thinking and feeling the same. Piaget called this egocentrism, an inability to decentre from our own perspectives. To assess this Piaget devised the now famous three mountains experiment in which the child was shown three papier mâché mountains, one with a cross on the top, one with snow and one with a hut. The child was then shown a number of photographs of the mountains from different perspectives and viewpoints. A doll was placed in a variety of positions around the mountains, and the child was asked to assess which of the photographs best demonstrated the doll's eye-view of the mountains.

Figure 1.2 *Piaget's three mountains experiment.*

Piaget's conclusion was that until a child reached approximately 7–8 years of age they were unlikely to be able to complete this task accurately, implying that below that age children were egocentric and unable to understand that others do not necessarily have the same beliefs about the world that they do.

Critics of Piaget

There has been much criticism of Piaget's theory and a number of other studies have tried to replicate the findings; Hughes (1975) adapted the experiment and showed that children much younger than 7–8 years of age could take an alternative perspective, possibly as young as four years old. Controversially, scientists at Yale University in the United States of America – Hamlin, Wynn and Bloom (2007) – claimed that babies as young as six months demonstrated a degree of empathy, which they claimed was a related concept. Whatever the truth of this, it is clear that it is a gradual developmental process, and children's language acquisition is likely to play an important role in this transition, as it affects the child's ability to interact with others. This ability sees the child's language move from what they want, need and feel, to talk about what others think and know, their opinions and viewpoints. As children with better developed theory of mind are likely to be better communicators, their social functioning is also likely to be better, and this could have a beneficial effect on their later academic success. The rate of development of theory of mind could be impeding the rate of language development, but equally varied and enriched parental cognitive talk could also facilitate theory of mind development. However, Wilde-Astington and Edward (2010) warn that children with a better developed theory of mind can also use it in an anti-social manner, by bullying and teasing, as they better understand their power over their ability to influence what others see and believe of themselves, changing their motivational states and intentionality.

Biological roots

Wilde-Astington and Edward (2010) claim that the theory of mind has biological roots and develops without specific teaching, but can have some environmental influences to its development. It is interesting that in the case of the feral children already discussed, such as Genie and Victor, not only did their deprivation appear to affect language development, but also their development of metacognition. It has been claimed that these children remain at a largely egocentric stage, as they are unable to interpret the world beyond their own perspectives. This may indicate that we need to see the development of theory of mind as more of a continuum than a switch on/off transition. This could account for the wide variation in the ages and abilities to which this cognitive process is attributed by the research. It certainly highlights the problem that researchers have with the development of thought and the development of language, and how these are not discrete processes, but the product of a complex interaction which is far from well understood.

Teaching versus learning

While teaching and learning are not mutually exclusive, what does appear to be the case is that most normatively intelligent children, across the world, learn their first language, but they are not taught this language. When you go to school the teachers attempt to teach the past participle, relative clauses, the imperfect tense etc, but how many parents have the grammatical knowledge and skills, or even the will, to explain this to their three year-old?

Many people in the world are either illiterate or have extremely low literacy skills, but most have a complex knowledge of spoken and gestural communication. A UNICEF survey in 2001 conducted for UNESCO estimated that illiteracy threatened over 900 million adults worldwide, that is one in every five people in the world, two-thirds of whom are women. Even in the United States of America, which we normally consider to be a First World country, it is estimated that over 93 million people have basic or below basic literacy skills. According to Smith (2004), Chomsky rather controversially claimed that we did not *learn* language, and neither was it acquired, but grammar *'grows in the mind'* (Smith, 2004, p 120). This suggests that language could be maturational, and therefore acquired in roughly the same way, in the same order and at the same rate across the world, irrespective of the language to be acquired. Smith (2004) examines the research for this and concludes that there is indeed striking evidence that this is so, and that maturation, and therefore genetic determination, is an important feature of the attainment of any language.

> *This means that children go through a stage in their language acquisition in which functional categories are absent and that these then mature, or come 'on-line' at a particular stage, when children are roughly two years old.*
>
> (Smith, 2004, p 127)

Chapter reflections

With deference to the song by Cole Porter in the 1920s 'birds do it, bees do it even educated fleas do it'…What do they all do?…They communicate, whether by voice, movement or by gesture. Of course, as we have already discussed, this is probably not language at all, but it is likely that these differing methods of communication are the bedrock of our current vocal communication systems. Indeed would you want the animals to talk in a Dr Dolittle kind of way? Could they really represent thought, symbolically in the way that humans do, or would you discover that they have very little to talk about and their intellectual capacity was deficient? Could the animals really appreciate aesthetics, poetry and narrative?

Clearly we do not know for certain how human language developed, as there are no tape recordings or even cave drawings which enable anthropologists and archaeologists to achieve hard evidence. All the perspectives and hypotheses that you have read about in this chapter have been largely conjecture and guesswork. They have, however, certainly been about an interaction between their ontogenetic (development of the individual) and phylogenetic roots (evolution of the species), in other words the interplay between initial gestures, shared intentionality, social development and the anatomical development of the vocalisation organs.

Chomsky (1972) summed it up well when he said:

> Human language appears to be a unique phenomenon, without significant analogue in the animal world. There is no reason to suppose that the 'gaps' are bridgeable. There is no more basis for assuming an evolutionary development from breathing to walking.
>
> (Chomsky, 1972, pp 67–68)

So where does all this leave us? This really is so hard to answer as despite thousands of years of language, and hundreds of years of enquiry into language development and decades of intense research into language acquisition, we still have no solutions. We are probably no nearer to solving the riddle of how we attain language or where it originated from, but despite this, millions of people worldwide complete the process apparently easily and effortlessly in approximately the same order and rate of progression. I suggest that it is the greatest achievement of the first three years of our lives, from crying to babbling to expressing complex sentences and meaning. What you can be sure of though is that as adults responsible for the care and education of the young, you have a vital role to play in this development and the more knowledgeable you are about these early beginnings, the more you can help these children along their path to competency, stable relationships and a fulfilled and rewarding existence.

Critical thinking activity

Now that you have read this chapter try to consider some of the following questions. To start with you might find it helps to work on this with a colleague and bounce ideas off each other. Do not be afraid of how unconsidered this might be at the beginning; you will find that through discussion your ideas will take better shape, and you will see the need for evidence to support your premise.

» *What do you think was the main purpose of writing this chapter?*

» *What do you think was the key question that the chapter was trying to address? If you feel that there is more than one, try to consider them in order of importance.*

» *Where do you think that the evidence has come from to write this chapter? Consider general sources, not specific texts...research papers, personal observations, statistical reports, primary research, letters, newspapers etc.*

» *Do you think that anything has been taken for granted when writing this chapter, for example the experience of the readers, the knowledge of the readers, literacy skills etc?*

» *Having read the chapter, you can probably see that there are no real answers to the questions which were originally posed. Can you see any implications for further research or future thinking? What do you think needs to be done to draw some more definitive conclusions? How possible is this and what ethical implications might there be?*

Further reading

Tomasello, M (2008) *The Origins of Human Communication.* USA: Massachusetts Institute of Technology Press.

Although this is a rather dense book grounded in empirical research, it is also very readable and takes you through a coherent account of the evolutionary origins of human communication. Tomasello examines a range of alternative explanations, while at the same time challenging many of the received views on language acquisition. This text offers you a compelling new vision for the study of communication, and although it probably creates more questions than it answers, it is both stimulating and thought provoking.

References

Ambridge, B and Lieven E (2011) *Language Acquisition: Contrasting Theoretical Approaches.* Cambridge: Cambridge University Press.

Baron-Cohen, S, Leslie, A M and Frith, U (1985) Does the Autistic Child Have a Theory of Mind? *Cognition*, 21: 37–46.

Bates, E and MacWhinney, B (1982) Functionalist Approaches to Grammar. In Wanner, E and Gleitman, L (eds) *Language Acquisition: The State of the Art.* Cambridge: Cambridge University Press.

Bickerton, D (1984) The Language Bioprogram Hypothesis. *Behavioural and Brain Sciences*, 7: 173–222.

Bruner, J S (1960) *The Process of Education.* Cambridge, MA: Harvard University Press.

Carroll, L (2013) (originally published 1871) *Through the Looking Glass and What Alice Found There.* New York: Createspace Ltd.

Chomsky, N (1959) A Review of B F Skinner's 'Verbal Behaviour'. *Language*, 35: 26–58.

Chomsky, N (1964) *Current Issues in Linguistic Theory.* The Hague: Mouton.

Chomsky, N (1965) *Aspects of the Theory of Syntax.* Cambridge, MA: MIT Press.

Chomsky, N (1972) *Language and the Mind.* New York: Harcourt, Brace, Jovanovich.

Corballis, M (2002) *From Hand to Mouth: The Origins of Language.* New Jersey: Princeton University Press.

Gardner, H (1993) *Multiple Intelligences: The Theory in Practice.* New York: Basic Books.

Hamlin, J K, Wynn, K and Bloom, P (2007) Social Evaluation by Pre-verbal Infants. *Nature,* 450: (7169) 557–559.

Hughes, H (1975) *Egocentrism in Pre-school Children.* Unpublished doctoral research, Edinburgh University.

Karmiloff-Smith, A (1992) *Beyond Modularity: A Developmental Perspective on Cognitive Science.* Cambridge, MA: MIT Press.

Kipling, R (2010) (originally published 1894) *The Jungle Book.* London: William Collins.

Kuhl, P K (2004) Early Language Acquisition: Cracking the Speech Code. *Nat Rev Neuroscience,* 5: 831–843.

Lenneberg, E (1967) *Biological Foundations of Language.* New York: Wiley.

Lenneberg, E (1969) On Explaining Language. *Science,* 164 (3880): 635–643. www.biolinguagem. com/ling_cog_cult/lenneberg_1969_on_explaining_language.pdf (accessed 15.10.15).

Levey, S and Polirstock (2011) *Language Development: Understanding Language Diversity in the Classroom.* London: Sage.

Liebermann, P, (1998) *Eve Spoke: Human Language and Human Evolution.* New York: W.W. Norton.

McNeill, D (1970) *The Acquisition of Language: The Study of Developmental Psycholinguistics.* New York: Harper Row.

Piaget, J (2007) (originally published 1923) *The Language and Thought of the Child* (translated by Gabain, M and Gabain, R). London: Routledge.

Pinker, S (1994) *The Language Instinct: How the Mind Creates Language.* London: Penguin Books.

Ploog, D (1984) Comment on J Leiber's Paper. In Harre, R and Reynolds, V (eds) *The Meaning of the Primitive Signals.* Cambridge: Cambridge University Press.

Prince, A and Smolensky, P (1993) *Optimality Theory: Constraint Interaction in Generative Grammar.* Maldon: Blackwell.

Project Nim (2011) directed by James Marsh. UK: ICONfilm.

Prüfer, K and Pääbo, S (2012) The Banobo Genome Compared with the Chimpanzee and Human Genomes. *Nature,* 486: 527–531.

Schlesinger, H S and Meadows, K P (1972) *Sound and Sign.* Berkeley: University of California Press.

Singleton, D (1989) *Language Acquisition: The Age Factor.* Clevedon, UK: Multilingual Matters.

Skinner, B F (1957) *Verbal Learning.* New York: Appleton-Century-Croft.

Smith, N (2004) *Chomsky: Ideas and Ideals* (2nd ed). Cambridge: Cambridge University Press.

Tomasello, M (2003) *Constructing a Language.* Cambridge, MA: Harvard University Press.

Tomasello, M (2008) *The Origins of Human Communication.* Cambridge: Massachusetts Institute of Technology Press.

UNESCO (2001) *Adult Literacy.* www.unicef.org/specialsession/about/sgreport.pdf/07_Adultliteracy_
D7341insert_English.pdf (accessed 10.09.14).

Vygotsky, L (1935) *Mind in Society: The Development of Higher Psychological Processes.* Cambridge,
MA: Harvard University Press.

Wells, G (1986) *The Meaning Makers: Children Learning Language and Using Language to Learn.*
Sevenoaks: Hodder and Stoughton.

Wilde-Astington, J and Edward, M (2010) *The Development of Theory of Mind in Early Childhood.*
www.child-encyclopedia.com/documents/astington-edwardsgxp.pdf (accessed 12.09.14).

2 Receptive language and listening

Some people talk to animals. Not many listen though. That's the problem.
(A A Milne, 2006, first published 1926: *Winnie the Pooh*)

Introduction

Research into receptive language development in young children does appear to be the Cinderella of the literature on language development. Although it is generally acknowledged that receptive language is a necessary pre-requisite for the development of speech and literacy, it is the area that is afforded the least attention in the writings on language development. Except for literature on deafness and hearing loss, the majority of the information focuses upon the child as a speaker and the child as a reader. This chapter examines in detail some of the issues that surround the development of receptive language from the anatomical to the neurological, and offers a taster of the topic areas and their implications for those working with young children.

What is receptive language?

Unlike words written down and read, spoken words 'disappear' as soon as they are said. Taking what you hear into your brain and translating it into action is something that has to be done instantly. The sound must be committed to the memory (either short term or long term), and meaning extracted from it. This involves an ability to analyse and process the stream of sound that hits your ear.

Receptive language is indeed at the heart of all other aspects of learning language, whether it is your first language or a subsequent language acquisition. It is essential that a child is able to recognise sounds, and differentiate words, to follow instruction, and learn sentences, rhymes and songs. Without this, a child's ability to develop social relationships, build spoken language and generally develop as a literate and numerate individual will be seriously affected, as will be their future academic success.

Conversational process

To understand the mechanics of a conversation you have to start with the simple premise that it always requires at least one speaker and one listener; further that they have the understanding of what a conversation is, to know when to swap these roles. It is probably true to say that you talk about something of interest only if you have someone to listen to you, but this ability to swap roles between speaker and auditor is vital to the language process, to avoid simultaneous talking, which would prevent mutual comprehensibility.

Children learn their native language in an apparently effortless way without formal teaching, and possibly because of this, over the years receptive language has tended to be rather neglected by professionals and researchers. This could also be compounded by the fact that learning language usually takes place before the age of three, and therefore before the child attends a school based nursery or Reception class. In the past most government attention focused upon reading and writing elements of language. However, in more recent times, and with the immense increase in numbers of very young children attending day care settings, receptive language has received a much higher profile. Professionals have now begun to understand the importance of receptive language to the whole language, literacy and communication debate.

Receptive language and policy

In 2008, with the introduction of the Early Years Foundation Stage (DCSF) in England, listening and speaking became a compulsory part of the framework for the education of the young child, and in Wales it appears in the Early Years Foundation Phase (2008) as a vital part of language and literacy learning. The Rose Review (2006) also emphasised the importance of supporting children's expressive and receptive language in their literacy teaching and learning. In the latest review of the Early Years Foundation Stage (DfE, 2014) the Department for Education highlights the importance of communication and language, by defining it as one of three Prime Areas, which are vital building blocks for learning within the whole of the framework.

> *Communication and language development involves giving children opportunities to experience a rich language environment; to develop their confidence and skills in expressing themselves; and to speak and listen in a range of situations.*
>
> (DfE, 2014, p 8)

The Welsh Early Years Foundation Phase refers to this within the 'Oracy' section of the framework, but still the emphasis is upon the ability to receive and understand language, but in this instance in both English and Welsh, with the skills learned in one language supporting the development and advancement of the other.

> *They should be encouraged to listen and respond to others, to the variety of life experiences that their peers bring to the learning environment, and to a range of stimuli, including audio-visual material and ICT interactive software.*
>
> (Yr Adran Plant, Addysg, Dysgu Gydol Oes a Sgiliau, 2008, p 19)

CASE STUDY

Siobhan

Siobhan has difficulty with receptive language and attends nursery part time, four days a week. The nursery worker told Siobhan, who is four years old:

Go and put your coat on.

Siobhan was able to hear and understand this instruction and process the information and it resulted in her action of collecting her coat and putting it on.

When her coat was on, the nursery worker said:

Well done Siobhan. Please <u>collect your boots from under your table</u>$_1$ and then <u>take them to the front door</u>$_2$. Then you can <u>put them on</u>$_3$ ready to go out to play.

Siobhan was later found wandering outside the nursery, not having acted upon these instructions.

In the first example there is one instruction to consider, and Siobhan was able to listen, process, understand and act upon it. However, in the second example there are *three* pieces of information with instructions, and these need to be followed sequentially. This requires Siobhan to commit parts of the instruction to memory, and to retrieve that memory in a pre-determined sequence, to enable her to fulfil all the instructions.

Critical question

» *How could the nursery worker adapt her practice to ensure that children like Siobhan are able to understand and process the information that they are given?*

When you, as a practitioner, work with young children, you generally assume that even very young babies are listening when you talk to them, and they become conversational partners. You talk to them as though they understand and have the potential to respond. If you listen to other adults talking to babies you hear them starting to take turns in the 'conversation', leaving spaces for a potential response. As the baby lies in the cot, s/he hears adults talking, even when this is not addressed directly to her/him. This secondary exposure to language is likely to be fully adult conversation, not limited by the adult's perception of the child's age or stage of development. What the baby hears is a stream of sound from one partner in the conversation then a gap, which is interjected by the other conversation partner. This goes on for a while as the partners take turns to speak and listen. Of course the baby does not at this stage understand that the conversation depends upon the listening partner, but hears the process of language taking place in the home, the shops, the baby clinic etc.

Do you hear what you think you hear?

Before babies can begin to acquire recognisable language they need to be able to discriminate speech sounds and hear these as distinct and individual. Trehub and Rabinovitch (1972) showed that as early as one month of age, a baby can discriminate between sounds such as 'pa' and 'ba' and will turn its head in response. By six months babies can distinguish between two syllable sounds such as 'baba' and 'baga'.

Pinker (1994) talks about *'sine-wave speech'* (p 158) sounds that are unlike speech sounds but follow similar contours, patterns and rhythms of the sounds in a sentence. When his researchers played such patterns of sound to adult volunteers they described what they heard as language, even though they *'couldn't quite make it out'*. Some said that they had heard recognisable words, and some even wrote down whole sentences that they *believed* they had heard. The brain appeared to be 'searching' for language in the sounds that they heard; it seemed to be searching for meaning. So we can perceive sounds as speech even when they are not. Pinker (1994) calls this phonetic awareness a 'sixth sense'.

> *When we listen to speech the actual sounds go in one ear and out the other; what we perceive is **language**.* (p 159)

If you return to the discussion in the previous chapter, on the remarkable imitative abilities of birds to articulate speech sounds, this is what is happening. When the parrot uses the valves on each bronchial tube to make two wavering sounds, your brain tries to interpret this as talking, even if it is not, as the parrot has no intention of communicating with you.

Word segmentation

Pinker (1994) describes language as an illusion; what you are listening to when you listen to someone talking is a continuous stream of sound with no spaces. Spoken language, unlike written language, has no spaces between the words, but your brain segments the sounds into separate words, giving the words boundaries. These word boundaries are there only as the seamless sounds that you are listening to start to take on meaning. In other words they are recognisable, due to previous exposure to the sounds' individual patterns, within the sound strings. Common misunderstandings can be made of interpretation of these sound strings, which are called 'oronyms'. An oronym is a string of words that sound the same as another string of words but are spelt differently.

> *The parcel was secured by grey tape.*
>
> *The parcel was secured by a great ape.*
>
> *The stuffy nose can lead to problems.*
>
> *The stuff he knows can lead to problems.*

These are often prompted by 'homophones', which are individual words that sound the same but are spelt differently and mean different things. The following is a well-known poem written with oronyms and homophones which may help you to understand:

Eye halve a spelling chequer

It came with my pea sea

It plainly marques four my revue

Miss steaks eye kin knot sea

Eye strike a key and type a word

And weight four it two say

Weather eye am wrong oar wright

It shows me strait a weigh.

As soon as a mist ache is maid

It nose bee fore two long

And eye can put the error rite

Its rarely ever wrong.

Eye have run this poem threw it

I am shore your pleased two no

Its letter perfect in it's weigh

My chequer tolled me sew.

(Source unknown)

You can perhaps better recognise the seamless nature of speech sounds when you listen to an unfamiliar language, particularly one which has a very different rhythm and pattern from your mother tongue. Sounds such as those from an East Asian language, for example Mandarin Chinese, illustrate this well. When you listen to two fluent Mandarin speakers conversing it is very difficult to distinguish individual words or even sentences. As a proponent of language innatism, Pinker (1994) describes this blurring of sounds and speech perception as a *'biological miracle, making up the language instinct'* (p 161).

Hearing or listening?

Hearing and listening are terms that are frequently interposed in everyday language, so we might say:

Can you hear that?

Listen to that.

However, hearing and listening are not the same thing. You are surrounded with noises in your environment which you hear, whether you want to or not. You can then *choose* to listen to some of them and block out the others. So listening is an active process requiring you to hear and use your brain to interpret the messages received by your ears. It is vital for all children's future learning that they are able to filter out the distractions and focus upon particular things. You cannot extract meaning from the things that you hear, unless you actively engage and listen to them.

The mechanics of the hearing process

Sound waves are channelled into the ear by the pinna, the external part of the ear that you can see and are familiar with. This initiates a series of movements and vibrations in the components of the inner ear. This in turn generates electrical energy or neural signals that result in the brain recognising the sound in the auditory cortex. As the channelled sound reaches the ear drum (tympanic membrane), it causes the drum to vibrate in the same way as the skin across a musical drum will vibrate when struck. This vibration moves the three smallest bones in your body, the hammer, anvil and stirrup (so called because this is what they look like). In turn this movement compresses fluid in the cochlea; this activates hair cells which are connected to the auditory nerve fibres. The amount of activity produced in these parts of the auditory mechanism depends upon the frequency of the auditory stimulation.

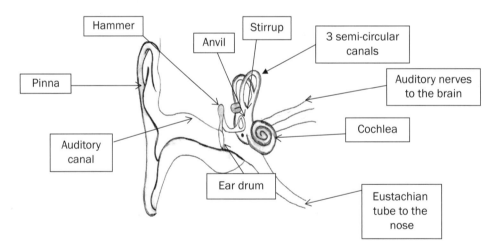

Figure 2.1 *Diagram of the structure of the ear.*

These hearing mechanisms develop in the foetus at approximately 16 weeks of gestation, although the ear is not fully developed until 24 weeks, implying that babies can hear language even before birth. Researchers at the University of Helsinki in Finland (Partanen et al, 2013) played to a number of pregnant mothers a tape of nonsense words and repeated these up to 71 times at different pitches. A second group of mothers formed the control group and had no tape played to them. They examined the babies at birth for normal hearing and then used an electroencephalograph (brain scan) to see if they responded to the nonsense words and different pitches. They showed that the babies that had been exposed to the nonsense words had greater electrical brain activity when the words were played after birth than the control group. This research also showed that not only did the babies hear the words in utero, but also could detect subtle changes and process complex information, for example loudness; the non-exposed babies were unable to do this.

Interestingly, in 1998, Hepper's research showed that babies of mothers who watched soap operas on the television throughout their pregnancy recognised the signature tunes and musical cues when these were played to them shortly after birth. These babies were also able to distinguish vowel sounds and pitch changes; this was strongest in the babies with the most exposure. Pregnant mothers frequently claim that their babies move more in the womb in response to certain sounds, and loud noises have been shown to startle the foetus and provoke activity. However, Partanen et al (2013) say that there is no evidence that exposure beyond the normal everyday sounds of life offers any long-term benefit to baby; in fact it is possible that it may overstimulate the foetal ear and auditory system by disrupting sleep cycles.

Critical questions

With a partner consider the following.

» *Should we be deliberately exposing all babies to more sound in utero?*

» *As the unborn child is unable to 'have a say' in what they are exposed to, what are the ethical and moral implications for this?*

Listening caught or taught?

Many practitioners and teachers believe that listening develops naturally, and it cannot be 'taught'. As a consequence the skill of listening is often neglected. It is probably true to say that it is an area which receives very little attention in the training of those working in early years, so practitioners are not always aware of its importance, or how to teach this vital initial component of language and literacy development. As a consequence children are frequently not encouraged to, or even given a purpose for, listening. Such purposes could be:

1. identifying the main purpose of an item;
2. distinguishing between the main purposes and supporting material;
3. detecting emotional nuances within language;
4. differentiating fact from fiction;
5. identifying descriptive vocabulary.

To provide purpose and guidance for the listening experiences that you offer children, you should not just be encouraging children to listen *to* something, but you should be indicating to them what they should be listening *for.* An example of this would be determining the tone and emphasis of a speaker's voice, to ascertain meaning:

> *Are <u>you</u> really going to wear that dress?*

> *Are you <u>really</u> going to wear that dress?*

> *Are you really going to wear <u>that</u> dress?*

In this case, by the emphasis in the sentence, we assume that the speaker could be angry, incredulous, joking etc. It is vital that the listener can detect this nuance of meaning to their response, and so to their relationship with the speaker.

Sounds and language

According to psychological research at Bristol University (Kazanina, 2008), in the first nine months of life the brain is programmed to recognise key sounds of language. Kazanina (2008) suggests that at birth a baby can distinguish all speech sounds that are made across all languages, but as we mature this ability gets less, and by six months of age we only recognise the vowel sounds from our mother tongue, and by eight to nine months of age we only recognise the consonant sounds. This potentially restricts the baby to the ability to learn only its native language. However, babies exposed to more than one language in the home do retain the ability to recognise all the sounds that they hear. Kazanina (2008) proposes that this is why English speakers find it so hard to learn French (which is the most common modern foreign language taught in our schools), compared to Italian and Spanish speakers who have more similar language sound patterns in their native tongues. This also accounts for why English learners from China and Japan find it so hard to distinguish between the 'R' and 'L' sounds when learning English, as these are not sound patterns that appear naturally in their native tongue. Kazanina (2008) suggests that as languages such as German and Swedish share many of our English sounds, in theory, these should be easier languages for us to learn as a second or subsequent language.

Werker and Tees (1984) undertook a comprehensive study of 12 babies and their ability to discriminate sounds. They divided their sample into three groups of babies: 6–8 months old, 8–10 months old and 10–11 months old. They showed that when exposed to speech sounds in English, Hindi and Salish (North American Indian), at 6–8 months the babies could discriminate between all languages, even those that were unfamiliar to them, but by 12 months they could not.

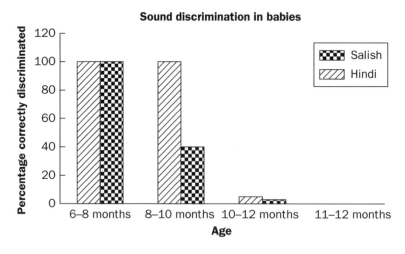

Figure 2.2 What happened to the longitudinal sound discrimination ability of six babies, adapted from Werker and Tees (1984, p 61).

These findings were later replicated by Kuhl (2014), who researched the exposure of American children to Mandarin Chinese, and showed that at nine months of age the children were able to distinguish phonetic elements of the Chinese language, when exposed for less than five hours. Controversially, Kuhl's experiments also exposed a separate sample of nine-month-olds to the same Mandarin Chinese on DVDs and audio tapes, but without the social, human interaction, this same ability to distinguish phonetic units was not repeated. She suggested that the human interaction was therefore a vital element in the learning of language. However, although this is well documented Khul believes that this phenomenon is still unexplained.

Critical question

Kuhl's theory was that we need exposure to face-to-face human interaction.

» *What does this say for those of you who try to learn a second or subsequent language through distance learning DVDs and audio tapes?*

Bee and Boyd (2011) suggest that this could be consistent with early development of brain synapses, which is then followed by what they call 'synapse pruning'. In other words lots of neural pathways are initially created, but as the child is using only a small percentage of these regularly, the remainder are redundant pathways and become defunct.

What are neural pathways?

Clearly the working of the brain is extremely complex and still poorly understood; however, in very simple terms psychologists believe that for learning to take place connections need to be created between neurons in the brain, and these connections are called neural synapses. When you are first confronted with new learning, it is a rather chaotic process, and something that as an adult you would find very simple to do, such as accurately picking up a pencil from a table, the baby will find hard as the pathways have not been appropriately created to 'instruct' the muscles to move in a particular way. So for the pathway to be created from A to B, initially the electrical activity will be random and disordered.

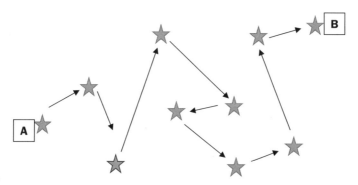

Figure 2.3 Chaotic and random nature of the creation of neural pathways.

This is clearly quite inefficient and makes no real sense. However, as the child repeats the action again and again the brain becomes more efficient and streamlined.

Figure 2.4 *The most efficient neural pathway established.*

This can best be described as like walking through a field of long grass; when you first walk through from A to B it can be quite random, as you zig-zag across the field to find the gate on the other side. However, as you do this every day you become more efficient, and the pathway becomes more established and worn, until it is clearly marked across the field, and others can follow your path easily.

With modern technology, it is now possible to monitor the activity of neural networks firing in a co-ordinated fashion and measure the electrical charges in the neural cortex by placing electroencephalograph sensors across a baby's head. Magnetoencephalography is another brain imaging technique; this localises the electrical activity when a sensitive helmet is placed over the baby's head, while they are performing sensory motor, or cognitive activities, such as phonetic discrimination when they are exposed to speech sounds. These tests, combined with Magnetic Resonance Imaging (MRI) scans, can show anatomical differences in brain regions, highlighting the areas of the brain responsible for these differing tasks.

Do we acquire language through the eye or the ear?

When you listen to someone speaking, you are not only taking in information from your hearing and auditory processing, but you are also watching them, their physical gestures and mouth movements. Without this capacity to combine the visual sense with the auditory, you would be limiting your ability to understand the information from the receptive language. This combining of information across the senses is called 'intermodal perception' or 'intermodal co-ordination'. One example of this is your ability to understand who is speaking when you hear spoken language.

Most humans are much slower than a computer at numerical calculation or recalling numbers or facts, but humans far surpass computers at language related tasks. Pinker (1994) suggested that the ear, as miraculous as it is, acts like an 'information bottleneck' constricting the hearing process. In the 1940s engineers attempted to produce a reading machine for blind and partially sighted people, but discovered that merely isolating the phonemes in words and then sticking them back together again in an infinite number of ways to form words was completely useless. As real speech is understandable at between 10 and 50 phonemes a second, this showed that it was not possible for you to 'read' speech in this way, at approximately three phonemes a second (approximately the same speed as a ship's radio officer 'reading' Morse code). To illustrate this, when we hear the tick of a clock we hear each individual sound, and if this were speeded up to 20–30 ticks per second it would sound to the human ear as a continuous sound, as the spaces between the ticks would be indistinguishable from each other.

> *Speech is a river of breath bent into hisses and hums by the soft flesh of the mouth and throat.*

(Pinker, 1994, p 163)

When you consider this, you begin to understand how a series of phonemes strung together as speech sounds appear to the human ear as a continuous noise. Add to this the differences of sounds that you hear when listening to various dialects. For example, imagine two people discussing their work. As John lives in Liverpool and Adah in London they may pronounce these words very differently:

Book $\longrightarrow$ BƱk $\longrightarrow$ Bu:k

Garage $\longrightarrow$ Gara:ʒ $\longrightarrow$ Garidʒ

Grass $\longrightarrow$ Gra:ss $\longrightarrow$ Grass

As you hear each of these different pronunciations your brain has to process these as similar words and not as different, even within the same conversation. Now add Mike to the conversation who is from Glasgow and you begin to see the difficulties and complexities of this process. One way to explain this phenomenal feat is that when you hear speech, your brain narrows down the possibilities of what might be said. For example, consider what a child might say in the playground, playing on the swing. A word such as 'rhinoceros' is unlikely to come into the conversation, but if you go to the zoo and stand looking at a rhinoceros in a pen, this word is highly likely to occur in the sentence. This could also account for the number of times that we hear what we want to hear, rather than what is actually said. Perhaps we are hearing and guessing, without really listening. However, if you take this guessing premise further you are implying a top down model of speech recognition rather than the bottom up model, which is what the computer model described earlier was trying to do.

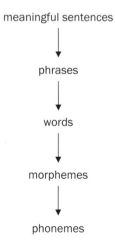

Figure 2.5 Top down model of speech recognition.

However, language is not always that predictable; you *do* say things to others that are entirely out of context, or with an unusual phrase structure, which we nevertheless can still hear, interpret and usually understand.

Critical questions

Hearing and listening are unseen activities; you cannot 'see' the listening process; you cannot 'see' your children listening to you. With a partner, consider the following questions which may influence your practice. These questions could form the basis for discussion in your next staff meeting or an online forum:

» *How do you know that children in your care are listening and understanding?*

» *How do you engage children with listening activities?*

» *Does it just depend upon what you are talking about?*

» *Does it depend upon the way you are talking?*

» *Does it depend upon whether you are listening?*

» *Does it depend on how you are listening?*

» *How can you show children that you are listening to them?*

» *What is 'active listening'?*

» *When talking with the children how much of the conversation is yours and how much belongs to the child?*

» *Is your conversation child or adult initiated?*

» *Is your conversation child or adult directed?*

Attention

As you read earlier in this chapter, babies respond to a wide range of sounds even before birth. What is particularly interesting is that they appear to be 'hardwired' to respond and pay attention to speech type sounds, more than any other noises.

> *They react most noticeably to sounds in the frequency range (pitch) of 1,000 to 3,000 Hz, the range in which most speech occurs.*
>
> (Siegler and Alibali, 2005, p 165)

Sounds in this range and frequency appear to interest them more than any other; this may be backed up with visual attention to the movement of the lips and facial gestures. Mandel, Jusczyk and Pisoni (1995) found that in their research on the babies of four months, they were particularly receptive to their own name, and babies as young as three days old could identify their mother's voice, affording it more attention than any other voice. Of course we know that they have been listening to their mother for the last nine months, so this may not be so surprising, as the pitch and tone of this will be very familiar to them already.

When speaking to young children, adults around the world often use a high tone, w. gerated intonation and lots of repetition. In the 1970s this came to be known as 'motheres. perhaps today you would more correctly refer to this as 'parentese', as it is a phenomenon seen in most adults when they are talking to children. Stern, Spieker and Mackain (1982) showed that 77 per cent of the language that adults used with children fell into this category, and it would appear that this is the case across cultures and languages. This research also appeared to show that attention from the baby to the adult was greater when 'parentese' was used, possibly due to the higher and more accessible pitch.

This ability to focus upon a particular sound, person or item is called 'attention' or concentration. As you mature and develop, your ability to focus and attend to something gets greater, even in things which we are not particularly interested in. I am sure that most of you will remember studying at college or university and finding it hard to concentrate upon a particular element of your programme that you did not find interesting. For you to be able to concentrate you need certain rewards, or some element of reinforcement, and in the early years these rewards need to be instant. A young child will only listen to a story if they are enjoying its content, it is fun and instantly gratifying; otherwise their attention will wander and they will cease to listen. As you mature these rewards can be delayed, and you might study your degree or college course with the reward of success not appearing for two or three years. This is called 'delayed gratification' and Mischel, Ebbesen and Raskoff Zeiss (1972) showed that this ability to increasingly delay gratification was an essential element to all future learning.

It is interesting that Gaertner, Spinrad and Eisenberg (2008) found very limited evidence for any difference in the *ability* to concentrate and attend between genders, although females did appear to exhibit slightly more incidents of focused activity than males. What was more apparent in the Gaertner et al (2008) research was that negative emotionality had a significant effect upon a child's ability to focus, and overarousal from frequent or intense periods of distress made it difficult for children of both genders to focus. This same research showed that praise had a significant effect, when it was demonstrated to the child on engagement with a task, or that adults showed that their efforts were valued. However, it should be noted that their research was largely conducted on white, middle-class children, and it is possible that cultural influences, parenting practices and levels of socialisation could impact upon the child's attentional ability, so more widespread research into this needs to be undertaken.

Joint attention and mutual knowledge

Joint attention is described by some researchers (Carpenter and Call, in Metcalfe and Terrace, 2013) as the ability to share attention; this is the child who follows the gaze of their parent when they are looking at a toy or other object. The child may then alternate the gaze between the parent and the toy. In other words both partners 'know' that they are attending to the same thing, and they have mutual knowledge. This then involves a triadic relationship between two people and an object or subject of mutual interest (Bakeman and Adamson, 1984).

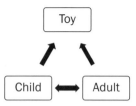

Figure 2.6 *Joint attention.*

However, not all researchers would agree with this definition (Tomasello, 2008), and the term 'joint attention' is not always clearly defined. For some, it is sufficient to look at the same thing together to conclude that joint attention has occurred (Leavens and Racine, 2009), but for others more is demanded, and in particular the sharing of that attention (Tomasello, 2008), rather than just parallel gaze. If you relate this to children, joint attention could be just looking at the same thing, for example a television programme. However, how do you know that there is mutual understanding if you just watched together? If you watch and discuss the programme afterwards, then there can be an acknowledgement that there is a sharing of understanding and shared attention.

What does seem to bring the various researchers together in agreement is that children start to exhibit joint attention at approximately 9–12 months of age. They also agree that the development of joint attention is essential to language development, and in particular the development of receptive language and the building and sustaining of vocabulary. The child needs to understand what the adult is focusing upon in mutual understanding before they can respond, so for example:

ADULT POINTING: *Oh! Look at that lovely teddy!*

Child looks to where the adult is pointing and gazing.

ADULT: *Can you give me the teddy?*

Child understands where the attention is focused and passes the teddy to the adult.

Of course this may not always be so straightforward and the adult may point to a dog trotting down the street and say 'dog'. How is the child to know what to focus upon? Could the word 'dog' refer to the whiskers, legs, tail, colour, trotting action, fur etc? Communication whether verbal or non-verbal allows you to share further knowledge about something instantly – this might be as simple as a smile, pointing or eye contact between you – to indicate something. This simple interaction shows that you are both focused on the same thing and both agree what that is.

Information processing and memory

To attain any level of understanding of the language that a child hears, they need to be able to process that language in the brain, thereby relating this to their previous understanding and memories. They then have to be able to recall those remembrances at a later date either from their short-term or long-term memory, and transfer that information to a working memory. They then probably need to take that understanding to other areas of the brain to formulate a response. The more words that a child hears and needs to learn, the larger the capacity of the vocabulary available to them. Schneider and Pressley (1989) noted that this capacity to remember words increases with age, but suggested that rather than any physical change in information processing capacity, this could be attributed to the speed of the processing, as the neural synapses develop and the child has more experience of using strategies to remember and recall. If you consider the complexity of this chain of events, you can probably understand how one small hiccough in the process could cause a child difficulties with their receptive language processing, for example in their short-term memory, auditory sequencing problems etc. Clearly such a problem can affect all their future language abilities, and hence their entire development and academic success.

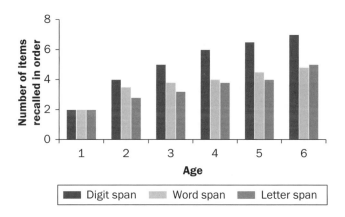

Figure 2.7 *The number of items that children are able to remember at different ages, adapted from Dempster (1981).*

There is clearly a lag between the acquisition of receptive language and the development of expressive language, and Menyuk, Liebergott and Schultz (1995) suggest that this is approximately five months. At about 13 months of age the child will comprehend almost 50 words, but they may not produce that number in expressive language until roughly 18 months of age. This could be because receptive language requires the child to recognise and comprehend a word, but for expressive language they need to recognise, comprehend and then recall the word.

As the child hears a new word, to add to their lexicon, they are comparing and contrasting how this new word fits into their existing word knowledge, what they can already remember and recall. For example, the child hears the word bicycle and needs to be able to categorise it, and subject it to their prior knowledge, which might be:

- things that move;
- outside toys;
- things that have wheels;
- metal objects.

able to categorise in this way the child needs to be able to see the 'big picture', and *then* consider the details. This ability is called 'Central Coherence'. Interestingly, it is thought (Pina et al, 2013) that children on the autistic spectrum and children with Attention Deficit and Hyperactivity Disorder (ADHD) have poor central coherence, in other words they consider the fine detail, without being able to see the big picture. To illustrate this, if you return to the bicycle example, when the child is able to see the big picture they will see a mode of transport, fun to use in the outdoors. If the child is unable to see this, they could get obsessed with the minor issues such as the size of the spokes, how the pedals go round, what the bell does etc.

Categorisation such as this could take the form of a schema. A schema, according to Siegler and Alibali (2005), was what Piaget (1952) referred to as a collection of information, concepts or events which the child already has in mind, but they are often incomplete and flawed. New information needs to be taken into the basic schema, assimilated and accommodated to refine the neural picture or script.

CASE STUDY

Sian

Sian is two years old; she lives in a rural part of Wales and is familiar with the cows on the farm around her. When she sees a cow in the field she gets excited and shouts:

> Cow, cow!

However, one day the cows are not out and instead there is a black and white horse. She shouts:

> Cow, cow!

Her schema for a cow is a four legged, black and white creature with a tail that stands in a field eating grass.

When she is told that it is not a cow but a horse, she has to adapt her schema to accommodate and reconstruct this new information.

Not all theorists (Pinker, 1994) would accept this idea of schemas as it does imply a top down approach to language and thought. This approach suggests that first there are thoughts, and then language is put to those thoughts in a form of labelling. Alternatively, Pinker suggests that thoughts come into existence through language and language is a way for children to make sense of the world around them. Through language the child develops as a thinker and a learner.

If you examine how we understand receptive language you will see that there are generally two types of comprehension.

1. **Literal comprehension**: This is how you understand the concrete information that you hear. This tends to be the 'who, what, where, when' of a subject. You can assess a child's literal comprehension by asking questions such as:

- Who are we talking about?

- What were they doing?

- Where are they?

- When are they coming?

2. **Inferential comprehension**: This is a more difficult form of understanding and usually develops at a later stage of development. This is the understanding of things that are not explicitly stated, so the child needs prior knowledge with which to reference the new information. You can assess a child's inferential comprehension by using questions that start with 'What if? Why? How do you think? What happens next?' etc.

- What if Rapunzel had had her hair cut the night before?

- How do you think the prince climbed her hair?

- Why couldn't he use the door?

- What do you think happened after Rapunzel escaped?

Receptive language and technology

Increasing levels of engagement with technology such as television, social media, computer games and audio devices appear to be incontrovertible. Children are more and more engaged with their devices and are less physically active, but this also means that they are bombarded with complex noise and language sounds. In an American report by Clinton and Steyer (2012), they estimated that:

- more than 7.5 million American children have joined the social media site Facebook;

- by two years of age more than 90 per cent of all American children have an online history;

- by five years of age more than 50 per cent regularly interact with a computer/tablet;

- by 7–8 years of age children regularly engage with computer games;

- teenagers text an average 34,000 times a month;

- By the time they leave school, American teenagers have viewed approximately 20,000 hours of television (which is more than the entire number of hours in a classroom).

This could imply that these children are spending more time listening to and interacting with their multimedia devices than they spend listening to and interacting with their parents, peers and other adults. However, research into the effects of television viewing has been inconclusive, and Close (2004) suggests that although there is no established causal link between television viewing and restricted language development, if viewed extensively, it was likely to be detrimental. The issue here could be the term 'extensively'. How much television is too much television? A comprehensive review of television watching in 329 four-year-olds by Christakis et al (2009) did show a direct link and proportionality between the time that young children watch television, the detrimental effect on their receptive language and risk of the following:

- obesity;
- poor cognitive development;
- poor language development;
- their inability to pay attention;
- poor psychosocial health;
- diminished feelings of well-being;
- hyperactivity;
- lack of self-control.

The research done by Christakis et al (2009) showed that for every hour that the television was on, babies heard approximately 770 fewer words from an adult; that is a 7 per cent decrease. Conversational exchanges between the child and parent dropped by approximately 15 per cent, and children spent more time in silence than in active interaction. This study also noted that in America, 30 per cent of families had the television on for most of the day, even when they were not engaged with it. The ability to block out extraneous background noise and focus upon on attentional aspect is probably not well developed in very young children until approximately ten years of age, so this is likely to have a detrimental effect on their overall learning as well as their language acquisition.

Critical questions

Most young children are expected to work and learn in busy and noisy nursery settings and classrooms.

» *If they find it difficult to ignore the background noise and focus upon a task, how do you think it should influence the teaching of young children in nursery and Reception classes?*

» *If television and audio equipment constantly form a backdrop to some children's lives, how can you help them to focus and develop the attentional skills that they need?*

Chapter reflections

Receiving language and understanding is an unseen activity and because of this it is hard to research with confidence, especially in the initial stages of life, before expressive language develops. With increased technology and neurological scanning, researchers can now note when and where there is brain activity, but until such time as they can really 'see' what we are thinking, and this is no longer just science fiction, it is not possible to understand the cognitive processes which are in play. However, cognitive neuroscientists, led by Nathan Spreng, at Cornell University in the United States are currently working on this. According to Choi (2013), in an article in the online technology magazine Txchnologist, this research uses brain scans to tell what a person is thinking. These researchers claim to be able to decode imagery to know what number a person is thinking of, or a person that they are considering. Clearly this is very exciting, cutting-edge research, which if correct will open up numerous possibilities for 'mind reading' and greater understanding of the human brain as it develops.

Practitioners need to better understand the value and importance of helping children to develop their ability to receive and comprehend language, and see that they can have an important role in this process. Listening is a vital skill which sets the basis for all other language development, and you can assist this by valuing a child's attempts to listen and comprehend and also to demonstrate what 'good' listening really is and the circumstances under which it can be enhanced. Without a visible product this can be difficult to justify to colleagues, and can be achieved only if you have a sound knowledge and awareness of what active listening really is, and how to support this in the babies and young children that you work with. This involves allowing children time to listen, respecting their choices of what to listen to, and creating shared experiences for listening which generate confidence in the children to take their listening to the next stage, and take the risks involved in expressing their thoughts.

This chapter leads you seamlessly into the next, which focuses upon the development of expressive language, moving the child from the ability to listen to and understand what they hear, to the more complex ability to express their thoughts and feelings in a creative and resourceful manner. The move from active comprehension to verbal communication is a complex one, but also fascinating as you will see.

DEVELOPING CRITICAL THINKING

Critical thinking involves reasoning, which is not difficult in itself, and on one level you probably do it all the time in your everyday life. It really just means that you know your reasons for doing something, for example:

Why are you applying for that new job?

- It is closer to home.

- It can earn you more money.

- It means shorter hours.

- It gives you more status.

- It is a springboard to better opportunities etc.

I am sure that you could identify all of these and more in your daily life. However, sometimes you are perhaps not as aware of your reasons for doing something. Perhaps you have not had the time or the inclination to consider them in detail, or they involve areas of your life that are so routine you have not thought it necessary to think about them. This may apply to you in your practice with young children, for example why do you organise snack time in the way that you do? Could it just be that you have always done it this way, and have fallen into a predictable pattern that you have not taken time to consider before?

Examining your reasons for actions could go much deeper than this, and if you have to examine the reasons for things like your beliefs, your faith, or lack of it, this can be much more challenging. This will require you to weigh up the different arguments for and against what you think you believe; but more than that, to be prepared to change your beliefs on the strength of these arguments.

Critical reasoning also involves your ability to articulate these arguments, and be able to explain to someone else why you have come to the conclusions that you have. Going further, you need to explain why you might need to change your practice or follow a particular line of action.

For your academic work, critical reasoning also means trying to follow other people's reasoning, when they purport a particular belief or theory. In this way you can attempt to unravel their thought processes when putting forward a particular construct, thereby assessing whether the evidence for their reasoning supports their conclusions.

Critical thinking activity

Now critically consider the following questions.

» *Is it important for practitioners to understand the competing theories of how children receive and experience language? Explain your ideas to a colleague.*

» *How could it help you to develop your own practice?*

» *Some practitioners, especially those working in areas of poverty and deprivation, tell me that their initial training did not adequately prepare them to identify and work with the numbers of children that they see with receptive language difficulties. What are your views on this?*

» *The concept of 'theory of mind' (discussed in Chapter 1) has featured prominently in the research into receptive language. Why do you think this idea is of such interest to the theorists?*

» *What influence could it have on practice in an early years setting?*

Further reading

Pinker, S (1994) *The Language Instinct: How the Mind Creates Language*. London: Penguin Books.

This is a classic and comprehensive text which is a 'must read' for anyone seriously interested in language development. Pinker takes the reader through the origins of language, the production and reception of speech, neurology of the brain and the pathology of language disorders. This book is well scripted to enable the general reader to be able to access some complex and difficult concepts. Pinker is renowned as an innatist theorist, but this book offers the reader a full range of theoretical alternatives, to enable you to decide between them and reach your own conclusions.

References

Bakeman, R and Adamson L (1984) Coordinating Attention to People and Objects in Mother-Infant and Peer-Infant Interactions. *Child Development*, 55: 1278–1289.

Bee, H and Boyd, D (2011) *The Developing Child* (13th ed). Cambridge, MA: Pearson.

Carpenter, M and Call, J (2013) How Joint Is the Joint Attention of Apes and Human Infants? In Metcalfe, S and Terrace, H (eds) *Agency and Joint Attention*: Oxford: Oxford University Press.

Choi, C (2013) *Brain Researchers Who Can Detect What We Are Thinking About*. Txchnologist, March 2013. www.scientificamerican.com/article/brain-researchers-can-detect-who-we-are-thinking-about/#commentsinking-of-somebody-brain-researchers-know (accessed 26.10.14).

Christakis, D, Gilkerson, J, Richards, A, Zimmerman, J, Garrison, M, Dongxin, X, Gray, S and Yapanel, U (2009) *Audible Television and Decreased Adult Words, Infant Vocalisations and Conversational Turntaking*. Archives of Pediatrics and Adolescent Medicine, 163 (6) (June): 554–558.

Clinton, C and Steyer, J (2012) *Is the Internet Hurting Children?* www.edition.cnn.com/2012/05/21/opinion/clinton_steyer_internet_kids/ (accessed 23.09.14).

Close, R (2004) *Television and Language Development in the Early Years: A Review of Literature*. London: National Literacy Trust.

Dempster, F N (1981) Memory Span: Sources of Individual and Developmental Differences. *Psychological Bulletin*, 89: 63–100.

Department for Children, Schools and Families (DCSF) (2008) *Statutory Framework for the Early Years Foundation Stage*. Nottingham: DCSF.

Department for Education (DfE) (2014) *Statutory Framework for the Early Years Foundation Stage: Setting the Standards for Learning, Development and Care for Children from Birth to Five*. www.gov.uk/governmentpublications (accessed 23.10.14).

Gaertner, B, Spinrad, T and Eisenberg, N (2008) Focused Attention in Toddlers. *Infant Child Development*, 17 (4) (August): 339–363.

Hepper, P G (1998) Foetal 'Soap' Addiction. *The Lancet*, June: 1347–1348.

Kazanina, N (2008) Infant Exposure to Language Improves Later Learning. *Language Magazine*, 7 (11) (July): 12.

Kuhl, P K (2004) Early Language Acquisition: Cracking the Speech Code. *Nature Reviews Neuroscience*, 5 (November): 831–845.

Leavens, D and Racine, T (2009) Joint Attention in Apes and Humans: Are Humans Unique? *Journal of Consciousness Studies*, 16 (6–8): 240–267.

Mandel, D, Jusczyk, P and Pisoni, D (1995) Infants' Recognition of the Sound Patterns of Their Own Names. *Psychological Science*, 6: 314–317.

Menyuk, P, Liebergott, J and Schultz, M (1995) *Early Language Development in Full-Term and Premature Infants.* Hillsdale, NJ: Lawrence Erlbaum Associates.

Milne, A A (2006) (originally published 1926) *Winnie the Pooh.* GB: Egmont.

Mischel, W, Ebbesen, E B and Raskoff Zeiss, A (1972) Cognitive and Attentional Mechanisms in Delay of Gratification. *Journal of Personality and Social Psychology*, 21: 204–218.

Partanen, E, Torppa, R, Pykäläinen, J, Kujala, T, Huotilainen, M (2013) Children's Brain Responses to Sound Changes in Pseudowords in a Multifeature Paradigm. *Clinical Neurophysiology*, 124 (6) (June): 1132–1138.

Pina, F, Flavia, M and Patrizia, O (2013) Relationship between Weak Central Coherence and Mental States Understanding in Children with Autism and in Children with ADHD. *Mediterranean Journal of Clinical Psychology (MJCP)*, 1 (1): 1–19.

Pinker, S (1994) *The Language Instinct: How the Mind Creates Language.* London: Penguin Books.

Rose, J (2006) *Independent Review of the Teaching of Early Reading.* Nottingham: Department for Education and Skills.

Schneider, W and Pressley, M (1989) *Memory Development between 2 and 20.* New York: Springer.

Siegler, R and Alibali, M W (2005) *Children's Thinking* (4th ed). New Jersey: Pearson Education International.

Stern, D, Spieker, S and Mackain, C (1982) Intonation Contours as Signals in Maternal Speech to Pre-linguistic Infants. *Developmental Psychology*, 18: 727–735.

Tomasello, M (2008) *The Origins of Human Communication.* Cambridge, MA: Massachusetts Institute of Technology Press.

Trehub, S E and Rabinouitch, M (1972) Auditory-Linguistic Sensitivity in Early Infancy. *Developmental Psychology*, 6: 74–77.

Werker, J and Tees, R (1984) Cross Language Speech Perception: Evidence for Perceptual Reorganisation during the First Year of Life. *Infant Behaviour and Development*, 7: 49–63.

Yr Adran Plant, Addysg, Dysgu Gydol Oes a Sgiliau (Department for Children, Education, Lifelong Learning Skills) (2008) *Framework for Children's Learning for 3–7 Year Olds in Wales.* Cardiff: Llywodraeth Cynulliad Cymru (Welsh Assembly Government).

3 The oral tradition

Alice thought to herself, 'Then there's no use in speaking.' The voices didn't join in this time, as she hadn't spoken, but to her great surprise, they all thought in chorus (I hope you understand what thinking in chorus means – for I must confess that I don't). 'Better say nothing at all. Language is worth a thousand pounds a word!'
(Lewis Carroll, *Alice through the Looking Glass*, 2015, pp 43–44)

Introduction

How children learn to speak is a truly remarkable phenomenon, and an amazing feat of complexity which we do not yet fully understand. Imagine for a moment the cacophony of noise that hits the ear of a newborn baby as s/he emerges into the world. Now close your eyes and consider the sounds that you hear right now: it could be a car going past, a clock ticking, workmen drilling or hammering, the fridge whirring or the radio playing; from this discordance of sound a baby needs to isolate speech sounds, break them down into words, understand what they mean and when all of that is under way, to work out how to reassemble the words into creative and recognisable language...wow! This chapter examines the process of sound production that allows the formation of human language, and the cognitive development that ensures meaningful communication.

Origins of expressive language

Expressive language probably only evolved because it was in some way an evolutionary advantage to the early hominids. What these advantages were we can only speculate, as there is no concrete archaeological evidence to prove this. However, Corballis (2002) provides a well-reasoned series of hypotheses that are based on the idea that sound is more accessible than gesture. Corballis (2002) suggests that some of these advantages include that speech can be effective in the dark, or when we cannot see each other (when in another room or when our back is turned). This allowed early man to hunt at night or at a distance from the pack. On the contrary, sound and speech can also be a disadvantage, alerting prey as to your whereabouts, whereas silent gesture does not. Corballis (2002) also suggests that speech frees up our hands to do other things. In today's terms, it allows us to communicate while holding the baby, carrying the shopping or driving the car etc. Corballis (2002) also proposed, somewhat controversially, that the remarkable ancient cave drawings discovered by archaeologists are the result of the advent of speech, freeing the hands to draw and use tools more effectively.

> *The final achievement of autonomous speech freed the hands and opened up the full potential for manufacture, pedagogy, and cultural transmission of information. But this achievement is unlikely to have depended on a sudden biological change. Rather, the adaptations necessary for autonomous speech were probably in place 100,000 years earlier with the emergence of Homo Sapiens in Africa. Vocalization must have played a prominent role in language even then, for otherwise the biological adaptations necessary to produce sounds would scarcely have evolved. Nevertheless my guess is that language still depended in part on manual and facial gestures as well as on vocal accompaniment, perhaps as recently as 50,000 years ago.*
>
> (Corballis, 2002, pp 97–98)

You have already read in Chapter 1 how special language development is, and it is unique to humans, having evolved alongside our more general cognitive, neural and social development. However, the special nature of language is that we seem to have an overwhelming need to 'get in touch'; it is like a compulsion in us, unlike any other species on the planet. This desire to communicate appears to go beyond a survival technique, and is just for the apparent enjoyment of the process. It seems that we do it because we can!

Anatomy of vocalisation

The muscular control required to create words and sounds is impressive. In fact all you are doing when you talk is pushing air through a series of tubes and spaces of different lengths and diameters. It is a bit like the difference between blowing through a thin plastic tube or down a piece of guttering. However, as you speak, you have to change the pitch and frequency of the sound, and this produces the intonation which distinguishes human speech from that of robots and computers. This is particularly important in 'tonal languages' such as Mandarin Chinese and Vietnamese, where the change in the tone of a word can change its meaning, even if it is pronounced in the same way.

It is generally accepted that there are seven vocal articulators needed to produce speech:

1. the pharynx;
2. the soft palate, which closes off the nasal cavity and enables us to breathe and eat without choking;
3. the hard palate, which is the roof of the mouth;
4. the alveolar ridge, situated behind the teeth;
5. the tongue;

6. the teeth;

7. lips, which can readily change the resonance of the speech sounds.

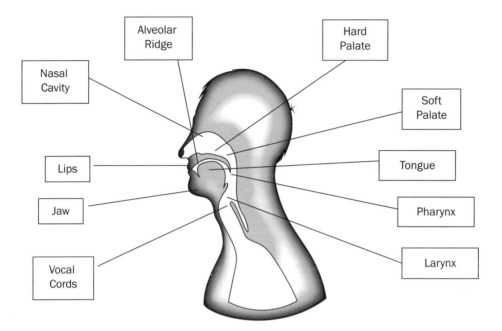

Figure 3.1 *Vocal articulators.*

However, there are also three other areas which can contribute to the changing sounds which are not usually described as articulators:

1. the jaw;

2. the nose and nasal cavity;

3. the larynx, the primary function of which is to stop food from getting into the lungs and causing choking.

Pinker (1994) suggests that the tongue is the most important organ of speech. The tongue is one large muscular structure, capable of making movements both vertical and horizontal at the rate of up to nine per second. Pinker (1994) describes the tongue as three organs in one:

1. the hump or body, with a blade front and back;

2. the tip;

3. the root.

The tongue allows the exit of the air from the lungs to be channelled for longer, or down a narrower outlet, by changing the shape of the throat and mouth. The flow of air can also be interrupted by the teeth or the lips.

> *To articulate a phoneme, the commands must be executed with precise timing, the most complicated gymnastics are called upon to perform.*
>
> (Pinker, 1994, p 171)

It should be remembered that the articulation equipment in a baby is very different from that of an adult or an older child. In the first instance there are likely to be no teeth, and the cavities are smaller and not always shaped in quite the same way.

Vitally, the production of speech and its understanding requires the brain to extract the meaning from a highly variable acoustic signal, taking into account the variability of speech sounds, including the difference between male and female pitch, tempo, accent and dialect. The brain also needs to counteract such contextual features as background noise and competing speech messages. Because you do this all the time, and usually do not give it a second thought, it is tempting to think that the co-ordination of the muscles required for articulation is easy. In fact, speech is such a complex human motor activity involving the co-ordination of breathing, voice, resonance and pitch, it requires hundreds of muscles to work within millisecond timing.

> *Speech is unique to humans and there are significant specialisms that have evolved for speech processing in the human brain that cannot be readily studied in animal models.*
>
> (Pasley and Knight, 2013, p 4)

Language and the brain

The language system of the brain is divided into two main areas, the Wernicke's area and the Broca's area. These two areas are connected to each other by nerve fibres called the arcuate fasciculus. This produces a loop from one area to the other, often referred to as the 'language loop'. This loop is usually in the left hemisphere of the brain (about 90 per cent of cases), but may occasionally vary if the child is left handed.

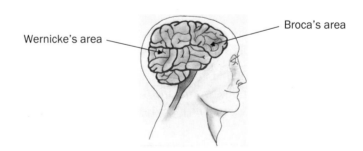

Wernicke's area

Broca's area

Figure 3.2 *Main areas of the brain for language development.*

We know this because in the cases where these areas have been damaged, aphasic symptoms can occur, with impairment to expressive and/or receptive language (Pasley and Knight, 2013). In receptive language, the brain's role is to convert sound to meaning. However, for expressive language to occur this has to go much further, and the articulatory representations are processed in the frontal lobe of the Broca's area, stimulating the activation of the muscles of the vocal organs. This can be augmented with higher level control of articulation, which involves gestures and lexical, syntactic and phonological information processing (Pasley and Knight, 2013).

Results from research by Pasley et al (2012), from the University of California, provide insight into the higher order neural speech processes, and suggest that it may in the future be possible to 'read out' intended speech directly from the brain. Participants in the research, who were all undergoing neural surgery for other medical conditions, were played a recorded single word (unknown to the researcher). The researcher then had to successfully predict the word based on the electrode wave recordings. They were then able to use these waves to reproduce an electronic sound, close enough to the original to be able to correctly guess the word. This emerging new work is a complex extension of neuroprosthetics where people control movement of prosthetic limbs with brain activity, simply by thinking of the action required. Clearly this is a very exciting step in technology, which could potentially help those with conditions such as locked-in syndrome, muscular dystrophy and motor neuron disease – like Professor Stephen Hawking – to communicate more easily.

Babbling

Over the years researchers have debated over whether babbling is just a type of oral motor skill, like crying and chewing, or whether it really is an essential precursor to language. Some writers, such as Santrock (2001), do believe that babbling is an important first stage to speech and articulation, exercising and honing the muscles of the lips, tongue, larynx and pharynx.

> *The purpose of a baby's earliest communication, however, is to attract attention from parents and others in the environment. Infants engage the attention of others by making or breaking eye contact, by vocalizing sounds, and by performing manual actions such as pointing. All of these behaviours involve pragmatics.*
> (Santrock, 2001, p 21)

Holowkas and Petitto (2002), through the use of close observation and electrode recordings, saw babies smiling, yawning, crying and also making the repetitive sounds of babbling. They noted that the language areas of the brain were active only when the babies were babbling, and thereby concluded that babbling was a fundamental linguistic activity. Pinker (1994) likened this stage in a baby to an adult who has been given a complex piece of audio equipment,

> *Bristling with unlabelled knobs and switches but missing the instruction manual.*
> (Pinker, 1994, p 266)

O'Grady (2005) suggests that although babies are undoubtedly born being aware of their mother tongue and the variety of sounds made by it (as you read in Chapter 2), it is most likely that it is the intonation of their home language and the frequency of sounds within that language that they recognise, rather than the actual words made. So if the 'P' sound is more frequent in one language than another, then the 'P' sound will occur more frequently in the babbling of the baby for whom it is their first language. Controversially, O'Grady (2005) believes that the idea that babies are born with the ability to produce all human language sounds is a myth, and that in fact they are at this stage not even able to produce all the sounds that will eventually be required of their home language.

First words

It used to be thought that recognisable language development began with the child's first words, but language specialists such as Corballis (2002) now realise that language development is not a kind of awakening, whereby one day the child says 'da da' and all language springs from this moment. Rather it is an emerging process starting with receptive language in the womb. As the understanding and comprehension develops, so does the apparently innate imperative to communicate themselves in a pre-linguistic stage.

Imagine yourself as a newborn baby emerging into the world; prior to birth you had been able to hear sounds and language, but this must have been muffled and dulled by the amniotic fluid in which you were floating. However, the moment of birth must produce a sensory overload as you hit searing lights and acute sounds, with often intense emotional excitement in those around you. Imagine for a moment how it might feel to cry out and for the first time hear your own voice. Initially it must be a really strange sensation, and you are probably not even aware that the noise that you hear is of your own making, or that you have the power to control that sound, even the on/off switch.

Eilers and Oller (1976) demonstrated how good babies were at identifying words from a string of sound. They played two minutes of speech type nonsense sounds to the babies, where the sounds were all run together:

> *Dapikutiladoturpiogolabu...dapikuturpiotiladogolabu...turpiodapikuttilodogolabu*

They then played some nonsense three syllable 'words'; some of these were not contained in the original tape and would be new to the children, but 'turpio' was in the original passage. Look again at the passage and see if you can find it. 'Turpio' appears three times, and the children focused more on this 'word' than on the new 'words'. Eilers and Oller (1976) concluded that this indicated that they were distinguishing this particular 'word' from the other string of sounds.

Crying as communication

Eventually baby discovers that making noise is satisfying, even fascinating, and that it produces interesting reactions in the other humans around them. Crying is probably their first primitive sound, frequently emerging at birth with a lusty cry. As an adult you often associate crying with distress, pain and unhappiness, but crying can at times be a satisfying experience. How many of you have cried at a 'weepy' film and then said how much you have loved it, or cried with happiness upon receiving a sentimental gift or watching children perform in the school play? As a child I loved to watch the TV programme 'Lassie', a rough collie that always 'saved the day', but I always had a good cry at the end of the show. Crying is probably an expressive experience, indicating extreme emotion, an external sign of inner feelings. Crying is very powerful even in adults, and an adult found crying will elicit controlling feelings in those around them, usually producing sympathetic behaviours on their behalf. Crying babies soon discover that this behaviour elicits instant reactions in their carers, not always positive, but reactions and attention nevertheless. Crying brings your carer running to you, often picking you up; cuddling, rocking and talking to you; giving you food; and paying you attention in the form of nappy changes, etc. This is a potential tool for interacting with the outside world; in fact at such an early age, it may be their only tool to manipulate their immediate environment.

Another important role of crying is to exercise the muscles of the lips, tongue, larynx and pharynx, which need to be finely tuned if speech is to be achieved. Instead of just opening your mouth and sound coming out, you need to be able to control that sound, control the speed at which the air passes over your tongue, between the teeth and around the hollow cavity of the mouth.

Vowels and consonants

Crying is the most common sound made by a baby in those first weeks, and it is not until approximately 1–2 months that laughing and gurgling emerge as the baby gains more anatomical control over the muscles of articulation. Listening to a young baby alone in a cot, cooing and gurgling to itself, you can almost imagine that they are practising their scales like a musician, as they change pitch, tone and volume. In these early stages the sounds made are largely open mouthed vowel sounds such as ooo, ooo, ooo, uuu, uuu, uuu, aaa. Baby plays with these sounds enjoying a newly found ability to hear their own voice. Some anthropologists, such as Saxton (2010), have suggested that one crucial difference between humans and apes is the ability to voice the consonant sounds, and to use the lips and tongue to produce the P, T, C, M and N, sounds. Certainly other primates are incapable of making these sounds, and as you read in the first chapter, the research undertaken on primate communication had to involve teaching sign language rather than attempting to train apes to talk.

Consonant sounds in humans do not usually appear before 6–7 months of age. At around this time you will also hear the baby combining these sounds to form speech-like noises, and the baby plays with sounds, repetition and echolalia...da, da, da, da, ma, ma, ma, ma etc. This is the babbling that is probably the precursor to speech, and the intonation which the baby puts to this can often be similar to the intonation in the child's future mother tongue. Bates and MacWhinney (1987, p 157) called this the 'learning time before the words'. It is also at this time that the two way process of conversation emerges, and you can hear in the babbling the rise in intonation at the end of sound patterns that is akin to adult conversation. When you are talking and expecting a reply, you pass over the baton of language to your conversation partner to indicate that you are now in receptive language mode, by raising the intonation of your voice; your partner recognises that this is their cue to respond.

Symbolism and representation

Before you can utter your first meaningful words you have to understand symbolism. This means that you understand that a sound can be a symbol, or a cognitive representation of a concrete object, that can be used flexibly across a range of appropriate referential situations. For example, the sound 'dog' can be applied when you see a dog walking down the road. In other words the sound is context bound. However, a huge developmental leap comes when you are able to use the sound even when you do *not* see the concrete object, and understand that those around you know what you are thinking about and referring to. Bee and Boyd (2011) suggest that most children make this leap of understanding at around 13 months of age.

Smith et al (2003) suggest that even if sounds are not conventional words, if the child uses a sound consistently to refer to a particular object, context or activity, it can be considered to be a word. This becomes particularly relevant when the adult carer also uses the word. So the baby that refers to their comforter as a 'Nu Nu' is requesting the comforter or labelling it in a way that is reinforced by the adult who asks *'Do you want your Nu Nu?'*

Holophrase theory

At this stage the child is using one word at a time, but according to the context, their physical gestures or their intonation and pitch as well, and this word can mean a variety of things. For example, the word *'dog'* can mean:

- *I can see the dog* (label);

- *The dog has taken my comforter* (information);

- *I want the dog to come here* (request);

- *Take the dog away* (demand).

From this small example you can see that a single word can condense a myriad of meaning. This is sometimes referred to as the 'holophrase theory', where single words imply whole sentences. As the child matures these one word utterances become 'telegraphic speech', which means combining words to refine the sense, for example *'Doggie go'* can mean:

- *The dog is going*;

  or

- *I want the dog to go.*

Although the development of overtly expressive language starts slowly, from this point on it begins to grow rapidly, and an explosion of new words takes place. At the height of the vocabulary spurt children are incredibly capable of learning one or two words an hour, week after week, often needing to hear them only once (O'Grady, 2005). This is a truly amazing rate of learning.

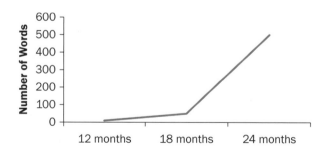

Figure 3.3 *Rate of vocabulary spurt, adapted from O'Grady (2005, p 8).*

Word strings

Alongside this vocabulary spurt comes a similar pattern in combining words into word strings or rudimentary sentences. Like learning individual words, this starts slowly but at about 15–18 months of age increases rapidly (O'Grady, 2005). O'Grady (2005) describes combining words into sentences as upside down trees with the branches that spread out endlessly, so that there is no limit to their length or combination.

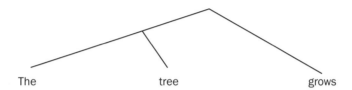

The   tree   grows

Figure 3.4 *Example of O'Grady's upside down word tree.*

You might be reminded of the children's rhyme, 'The House that Jack Built', where adding a new word each time means that the sentences get longer and longer.

> *This is the house that Jack built.*
>
> *This is the malt*
>
> *That lay in the house that Jack built.*
>
> *This is the rat,*
>
> *That ate the malt*
>
> *That lay in the house that Jack built.*
>
> *This is the cat,*
>
> *That killed the rat,*
>
> *That ate the malt*
>
> *That lay in the house that Jack built.*
>
> *This is the dog,*
>
> *That worried the cat,*
>
> *That killed the rat,*
>
> *That ate the malt*
>
> *That lay in the house that Jack built...and so on.*

These first combinations of words usually start with a one word 'hook', that is, one word that focuses the sentence, and then others appear either side of it to offer greater meaning. For example, you could gradually add prepositions, definite article, pronouns etc.

> *Go (the word hook).*
>
> *Daddy go.*
>
> *Daddy go car.*
>
> *Daddy go red car.*
>
> *No daddy go red car.*

Typically the first words expressed are objects and actions that are meaningful to the child and their life...mama, dada, juice, toast, gone, come etc. However, increasingly functional words begin to emerge, enabling the child to contextualise the meaning, and place emphasis where it is needed...more, happy, sad, give etc. Interestingly this appears to be consistent across continents and throughout history (Santrock, 2001 and Pinker, 1994).

Developmental milestones

While it is useful to see the order of language developmental milestones, it must be remembered that a chart such as the one in Table 3.1 is one of averages, and all children are different. Some will wait much longer before starting to talk, and they usually appear to be no worse off when they do talk than those who speak earlier. Controversially, according to Lenneberg et al (1965) and Corballis (2002), this is largely determined by biological maturation, and not influenced by reinforcement or their ability to hear, and even totally deaf babies go through a babbling stage. However, the very fact that such a chart can be produced recognises that the sequence of children's language development is usually predictable (although not always in a linear pattern), regardless of race, culture or social status. Several stages may emerge at the same time, alongside each other, or even overlap; however, it is true to say that almost without exception, babbling comes before single words, single words come before telegraphic speech and telegraphic speech comes before complex sentences, syntax etc.

Such a linear chart would make sense if language development was purely innately or genetically controlled, but as you read in Chapter 1, the environmental influences also take their place. Learning and social context undoubtedly play an influential role in the speed and path of language development. The risk with producing a developmental chart, such as Table 3.1, is that account is not taken of that environmental role, and the child can be labelled, and placed into an inappropriate 'pigeonhole' at a very early stage. This in turn can initiate the 'self-fulfilling prophecy', whereby if little is expected of a child, then little will occur. It may also trigger expensive intervention programmes, which may be totally unsuitable or unnecessary. Such charts usually take no account of gender differences, cultural or social contexts.

Table 3.1 Language milestones.

Estimated age	Language related behaviour	Stage
Under 1 month	Crying, gurgling, coughing, grunting and sneezing.	Phonation stage
1–2 months	Laughing, cooing and fussing. Vowel sounds apparent.	
3–5 months	Squeals, grunts, yells, raspberries and whispering. Consonant sounds appear.	Canonical stage
6–7 months	Starts to 'play' with sounds. Babbling and echolalia.	
8–9 months	Starts to combine consonant sounds with vowels. Gestural language developing alongside verbal communication.	
10–12 months	Receptive language develops, and an understanding of the symbolic nature of language appears.	Integrative stage
12 months	Sounds that do not appear in the mother tongue begin to drop out.	
11–13 months	First individual words appear.	
13–17 months	Vocabulary of approximately 20–30 expressive words, but many more receptive words understood.	
17–23 months	Vocabulary of approximately 100–200 expressive words. Two word utterances appear. Telegraphic speech common.	
24–27 months	Three and four word utterances appear.	
28–36 months	Start of a morphemic structure to language with endings such as *ing* and plurals.	
36–48 months	Questions are prevalent.	
40–46 months	Simple sentences and tense appear.	
42–52 months	More complex sentences. Contractions such as isn't, couldn't etc.	
5–6 years	Vocabulary of approximately 14,000 words, both receptive and expressive. Full phonological proficiency.	
6–18 years	Could be learning up to 20 new words a day.	
18 years	Typically at this age there will be a usable vocabulary of approximately 60,000 words.	

Parentese

The one thing that we do know is that parents the world over do want to communicate with their babies, and are usually prepared to do what it takes to instigate that communication. Parentese is a manner of speaking which you have already come across in Chapter 2, and involves an element of 'baby talk'. The pitch is higher, the pace is slower, with short, grammatically simple sentences, and key words are placed at the end of sentences for emphasis, and it is highly repetitive usually referring to objects or people who are immediately present. Bee and Boyd (2011) suggest that babies are attracted to the high pitch, and can distinguish between this and adult directed speech.

Despite the fact that most adults (and older peers) do use this form of adapted language code, there are some communities and cultures where it is not seen in use (Heath, 1983). This would imply that although possibly useful for learning to speak, it is not an essential element. Heath (1983) showed that in one Afro-American community, the adults did not even have 'conversations' with babies or young children, yet these children still learned their home language, without any special help. O'Grady (2005) suggests that children will learn language on their own when they are ready, in the same way that they will learn to sit, stand and walk. What they need is the opportunity to do so, and exposure to a language rich environment which puts words into an understandable 'here and now' experience, with repeated exposure to the adult use of words.

Phonology

The term phonology is used to describe the way that sounds are stored and organised in the child's brain, and their knowledge of the rules of sounds of words and their sequence within speech. The child will need to understand that sequences such as *sr* or *ta* are acceptable but *zx* or *qb* are unlikely. This understanding allows the child to construct thousands and thousands of words from a few dozen phonemes. Paul and Jennings' research in 1992 showed that children under three years of age, with poor phonological awareness, were at increased risk of slow expressive language development, resulting in deficiency in their later lexical, syntactical and phonological development. This in turn put them at greater risk of long-term language, academic and social difficulties.

Understanding that words can be broken down into individual sounds allows a child to develop more complex and higher level skills of articulation and understanding, such as:

*   Alliteration...Lazy lizards lie low.
*   Rhyme...King, fling, ring.
*   Phoneme deletion and isolation...What is slap without the 's'? (*lap*)
*   Phoneme reversal...What is *was* backwards? (*saw*)
*   Phoneme manipulation (adding or deleting sounds to form new words)...ton/to, at/cat, dog/log, etc.

Producing the range of sounds required for language is difficult both anatomically and neuro-logically and requires a great deal of practice and precise muscle co-ordination. Some sounds (such as sh...th...sr) do appear to be more problematic to produce than others and require more flexibility and manipulation of the sound-producing organs. Children prevented from prac-tising these movements, possibly for medical or dental reasons, are according to Siegler and Alibali (2005) temporarily unable to produce meaningful articulation, despite having normal understanding and receptive language. When they regain their muscle control, they have to exercise the muscles for some time before they have sufficient control to articulate normally.

Syntax

While the child learns individual words quite easily, it is clear that until they can string them together this is not language as we know it. The production of expressive language requires more than just the physical articulators, and language starts in the brain as a complex cog-nitive process. First, the brain needs to visualise and conceptualise what it is to say, which then needs to be converted to recognisable words from an appropriate language, a process known as 'lexicalisation'. Crucially these words need to be arranged in the right order, which is 'syntactic planning'. This is reminiscent of the late, great comedian Eric Morecambe in the television sketch in 1971, with Andre Previn (the internationally renowned musician and con-ductor). Morecambe played the piano very badly, and when questioned by Previn said that he was indeed playing all the right notes, just not necessarily in the right order! Words have to be in the right order for them to make sense. Groups of words have to be grammatically constructed or syntactical to ensure meaning and hence communication:

>
> *Dog with Bethan the walked.*
>
> or
>
> *Bethan walked with the dog.*

All languages have some form of grammar connected to them, and by grammar I am referring to a mutually agreed order for the words. This implies that syntax is only an issue for the child once they have reached the stage of putting two or more words together into word strings. According to Pinker (1994) we know that children understand a sentence, using syntax, *before* they are able to express the words. An example of this can be seen when reading a story to a child who is at the one word production stage, where they will probably understand the following:

> *The Hungry Caterpillar ate the chocolate cake...can you show me what he ate?*

The child will point to the cake, implying that they understand that the sequence of words is important, and that the cake did not eat the caterpillar.

$$\text{SUBJECT} \longrightarrow \text{VERB} \longrightarrow \text{OBJECT}$$

If you consider that there are an almost infinite number of words to choose from, and an equally infinite number of ways to combine these words, you can begin to understand the complexity of the process of generating grammar. Even with a very small number of words, there are several ways to combine them which might change their meaning.

Boy rides horse.

Horse rides boy.

Rides boy horse.

Boy horse rides.

Of these very simple three word examples, three are feasibly grammatically correct; however, only one makes contextual sense. So what this means is that sentences can be grammatically correct without making sense. You can return to Chapter 1 and Chomsky's contrived sentence which while grammatically correct makes no obvious sense:

Colourless green ideas sleep furiously.

If you increase the number of words in a sentence to 20 (probably a mean number for an adult communicator), the number of word combinations is breath-taking. Pinker (1994) estimates that the number of sentences that one person can create is ten[20] or a hundred million trillion!

At a rate of five seconds a sentence, a person would need a childhood of about one hundred trillion years (with no time for eating or sleeping) to memorize them all.

(Pinker, 1994, p 86)

Grammatical phases

In 1973, Brown divided the process of developing grammar into phases:

Phase 1: telegraphic speech

Very early words strings (two–three words) that consist mostly of nouns and verbs with some adjectives. The inflections, which give a sentence a grammatical context, are missing, for example 's' for plural, 'ed' for past tense, 'ing', auxiliary verbs, prepositions, the article, etc.

Phase 2: grammar

Inflection begins to emerge, although slowly at first. With this come questions and negatives. Rules for language production are clearly being adhered to, and even though these rules may not be correct, they are at this stage consistent. This produces the tendency for overgeneralisations or virtuous errors, so that having learned that by adding 'ed' to the end of the word it generally puts it into the past tense, the child may use a word that s/he has never heard, but nevertheless conforms to a logical grammar:

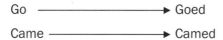

With the same logic the child learns that adding an 's' generally makes a plural:

Phase 3: later grammar

Overgeneralisations disappear and more complex sentence structures become evident.

In 1958 Jean Berko-Gleason conducted a research study into linguistic morphology which she called the 'Wug Test'. A Wug was an imaginary creature; she told the children that this was a Wug and then asked what would be the word for more than one Wug. By 4–5 years of age most of the children said 'Wugs'; however, children of 2–3 years of age were unable to do this and frequently said 'two Wug'.

Figure 3.5 *The 'Wug Test', adapted from Berko-Gleason (1958).*

Other language tests that Berko-Gleason conducted were:

> *'This is a man who knows how to SPOW. He is SPOWING. He did the same thing yesterday.*
>
> *What did he do yesterday?'*

> *'This WUG lives in a house.*
>
> *What would you call a house that a WUG lives in?'*

> *'This is a dog with QUIRKS on him.*
>
> *He is covered with QUIRKS.*
>
> *What kind of dog is he?'*

Critical questions

» *Does this test prove that children are able to make productive use of linguistic rules?*

» *How does this relate to Chomsky's theory of a Language Acquisition Device (LAD)?*

» *Do you think that the children's responses depend upon their rate of exposure to irregular words and correction by adults?*

There have been many critics of Berko-Gleason, and Taylor (2003) contends that the WUG test is a myth. The Berko-Gleason research was certainly not conclusive and did not appear to apply to all languages. Taylor's research (2003) was centred upon Japanese speakers, and he was unable to replicate the results of Berko-Gleason. He conducted experiments into children's knowledge of irregular words by presenting them to the children and asking whether they thought that they were 'silly'. The children frequently identified the overregularised words as incorrect, despite occasionally using them in their own direct speech.

Risk taking

Risk taking is something that you probably normally associate with physical activities, but all new learning involves risk, that is, the risk of not succeeding. A sensitive and empathetic practitioner will understand that a number of successful attempts are necessary for ultimate success, and will help to create an atmosphere where this can occur safely, both physically and emotionally. Risk in life is inevitable, and being able to take risks with language is as fundamental to good language acquisition as taking physical risks is to physical development.

Imagine that you are a Welsh language learner; in class you are doing really well, understanding the teacher when s/he speaks slowly and with simple terminology. You decide to go on holiday to Anglesey in an area where there are a large number of first language Welsh speakers. Before your holiday you are determined that this will be your great opportunity to use your new learning and extend your understanding of Welsh. The trouble is that when you get there and go into a shop, you feel too self-conscious to use your Welsh. You are unprepared to take the risk of the shop keeper laughing at you, belittling your attempts, ignoring you, or worse still being unprepared to take the time to listen carefully to your well thought through sentences. You tentatively say good morning 'Bore da' but get no further. This is not a lack of ability to process the language, but more a reluctance to respond and take the risk.

If I were to give you a new word, one that you are completely unfamiliar with both in its sound and meaning, you would need to remember that word tomorrow and be able to use the word, in context, and within conversation. That is just one word; imagine that I give you nine new words, and the next day another nine etc. I wonder how many you will remember by the end of the week, and how many you will continue to use from your lexicon? Do you feel comfortable about using new words or are you afraid that people will laugh at you if you get it wrong, or 'take the mickey' about you having 'swallowed a dictionary'? Put into this context you can see that a child learning language at this rate takes immense risks with their self-esteem and feelings of self-worth.

As the child grows and matures there will be an increasing number of people involved with them, from a widening circle of family and friends, to those involved in healthcare, welfare and education, and feeling able to take risks with the language used is fundamental to good language acquisition. At this stage the child needs to feel safe and secure, accepted, understood and valued. As a practitioner you need to consider what this means for your personal practice, and how you can create a climate within your setting that promotes responsible risk taking in the children. In other areas of development children are innately risk takers – the baby reaches forward into the unknown to touch the rattle, they take their first faltering steps – and this is one way in which they discover the world and learn.

However, failure, depending upon how it is managed, can also be an important aspect of the learning process for all of us. Risk taking involves decision-making choices. The child has to decide what to say in a given situation, but there is always uncertainty of the outcome and of the decision made. Statistically the more the child speaks, the more situations for potential failure they expose themselves to. Children need to try out their language, matching their skills to the demands of the environment, and if you try to create a completely risk free environment it is possible that children will become reluctant to take the risks. As a practitioner, you need to be aware not only of the uncertainty of a risk, but also of the importance of taking these risks to overall learning experiences. All children are different, with different temperaments and personalities, but you need to encourage all the children in your care to become thoughtful risk takers in all aspects of their life, including academic risk. The spin off from this is that the good, thoughtful risk takers are more likely to be confident, with increasing independence of thought, taking on new challenges and learning new things in all areas of their development.

Critical questions

Consider for a moment whether you have ever laughed at a child when they have used a word inappropriately and it has sounded funny. When children are first experimenting with their expressive language they often do make mistakes. How would you feel if that were you? Upset perhaps, embarrassed or humiliated. Would this encourage you to try again, or would you feel too self-conscious to try out the new word, unless you felt that you were in very safe company?

» *Work with a colleague to consider how best to approach this situation.*

» *How would you advise a less experienced member of staff that you heard laughing at a child's errors?*

» *Should you try to understand everything that a child is saying to you, or should you deliberately pretend not to understand, until they have said the word/sentence correctly?*

Managed risk

To create a setting with an environment where managed risk is seen as acceptable to children, it is important to consider five golden rules:

1. Encourage a positive self-image in all children.

2. Support all staff to develop a quiet, listening environment by allowing the children time to talk, valuing their contribution and speaking slowly and clearly to them.

3. Promote co-operative activities where children and adults can work together.

4. Foster a climate of independence and co-operative problem solving.

5. Inspire positive and respectful surroundings.

Some children despite all their efforts find expressive language difficult, and particular difficulties can occur with deafness and central processing disorders which are physical or neurological in origin. However, emotional and social effects can also inhibit expressive language, and one such disorder is selective mutism, which is a multidimensional childhood anxiety disorder, whereby children who have the *ability* to speak and communicate are unable to do so in particular social circumstances, for example nursery/school. It is important to emphasise that these children are not deliberately choosing not to speak, or being difficult or anti-social, but find themselves unable to do so because of anxiety and nervousness in that situation. These children fear speaking to others and taking the risks involved, and they are often very anxious children with inhibited temperaments.

CASE STUDY

Shona

Some years ago when I was teaching in a nursery class in a Liverpool school, a young girl joined the group of 20 other children. She was three years old and her mother did not intimate that there was anything amiss when she registered her.

Shona (as I shall call her) arrived on the first day and went straight to the dressing up clothes, where she donned a pair of high heeled shoes and a handbag. She then headed for the sand tray, where she stood for the whole morning, running the sand through her fingers. Despite my efforts, and that of the teaching assistant, to engage her in conversation, she did not communicate with either the adults or the other children in the class. At first I put this down to first day nerves, but as the days turned to weeks and months this ritual became the norm, and I felt that it was time to talk to the parent, who assured me that her daughter spoke fluently and frequently at home, but that she was just 'shy'.

Shona thwarted all our efforts to engage her with other activities, other children, other members of staff and other topics of conversation. This lasted nearly 12 months before the breakthrough, when she spoke one word in a whisper to the teaching assistant. By the time she left the nursery for Reception class, she was able to whisper one-to-one, to all the familiar full-time staff with whom she felt secure. However, she was still unable to speak in a group setting, at circle time or with the other children.

Critical questions

» As a practitioner with a child with selective mutism in your care, how can you balance the concern and anxiety that you and the family feel for this child, with the need to reassure them and develop their confidence and self-esteem?

» How can you reassure the parent of such a child?

» At what point do you think that specialist teaching should be deployed?

» How would you advise the other staff working with this child, if they are becoming frustrated with her?

» Should you explain to the other children if they ask why she is not participating in language activities?

Chapter reflections

Children do appear to learn to talk effortlessly and without formal teaching; however, it is important to remember that although children are autonomous constructors of language, they do need the adults who surround them, in the nursery and at home, to nurture and encourage them to use and express language. What children need is evidence for the need for language and its use; they also need feedback on their own *linguistic ability and opportunities to practise their skills in secure and pressure-free environments. Wells (1985) showed that exposure to the sheer quantity of language was what was important to produce a speaker, and in his research showed that the most competent speakers heard up to ten times more expressive language than the least competent.*

Learning to talk is arguably the greatest learning feat that a child ever accomplishes, but there is no one right way in which this will happen, and the diversity of language with different accents, dialects and language varieties is testament to this. All need to be respected and seen as a valuable resource upon which the child can build and grow, taking it into all other areas of their holistic development.

This chapter has focused upon the child's awareness of the significance of the communicability of language and the importance of being able to segment the speech flow into phonemes, words and identifiable units. It has also demonstrated the intercorrelation between lexical and syntactical development.

You have read about some of the key research areas of a complex and extensive topic, but this cursory glance may not have always done justice to an area that is sometimes difficult to understand, and contains technical vocabulary and new ideas. The basic concepts that you have read should now guide your further reading, and should encourage you to investigate further how you can use your own expressive language to guide and model for the children in your care.

In Chapter 2 you read about how hearing and understanding a sound or a word was so important, but of course this is not the same as creating one and speaking out loud. This is an enormous leap in the acquisition of language, and in the next chapter you will read about another great advance in the development of the language rich child, that of reading.

DEVELOPING CRITICAL THINKING

When you are reading an academic argument you must take nothing for granted. You need to question what you read in the light of what you have read before, and also from your own perspective as a practitioner.

Consider whether what you are reading makes sense to you from your own experience. If not, try to work out why not, for example your experience could be:

- limited to a particular area;
- limited to a particular age group;
- specific to a culture;
- within a narrow social class;
- because you are newly out of college and have limited experience etc.

You will also need to consider the arguments from the perspective of the researcher, for example perhaps their research has:

- been curtailed by a particular situation;

- illogical flaws in the arguments;

- been financially supported and sponsored; for example, a commercial manufacturer may be more likely to sponsor research that puts their product in a particularly good light, and thereby create bias;

- been conducted on a very small or skewed sample.

You need to consider the evidence offered by the researcher and weigh this up by considering whether there could be an alternative explanation for the findings given. Above all, when you are reading you need to keep an open mind and remember that just because it is written in a book or a journal (no matter how prestigious), it does not necessarily mean that it is correct. A writer may take many years to write a book, but that just means that the author has a 'bee in their bonnet' about the subject. In fact they are probably preoccupied and obsessed enough to continue researching and writing for many years; but it still does not necessarily mean that it is right. It is tempting to feel, as you probably did when you were at school, that if it is in a book it is 'gospel', but I suggest that if it is written down it is there to be challenged, subjected to rigorous scrutiny, by you and others with differing perspectives. Most academic authors write in the full knowledge that other academics will be critically analytical about their work, and write with the intention of engaging in dialogue with the reader. Do not be afraid to participate with that discourse.

Critical thinking activity

» *Make a list of what you believe to be the 20 key words from this chapter. Show these to a colleague who has not read the chapter and see whether s/he can understand what this was about. If not, return to the chapter and change some of your 20 words.*

» *Now write a paragraph to include all 20 words which will summarise the key points of what you have read.*

Further reading

O'Grady, W (2005) *How Children Learn Language.* Cambridge: Cambridge University Press.

This is a very accessible text which highlights much of the interesting research conducted into the acquisition of language, using easy-to-understand, non-technical words. It is designed to appeal to parents and students with limited prior knowledge of the field. This book looks at the issues from a range of perspectives, and you will find yourself engaged with psychology, sociology, philosophy, anthropology, speech therapy and education. The book links these divergent areas and will act as a springboard to those who wish to examine the area in more detail, through the exploration of the research papers and findings from which O'Grady meticulously draws his material.

References

Bates, E and MacWhinney, B (1987) Competition, Variation and Language Learning. In MacWhinney, B (ed) *Mechanisms of Language Acquisition.* Hillsdale, NJ: Erlbaum.

Bee, H and Boyd, D (2011) *The Developing Child* (13th ed). Essex: Pearson.

Berko-Gleason, J (1958) The Child's Learning of English Morphology. *Word*, 14: 150–177.

Brown, R (1973) *The First Language: Early Stages.* Cambridge, MA: Harvard University Press.

Carroll, Lewis (2013) (originally published 1871) *Alice through the Looking Glass.* USA: Create Space Publishing Platform.

Corballis, M (2002) *From Hand to Mouth: The Origins of Language.* Princeton, NJ: Princeton University Press.

Eilers, R E and Oller, D K (1976) The Role of Speech Discrimination in Developmental Sound Substitutes. *Journal of Child Language*, 3 (3) (October): 319–329.

Heath, S B (1983) *Ways with Words: Language, Life and Work in Communities and Classrooms.* New York: Cambridge University Press.

Holowkas, S and Petitto, L (2002) Left Hemisphere Cerebral Specialization for Babies While Babbling. *Science*, 297: 1515.

Lenneberg, E H, Rebelsky, F and Nicols, I (1965) The Vocabulary of Infants Born to Deaf and Hearing Parents. *Human Development*, 8: 23–37.

O'Grady, W (2005) *How Children Learn Language.* Cambridge: Cambridge University Press.

Pasley, B and Knight, R (2013) Decoding Speech for Understanding and Treating Aphasia. *Progress in Brain Research*, 207: 435–456.

Pasley, B, David, S, Mesgarni, N, Finker, A, Shamma, S, Crone, N, Knight, R and Chang, E (2012) Reconstructing Speech from Human Auditory Cortex. *PLoS Biology*, 10 (1) (January): e1001251.

Paul, R and Jennings, P (1992) Phonological Behaviour in Toddlers with Slow Expressive Language. *Journal of Speech and Hearing Research*, 002-4685, 35 (1) (February): 99–107.

Pinker, S (1994) *The Language Instinct: How the Mind Creates Language.* London: Penguin Books.

Santrock, J W (2001) *Child Development* (9th ed) (International Edition). New York: McGraw-Hill Higher Education.

Saxton, M (2010) *Child Language: Acquisition and Development.* London: Sage.

Siegler, R S and Alibali, M W (2005) *Children's Thinking* (4th ed). Upper Saddle River, NJ: Prentice Hall.

Smith, P, Cowie, H and Blades, M (2003) *Understanding Children's Development* (4th ed). Oxford: Blackwell.

Taylor, J (2003) *Cognitive Grammar.* New York: Oxford University Press.

Wells, G (1986) *The Meaning Makers: Children Learning Language and Using Language to Learn.* London: Hodder and Stoughton.

4 Foundations of reading

The more that you read, the more things you will know. The more that you learn, the more places you'll go.

(Dr Seuss, 1978, *I Can Read with My Eyes Shut!*)

Introduction

Man's ability to read is a relatively modern phenomenon. In the nineteenth century most people could not read and did not see that it was necessary; however, in the twenty-first century, the ability to read is crucial. Today there is a general *expectation* that all adults and young people can read. When you go into the bank to open an account, the cashier does not pass you the forms and ask whether you can read; you are expected to be able to fill these out and understand what is written on them. The mass of unsolicited post that comes through my letterbox each day is testament to an assumption from advertisers that each recipient can read.

This chapter builds upon the concepts of symbolism and representation, discussed earlier, to explore how children move from the recognition of signs and symbols to an understanding of the alphabetic code within the traditional orthography. Starting from the pre-literate stage of the baby, it will examine how you process information from the literate environment and present different theories for the acquisition of reading.

The current state of play

The National Literacy Trust (2014) suggests that less than 1 per cent of the adults in England are completely illiterate, but approximately 16 per cent (ie almost 5.2 million adults) are what they describe as functionally illiterate (achieving literacy levels that would be expected of an 11 year-old). A further 1.7 million adults have literacy levels below that expected of an 11 year-old. The United Nations General Assembly in 2013 reviewed the implementation of the 'Decade of Literacy', which was central to their ideal that literacy was a *'fundamental human right'* (p 4), and essential to ensuring a good quality of life and opportunity. This report showed that internationally, a child born to a reading mother was 50 per cent more likely to survive past the age of five years, and that physical and mental health for these children was significantly improved. UNESCO (2000) agreed to halve the level of world adult illiteracy by 2015 yet they acknowledge that there are still *at least* 781 million people in the world who are not literate and most of these are women.

The latest report for Save the Children Fund, written by Warren and Paxton (2014), showed that of the children on free school meals, 4 out of 10 were unable to read well by the age of 11 years, and entered secondary education already demoralised and humiliated.

> *This is the unacceptable consequence of child poverty in the UK which is exacting both a life sentence on these children and a terrible toll on our society.*
> (Dame Julia Cleverdon, Forward to Warren and Paxton, 2014)

Although most of you *can* read, you probably cannot remember how you did it, and the ability to read is an amazing feat of human endeavour. No other species on earth can interpret patterns of 'squiggly' marks and make meaning from them; we are unique in this respect.

Why is reading important?

The ability to read is vital not only to an adult's ability to secure and hold down employment, and hence their financial security, but also to their all-round social and emotional stability, their feelings of self-esteem and confidence to take on new challenges. The feeling of shame and inadequacy, frequently expressed by adults with low literacy skills, is often extreme. This can have a direct influence on their ability to establish and maintain relationships, and hence their opportunities to create and sustain secure family units. In 2012 Shah examined the relationship between adult literacy, educational attainment, self-harm and suicide, and while it is far from proven, Shah did find an apparently strong and significant link. Low literacy also appears to predispose to mental illness and anti-social behaviour, especially where there is a mismatch between levels of intelligence and literacy. This is an aspect of literacy that needs further research, as there is possibly an important public health and cost implication to sustaining a population with such low literacy levels. Put into these terms, you can see how important it is for children to make that leap from expressive oral language, to being able to interpret the written word and to read at least to a functional level.

So what is reading?

This may seem like a strange question to ask; surely you must know what it is because you are doing it right now. But is this what you want children to be able to do?

Reading can be loosely defined as a process which involves the recognition of the printed word, with accuracy and fluency, to facilitate comprehension. A report by Warren and Paxton (2014) for Save the Children Fund used a more precise definition of 'read well', that is, children who at the end of Year 6 in schools in England are achieving level 4b (the b indicates that they are working comfortably at this level) (DfE 2014). This implies that children are reading independently and fluently, with sound understanding of both fiction and non-fiction, in a range of genre and presentations.

> *'Reading well' by the age of 11 means that children should not only be able to read the words that are written down but they should also have a wider understanding of the meaning behind the stories and information and be able to talk about them and comment on them. As well as being able to read and understand books such as Treasure Island and Harry Potter, they should also be able to read a range of different materials including magazines and newspapers, relevant websites, letters and dictionaries.*
>
> (Warren and Paxton, 2014, p 4)

However you define reading, you know that this is a complex, multidimensional, multifunctional task, requiring a range of skills and abilities to achieve. Reading is an active, connective, critical process, requiring good receptive and expressive language before it can be achieved. However, reading is not something that you do once and it is achieved. I can learn to tie my shoelaces, and once it is done I can say that I can tie shoelaces and there is very little more that I need to know about it. But reading is not like that; I can probably never say that I have finished learning to read. Although I may well be able to read a good novel, give me a tax return form and I am like a child again. Although I can probably pronounce most of the words, my level of comprehension is limited. If I am going to be able to 'read' my tax return, I am going to have to piece together the information from the marks on the page into meaningful chunks of text.

One of the problems with defining reading is that it is an unseen activity. If I were watching you now, what would I see? I would almost certainly see you looking at the book, occasionally turning pages, I may even be able to track your eye movements, but I cannot **see** you reading. I wonder how many times you have picked up a book (perhaps you are tired or it is a little bit dry and boring), and you have got to the end of the first page and realised that you know nothing about what you have just looked at. To all intents and purposes you looked as though you were reading, but if reading is about a search for meaning and understanding, then you have not read.

Santrock (2001) offers a very succinct definition of reading:

> *Reading is the ability to understand written discourse. (p 328)*

However, a cognitive-psychological definition might be slightly different, with the view that reading is just decoding words, leading to meaning. However you define reading it appears to involve meaning and understanding, and if this is right then giving children a series of flashcards of unrelated words and asking them to 'read' them is a misnomer. Consider the following words that you might present to children who are learning to read:

him

the

saw

be

Children may be able to repeat these words, but on their own they do not mean anything, and cannot be described as a discourse or a conversation for meaning.

Reading aloud

Now consider the child sitting beside you 'reading' their reading book. What are they really doing? Whatever it is, it is not exhibiting mature reading behaviour. What you are doing, as a practitioner, is assessing the child's ability to speak words aloud accurately. They may have no fluency, and will probably be unable to tell you when they get to the end of the passage, what it is they have just said aloud. This has really only been about recognition, pronunciation and an act of elocution. I wonder how you would feel if asked to read aloud to your tutor, or even worse in front of your class? Some university students tell me that they get so nervous when they read aloud that they stumble over words, have no intonation and no idea what they have been 'reading' about. This sounds similar to the child reading aloud to an adult. In this context it is easy to see that the original question 'what is reading?' is not so easy to answer.

The eyes and the brain

When you consider what a reader *does* do, you can see that reading is not only about what the eyes are doing, but also what the brain is making of the information being relayed to it. Smith (1985) talks about reading from 'behind the eyes', the brain using the prior knowledge of the subject matter and knowledge of language, syntax, semantics, graphophonics etc. Armed with this knowledge the eyes look across the line of text and the brain *infers* meaning. When your eyes move along the text they do not move smoothly, and eye tracking devices have shown that they move in stops and jumps, and even go backwards or regress, across the text again. These are called fixations and saccades.

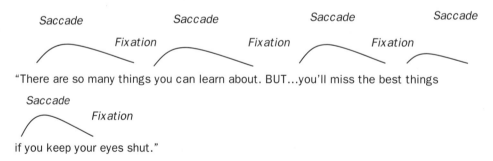

In the saccade the eye perceives a blurred image, so the information about the meaning of the text is largely gained from the fixations and the contextual, syntactic and graphophonic cues that the child knows. Oakhill and Garnham (1988) showed that the eyes continue in a left to right mode until the meaning is obscured; then the eyes will regress and scan the text again, often focusing upon individual words, with more frequent fixations until the meaning is achieved again. This can occur in as much as 10 per cent of the reading time, even in the most fluent readers.

Smith (1985) suggests that the brain can cope with only a limited amount of visual information at one time, and it is probable that at any one fixation the brain can only deal with four–five pieces of information. If that information is four–five individual letters this is going to make reading an impossible task.

$$\boxed{A \quad G \quad T \quad S \quad O}$$

However, the letters combined can form *one* piece of information.

$$\boxed{GOATS}$$

So if these letters are combined into recognisable words then the four–five pieces of information can become a whole sentence.

$$\boxed{\textbf{THE GOATS RUN AND PLAY}}$$

If the child tries to read this sentence word by word and fixate on each word, their reading will be laboured, and they will find it difficult to understand. Being able to absorb meaning from groups of words at any one time means that the brain is free to allow comprehension. Try to read the following passage and see what I mean; it is likely that your non-visual information is limited, in other words it is likely that you are unfamiliar with the content, and you will have to focus on each word as it appears. I suspect that by the end of the passage you will still be unable to understand what it means, despite all the visual information being present.

> Since the components of an eigenvector can be found from the eigenvalue equation only to within a multiplicative constant, which is later determined by normalisation, one can set $C^1 = C^2 = C$ in the equations.

This demonstrates the importance of prior knowledge and life experiences for the child as he/she begins to learn to read.

DEVELOPING CRITICAL THINKING

Critical thinking requires you to think 'outside the box', to come up with solutions to problems, however improbable they may appear to begin with. The problem is often that we see one solution to a problem, often suggested by what you have read or your existing knowledge, and this blocks out your capacity to see beyond that. If I were to ask you what you could do with a wooden kitchen chair, in all probability you would say 'sit on it'. However, if I ask you to really think about it, perhaps you would come up with:

*   use it to reach a high shelf;

*   cover it with a blanket to make a den;

*   use it as a barrier to prevent people walking through a space;

- chop it up to make firewood to keep warm;

- use it as a foot rest to tie your shoelaces;

- guard off tigers!

- use it as a door stop;

- hang your coat on it.

Can you think of any more?

Critical question

» *Using the same technique what solutions could you think of for the following problem? The first two have been suggested, but you can add more solutions to the diagram.*

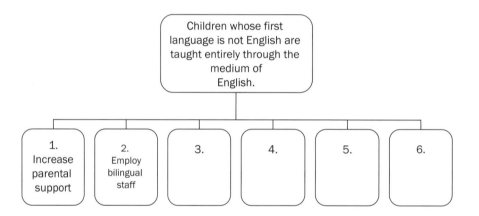

Environmental print and pre-reading skills

When you reflect on children learning to read, many of you will think of schools and reading schemes, implying that this is something that happens at around about five years of age upon entry to school. This could also suggest that learning to read is some kind of epiphany, one day you cannot read and the next you start. Certainly when I trained to teach in the 1960/1970s, the perceived wisdom was that a child had to be 'ready' to read and there was little point in 'teaching' reading until that moment arrived. Parents were discouraged from formally 'teaching' their children to read because clearly they would get it 'wrong'! The child would not be 'ready' until they got to school, where the teacher had the magical powers needed to teach a child to read! It was a mystification of the reading process which could be unlocked only by someone who had been to teacher training college.

I am pleased to say that this is a concept that has now been abandoned. Reading is now seen as a developmental and developing process which starts long before the child is able to recognise a symbolic word on a page, before they are able to understand the significance of the marks that they are surrounded by. Ultimately reading involves comprehension, going deep within a text, a problem solving experience which contextualises the words and makes links between those words, phrases and ideas. It relies upon a child's general knowledge, their bank of life experiences and emotional intelligence. This emphasises the importance of the pre-literate social experiences of the child in the very early years, such as story, visits, co-operative play and environmental print.

Reading and association

You live in a print saturated society; it is all around you, in the supermarket, in the bus, on the street, even in your cupboards and homes. You do not need a book or a tablet to find print to read. One way in which you learn is by association, and much early reading of environmental print is of this nature, because it serves your immediate needs. You go to the kitchen cupboard for a tin of beans and you have to be able to recognise the can, or you could find yourself pouring the cat food on your baked potato!

Even very young children recognise the golden arches of the McDonald's logo. It could be argued that they are 'reading' it, as it is clearly making meaning for them. Equally they learn to read food labels that they like, sweet packet labels and signs for the toilet, park signs and many other personally relevant words. In 1976 Clark's research in Scotland showed that some children do acquire reading quite naturally without formal instruction, in the same way as they acquire expressive language, but clearly many do not, and for these children the process of learning to read probably needs structure and organisation. One of the key elements of learning to read (as with most other learning) is motivation. Only when the child understands what reading can unlock for them can they start to achieve. This usually begins in the very early stages, long before reading books, teachers and methods. The youngest children need to be introduced to the idea that these strange 'squiggles' on the page have meaning, by surrounding them with text, immersing them in the written word in the same way that they have been immersed in the spoken word. Whitehead (2010) referred to this as their *drive* to make sense of things around them.

Symbolic representation

Print is a symbolic representation of meaning, and children have to understand that before they can read. Imagine for a moment that a cat has walked into the room and that it is fluffy, tactile, mobile, unpredictable, smelly, noisy and potentially dangerous, in fact a creature that assaults all of our senses. With time, each occasion that you say 'cat', the child learns that this sensory and visual experience is referred to as 'cat'. Now compare that sensory experience to a picture in a book, even a photograph of a cat, and you will begin to see how different they are. The picture is not a multisensory experience in the same way, and the child needs only visual skills to recognise this. Possibly the real cat that the child is familiar with is a black one, but the one in the picture may be a ginger cat, and the picture is not 3D but a 2D facsimile: is it any wonder that many children become confused? From this visual representation of a cat you expect the child to move to a diagramatic representation:

This looks nothing like the original cat and has very little of the sensory information that the child initially understood was the requirement of a cat. Now move this to the written word:

cat

Now you can begin to understand the numerous leaps of conceptual awareness that the children must make if they are going to learn to read. Now add to the mixture the different ways to represent that word:

Cat

CAT

cat

c*a*t

Cat

Cat

…etc.

You can see the monumental task ahead of the child and you probably marvel at how you ever achieved what you now regard as a simple task. This 'simple task', however, involves the mastery of phonology, morphology, syntax, semantics and graphophonics, a complex and at times overwhelming mission for the reader.

Directionality

The print that surrounds us ensures that most children do come to school understanding which way up to hold the print, and that print in this culture is read from left to right and top to bottom (of course this is not always so, and in some highly literate cultures they run bottom to top and right to left or both).

元来日本語は漢文に倣い、文字を上
から下へ、また行を右から左へと進
めて表記を行っていた。漢字と仮名
の筆順も縦書きを前提としており、
横書き不能な書体も存在する。

元来日本語は漢文に倣い、文字を上から下へ、また行を右から左へと進めて表記を行っていた。漢字と仮名の筆順も縦書きを前提としており、横書き不能な書体も存在する。

Figure 4.1 *Examples of Japanese writing.*

At this stage children understand that print, like the spoken word, has a particular order, and that order affects the meaning. Words, letters, sentences and paragraphs are also distinct and separate. They also learn that the 'scribbles' that they see on the page have a unique combination of vertical and horizontal lines, curves and diagonals which will fundamentally influence the meaning that they attach to them, for example:

b   d   p   q

Cunningham and Stanovich (1997) showed how important expressive language was to a child's eventual ability to learn to read and in particular the size of their lexicon. This implies that the more opportunities there are for children to talk and have experiences in their very earliest years, the better placed they are to be able to weave these into an oral narrative which will enable the child to read more easily.

For the very youngest babies, using and experiencing books of all sorts, shapes and sizes is a valuable first step to reading. First, they learn what a book can and cannot do:

•   Is it good to eat?

•   Can I put it in the bath?

•   Which way up do I hold it?

A book to a young baby is a whole sensory experience, tasting the paper, feeling the texture, seeing the shapes and colours, hearing the pages turn or tear and the voice of the adult reading. It is a comforting, secure experience, frequently involving warmth and cuddles. Introducing books to young children allows this exploration to take place and encourages the physical development that will be needed to turn pages, follow with the eyes and the sustained holding of a book in an appropriate manner.

CASE STUDY

Reading together

Imagine that you are a young baby, warm and sitting comfortably with your parent/carer and looking at a book together. The adult will cuddle you, making the whole experience pleasurable, and one in which attention is focused upon you. You are not really sure what the adult is doing, but they are certainly holding this paper and turning the pages while talking aloud, making noises with a variety of intonation in their voice and pointing to the squiggles while following the lines with their eyes. Eventually you begin to understand that the adult is gaining meaning from the patterns on the page.

Critical question

» *What else do you think that the baby is learning while 'reading' together?*

Most children love to hear the same stories over and over again and eventually they make the connection between sounds and the text, thereby developing an orthographic knowledge. Nutbrown (2006) described this as 'family literacy' with adult-to-child and child-to-child conversations and interactions taking place, allowing the young child to experiment safely with rhyme, alliteration, story structure etc. Nutbrown (2006) talks of these as 'important building blocks' for future literacy.

Approaches to teaching reading

Teachers and researchers have long debated the differing approaches to teaching reading, and perhaps the only constant in the debate is that they cannot agree. This is often referred to in the debate as the 'Reading Wars'. In essence they are looking at two major dichotomous arguments, a top down or bottom up approach, a break down or build up, small chunks or large chunks. This means either breaking down the whole word into smaller segments and then building it up again, or starting with the small segments and building them into words and sentences. Of course somewhere in the middle is a third way and many teachers recommend a more balanced and flexible approach by using both methods, a hybrid approach, according to the individual circumstances of the child.

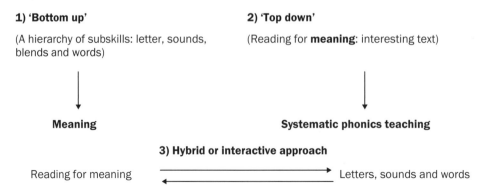

1) 'Bottom up'

(A hierarchy of subskills: letter, sounds, blends and words)

↓

Meaning

2) 'Top down'

(Reading for **meaning**: interesting text)

↓

Systematic phonics teaching

3) Hybrid or interactive approach

Reading for meaning ⟷ Letters, sounds and words

Figure 4.2 *Approaches to teaching reading.*

Within these approaches there are many adaptations which their advocates will swear by, insisting that *their* way is the panacea and the 'great breakthrough'. In truth there is no such miracle method which will suit every child and every situation. The wise practitioner is the one who keeps their mind open and adopts a 'designer approach', by focusing the method to the individual needs of the child. If one method is not helping, they have the confidence and the resources to change the methods to interest and engage the child, inspiring them to want to learn to read.

Now examine these approaches in more detail.

1.   First, there are the advocates of a basic skills (bottom up) approach which involves the use of phonics, attributing sounds to letters and then building up the sounds to make recognisable words and meaning, frequently called 'decoding'. Many of the reading schemes and approaches currently in use in schools work from such an approach, such as 'Letters and Sounds' (DfES, 2007) and the 'Oxford Reading Tree' (OUP, 2014). These encourage the child to decode simple, phonetically reliable words, to start building up in a stuctured manner to more complex words.

$$M - a - t \longrightarrow \quad Mat$$

This was the approach recommended in the Rose Review (2006) which stated that systematic, discrete phonics needed to be taught. This implies that readers translate visual print directly to sound, and only then to meaning.

2.   A whole language approach (top down) starts by exposing the child to complete text in real life experiences, in an effort to interest and motivate the child to want to learn to read, and promote a positive spin to the reading process. The whole language approach is focused upon making meaning rather than decoding and breaking down words in a constructivist approach. This is about looking at a whole text and predicting meaning from cues, such as context, syntax or graphics, sometimes called a 'guessing' or 'hypothesis' approach. So if the child sees an illustration of a cat with a word beneath it, they will assume that the word is CAT. There is an assumption by the reader that text is meaningful and has some regularity to it. Of course errors can occur; the word beneath the illustration could have been KITTEN, SIAMESE or FELIX. This is the basis of the Ladybird's Key Word Reading Scheme, where the child is required to sight read a number of key words before starting the books, or in the 'Real Books' approach in which children choose their own favourite books to read, rather than working through a graded scheme.

3.   The problem with these dichotomous approaches to reading is that they appear to pitch against each other, and the proponents of each model appear to have backed themselves into an entrenched corner, thereby oversimplifying what is such a complex and multifaceted task. According to Stainthorp and Stuart (2008), on their own neither of these models is sufficient for reading to take place, and it is probable that both are initially necessary. As the child becomes more proficient with the reading process, the balance between these methods changes, with the child having established a larger lexicon which they can recognise instantly, and more skilful approaches to decoding words with which they are less familiar. This hybrid or

interactive approach is also referred to as a *'balanced approach'* to teaching reading (UKLA, 2010) and in this meaning and decoding have equal importance and can be balanced out according to the needs of the child.

DEVELOPING CRITICAL THINKING

When you are reading critically it is important to distinguish whether what the writer says is fact or opinion. Sometimes this is hard to ascertain but consider the following and try to decide whether it is fact or opinion.

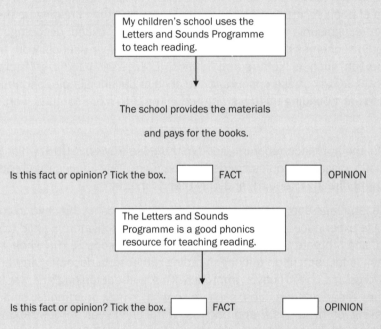

My children's school uses the Letters and Sounds Programme to teach reading.

The school provides the materials

and pays for the books.

Is this fact or opinion? Tick the box. ☐ FACT ☐ OPINION

The Letters and Sounds Programme is a good phonics resource for teaching reading.

Is this fact or opinion? Tick the box. ☐ FACT ☐ OPINION

This is more difficult and could fall into both camps, as it depends upon your definition of the word 'good' in this context. If you are saying that Letters and Sounds receives government support as a 'good' way to teach reading, this may well be fact. However, if you say that most teachers consider it to be good for their children, this is opinion.

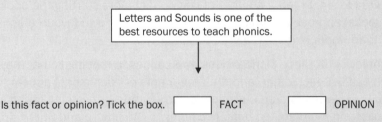

Letters and Sounds is one of the best resources to teach phonics.

Is this fact or opinion? Tick the box. ☐ FACT ☐ OPINION

If you have reliable and validated research statistics of the other phonics resource programmes, this may be fact. However, is this just your opinion having reviewed other literacy programmes?

Letters and Sounds is better than Jolly Phonics or Sparklebox.

Is this fact or opinion? Tick the box. ☐ FACT   ☐ OPINION

Now you need to consider the word 'better'. Better at what? Better in what way...helping with decoding, sounding out, more attractive etc?

You can see from this that critical reading requires a different approach from that of reading a novel or a magazine. You need to actively engage with the text in a sustained manner, to learn from it rather than simply be entertained by it.

Visually based retrieval

Cambourne (1988) equated the process of learning to read with that of learning to talk. He marvelled at the effortless way in which young children learn to talk and believed that they could learn to read in the same way. He put forward an eight point plan that he believed were the fundamentals of learning to read.

1. **Immersion**: The child needs to be surrounded with language and print, throughout their waking hours. This can be compared to the work of Glen Doman, the American who founded the Institute of Achievement for Human Potential in 1955 and famously wrote about teaching babies to read through flash cards and a whole word method (Doman and Doman, 2006).

2. **Demonstration**: The child needs to see adults making sense of print and acting upon it.

3. **Engagement**: The child is interested in the process and attempts to emulate what they hear and observe.

4. **Expectation**: The adults around the child believe that the child will be able to read eventually and they convey this expectation to them.

5. **Responsibility**: The child needs to be autonomous and make decisions about which aspects of the reading behaviour they observe will be adopted.

6. **Approximation**: When the child is learning to talk adults are very accepting of errors and usually try hard to understand. However, when listening to reading, adults expect accuracy and make no allowance for hypothesis or risk taking (something that was discussed in Chapter 3).

7. **Use**: Children need the opportunity to practise their new skills in naturally occurring situations.

8. The last one Cambourne calls **response and feedback**, but I will call *praise and encouragement*, giving time to the child for the task.

You can compare these eight fundamental aspects to that of Armbruster et al (2001) who suggested that there were five essential elements for learning to read.

1.   **Phonemic awareness:** the ability to hear and identify sounds in words.

2.   **Phonics:** linking the sound to the grapheme or shape of the letters and words.

3.   The size and range of the available **lexicon.**

4.   **Fluency:** reading and understanding accurately, at speed and with intonation.

5.   **Comprehension:** understanding what you read.

Comparing these two approaches, you can see how startlingly different they are. Put into Cambourne's (1988) terms, learning to read should be as seamless as learning to talk, but while I believe that his ideas have much to recommend them, from the numbers of children who struggle with the process it is clearly *not* 'The Whole Story'. Learning to talk is not the same as learning to read; you read in Chapter 3 that all human populations and tribes have some form of oral tradition, but more than half of spoken languages have no written form or literary tradition. Reading requires neurological elements and pathways that are not used when learning to talk. As you will read in Chapter 6, research into the origins of dyslexia has shown brain scans of children reading with very differing patterns from those of children talking. The visually based retrieval system for teaching reading implies that if you surround a child with a literate rich environment, then reading will be absorbed. My analogy for this would be that you could sit a novice driver in the best Rolls-Royce, Daimler or Porsche, but without an element of formal, graded teaching, they are unlikely to be able to drive!

Motivation

It is possible that the size of the task that reading presents is too great for the child to achieve without some assistance. It is possible that to reach the level of motivation that comes with success, the task needs to be broken down into smaller, manageable, 'bite sized' chunks. It then makes sense to grade these segments or sub-skills to become the building blocks for future success. This will involve skilful teachers and practitioners who understand the process of reading acquisition and who understand the individual needs of children. It is important to add that there is probably no optimal order for this grading, from simple to complex, as what is simple and easy to one child is complex and hard to learn for another. This explains why there are so many different graded schemes and reading kits developed, each claiming that they have 'the answer'.

Synthetic phonics

Since the publication of the Rose Review (2006), the British government has required all state funded schools to teach reading through synthetic phonics. While there was academic debate over the use of analytical phonics (analysing whole words by looking at the letters they see and their context), or synthetic phonics (synthesis of phonemes, the smallest units of sound and building up to make meaning), Rose (2006) adapted the 'Simple View of Reading', first put forward by Gough and Tunmer (1986). This formed the basis of the 'Search Lights Model' introduced in the National Literacy Strategy (DfEE, 1998).

> Children should have a secure grasp of phonics which should be sufficient for them
> to be fluent readers.
>
> (Rose, 2006, p 7)

This is the system currently advocated by the government through their Letters and Sounds
programme (DfES, 2007) and is the preferred option to analytical phonics.

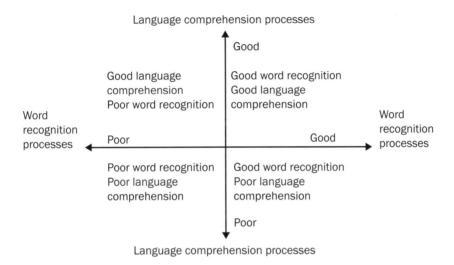

Figure 4.3 *The Simple View of Reading, adapted from Rose (2006, p 40).*

Synthetic phonics has a number of key features which distinguish it from other methods of
teaching reading.

* Children are taught letter shape and sound correspondence in a graduated
  sequence.

* This leads to blending sounds.

* Phonetically irregular words such as 'come', 'should' and 'people' are referred to in
  the Letters and Sounds Programme (DfES, 2007) as 'Tricky Words', but children are
  encouraged to sound out what they can, even if only the first letter.

In the early stages of the reading process children do need to be phonemically aware, that
is, sensitive to sound and to the structure of a word, with an ability to analyse the constitu-
ent sounds which make up that word. This comes long before the child knows the names of
the letters and can be as simple as sounding out their name, alliterative fun and words in
rhymes and songs.

Initial teaching alphabet

The ultimate phonetic approach to reading is the 'initial teaching alphabet' (ITA). This was
first developed in 1961 by James Pitman, the grandson of the inventor of Pitman short-
hand. Languages such as Welsh and Spanish are referred to as transparent languages, that

is, the symbol that you see is always sounded in the same manner wherever it appears in the word.

> The **ff** symbol in Welsh is always
> pronounced as an **F** as in the word 'fun',
> and a single **F** always as a **V** as in the word
> 'van'.

However, English is referred to as an opaque language as sounds are often represented in different ways, making the teaching of reading more challenging and demanding. Mosely (1990) showed that only one-third of the words used in most English initial readers was truly phonetically reliable:

> **f** as in fun.
> **ph** as in elephant.
> **ough** as in cough

Pitman's aim was to create a reliable sound/symbol regularity for the opaque nature of the English language, with 44 characters instead of the 26 letters of the traditional orthography. The principle behind ITA was that once children were able to understand what they were reading and writing, they would develop a motivation to read and would gradually and seamlessly transfer to a traditional orthography (TO). ITA was used extensively in England and Wales in the 1960–1970s but rather fell out of favour; however, it is still in use today in the United States and Australia, particularly with children with dyslexia and other reading difficulties.

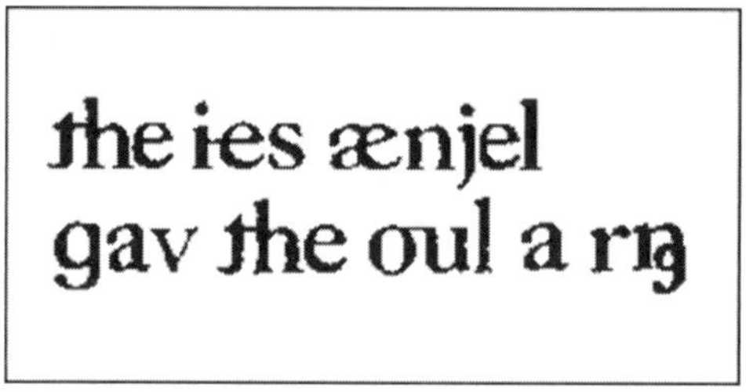

Translation: the ice angel gave the owl a ring

Figure 4.4 *Example of ITA (BBC, 2001).*

Fluency

You can learn the laws of physics that enable you to remain buoyant in water, how to move your arms and legs and when to breathe, to enable you to swim. However, when you jump into the water it is a very different matter, and some people are unable to stay afloat despite having the theoretical understanding. This is like fluency in reading; as the swimmers adjust their weight, body shape, speed and co-ordination of movement in the water, so the reader has to draw on a range of strategies to read. Like the swimmer, the fluent reader does this automatically, without having to think about a breakdown of their strategies. Only when the swimmer starts to drown do they think about technique and tactics to remain afloat. So as a fluent reader, you are not conscious of the approaches that you are using to read, until *what* you are attempting to read does not make sense. Only then do you stop and read each word on the page slowly and use your phonic knowledge to sound out and put it into context. This is the reading equivalent of preventing drowning!

Fluency bridges the gap between word recognition and understanding. Listen to a non-fluent reader and you will notice that word recognition becomes the all important element of reading. This comes at the price of being slow, laborious, without expression, and when asked at the end of a passage what it was about, they frequently cannot tell you. A fluent reader divides the text into chunks. Chunking allows the reader to pause, change pace and pitch and to give the text meaning and expression. So a fluent reader needs automaticity, which refers to accuracy and speed but also chunk and flow. This applies to both reading aloud and to more mature, silent reading.

Visio-spatial features of language

Ehri (1995) was interested in how mature readers were able to read so fluently with understanding. She suggested that this was due to their ability to recognise and understand words immediately. Ehri's (1995) research examined how children acquire this ability with sight words; she called this Sight Word Reading. She recognised that this placed a great demand on memory, and refers to Harris and Jacobson (1982) who calculated the number of words in some basic reading books. They estimated that children would need a sight word vocabulary of 10,240 words, just to read a basic text in this manner. Ehri (1995) emphasised that such a vocabulary was developed through a process of rote learning and not through any form of phonics approach. It places an almost impossible pressure upon memory retrieval as the child needs to remember what each word looks like, and at the end of Key Stage 2 the child would have to know over 50,000 words by sight.

> *The visio-spatial features stored in the memory might be letters, letter patterns, word configurations, or length.*
>
> (Ehri, 1995, p 137)

Ehri (1995) proposed a number of phases of sight word reading development. She emphasised that this was not a linear model or a stage theory, which is why she refers to these as *phases*, one phase *'morphing'* into another with transitional periods.

1. **Pre-alphabetic phase**: using visual or contextual cues to remember the words.

2. **Partial-alphabetic phase**: the children have some knowledge of the shapes and names of the letters and make partial connections with the letters in their memory.

3. **Full-alphabetic phase**: decoding and graphophonic knowledge.

4. **Consolidated alphabetic phase**: blending, letter sequences, use of onsets and rimes.

5. **Automatic alphabetic phase**: recognising most words by sight and able to apply a range of strategies to read unfamiliar words. This is the phase of complete fluency.

Interestingly, Rose (2006) does not discuss fluency, the speed of reading or intonation in his report, but implies that if children are good at decoding and phonics they will automatically be fluent. However, this may not be an appropriate assumption, and Parvin (2014) questions whether the decisions of the Rose Review are really founded on secure research evidence. Parvin (2014) questions the whole premise of synthetic phonics, suggesting that

> *The children's ability to understand what they read was not in line with their ability to decode.* (p 173)

Unlike the quotation at the start of this chapter, taken from the Dr Seuss book, you *cannot* read with your eyes shut, not unless you are reading braille! Reading is an intensely visual experience. However, your eyes are only light reflectors and the real work of reading is done in your brain, behind your eyes. So if you are a new reader, simply seeing the text, the squiggles on the page, is not enough. The reader and the non-reader can look at the same text together and what will have meaning for one will have no meaning for the other. Smith (1985) describes these as visual and non-visual information and he stresses that to be able to read you need both.

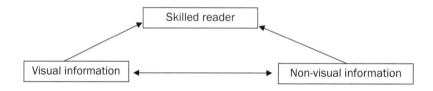

Figure 4.5 *Reading behind the eyes, adapted from Smith (1985, p 14).*

Smith (1985) suggested that the more non-visual information you have the less visual information you need to be able to read. For example, if you go to the library and select a book that has a cover picture of a hand run through with a dagger and blood dripping from it, the sorts of words that you might expect to read in that book will be:

» *blood*;

» *murder*;

» *death*;

» *investigation etc.*

Your brain would find it confusing to read words such as:

» *romance*;

» *love*;

» *heart*;

» *beauty.*

This expectation allows you to read at speed and develop fluency, because it means that the eyes do not have to do all the work. This would imply that the more knowledge and understanding of the world that the child has and the larger their memory lexicon, the more fluent they will become. That process of looking with the eyes and recognition within the brain probably does not happen instantaneously, as the brain needs time to take in the information and make decisions. When I go shopping I leave my car in a large supermarket car park. On my return I see all the cars and have to decide which one is mine. I use my visual information, which is lots of cars, shapes, colour, position, but also the non-visual information about the colour and shape of *my* car, where approximately did I leave it, the registration number, whether I left my coat on the back seat etc. The same process can be applied to reading, the eyes see the letters, but the brain groups these letters together into words and sentences. Rayner et al (2006) demonstrated that where there were transpositions of internal letters in a familiar word, the words still remained relatively easy to read, despite a decrease of 11 per cent in reading speed.

> *yuor ability to raed jmulbed wrods shwos teh imorptnace of non-vsiaul inrofmaiton to raednig.*

Reading versus readers

You may well ask what the difference is between reading and being a reader. How many of you can truthfully say that you often turn off the television, or leave the iPod, in favour of reading a good book? When I ask this question of university students, the response is always very low, possibly 1 or 2 in a group of 30 students, even though all of them can read proficiently. My definition of a reader would be someone who really enjoys reading for entertainment, knowledge, learning and understanding. In 1988, Cambourne stated that '*Teachers are prisoners of a model of learning*' (p 17). He described teaching as the act of establishing 'habits'. This habit formation of learning is based on a Skinnerian (Stimulus → Response) form of teaching which he claimed was destroying our enjoyment of reading. While he did not deny that children did learn to read in this way, his concern was that children were being 'turned off' books, and were seeing reading as something that you do in school but not as a lifestyle choice.

> *Of what use is teaching a skill like reading if it has such a low durability that it ceases to be used and in some cases is actively avoided when schooling is over?*
> (p 24)

In other words he believed that teachers were teaching reading, but not teaching children to be readers. I suspect that most teachers and practitioners when questioned would say that one of their main aims is to teach children to enjoy reading. Can it then be true that we are doing the very opposite, and while teaching children to read, we are inadvertently destroying their love of reading? If we are to enable children to be readers they need to be motivated and excited by the prospects of reading. That means reading for pleasure. For those of you who read avidly and enjoy the emotional experience that reading can bring, this could be seen as the ultimate motivation to read and enables you to join what Smith (1985) called the '*reading club*' with a passionate quest for meaning.

It is not clear in the Rose Review (2006) what his definition of a reader really is, but it certainly appears to include some aspect of the importance of phonemic awareness. Parvin (2014) suggests that this contradicts previous views which involve comprehension and understanding, but concedes that children need to be proficient at decoding before they can actively engage with what they are reading. This clearly produces a dichotomous approach to reading and readers, but such a segmented approach could be distorting the whole concept of reading, its nature and purpose.

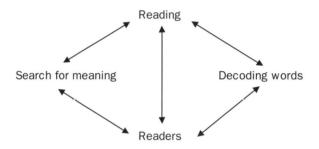

Figure 4.6 *Dichotomous approach to reading and reader.*

Chapter reflections

One conclusion that we can draw from this debate is that conclusive research into which method of learning to read is the most effective is almost impossible to obtain at this point in time. Designing and implementing such research is challenging and potentially ethically dubious.

The Save the Children Report (2014) written by Warren and Paxton describes the United Kingdom as 'One of the most unfair countries in the developed world' (p 1). It attributes this to a history of educational inequality. The report suggests that increasing literacy levels would contribute to a more socially mobile and overall fairer society.

The Bullock Report (1975) stated that:

> *There is no one method, medium or approach, device or philosophy that holds the key to the process of learning to read. (p 77, para: b)*

This statement is probably as true today as it was 40 years ago, when it was first written, and Willingham (2015) in his new book talks about the importance of 'balanced literacy'. Neither have we changed the basic premise of learning to read despite all the proponents of the 'miracle method'! It is probable that the main reason for this debate is that no one really knows what happens when we read or how we acquire the skill. Despite the National Literacy Strategy and all the initiatives that have followed, the number of children still leaving school with low literacy skills has not shown much overall improvement (Brooks, 2013).

In the next chapter you can read about the creativity of language as the child learns to write and script their own material.

DEVELOPING CRITICAL THINKING

Critical thinking is too difficult!

> *Thinking is the hardest work there is, which is the probable reason why so few people engage with it.*
>
> (Henry Ford, 1922, p 247)

Do not be afraid that you find critical thinking and evaluation a challenge; most people do; it is not a skill that many people possess naturally as it requires time, concentration and exactitude. Therefore it needs to be worked at and developed over a long period.

Critical reading requires you to concentrate upon an idea or a problem, so scan reading is unlikely to be deployed for this. Rather you need to focus upon what you read and pose questions in your head; it may even help to write them down or share them with a trusted colleague. Reading critically is a little bit like a treasure hunt: as you read an article try to understand where that author obtained their information.

Critical thinking activity

An important source of information is the reference list, yet so many students gloss over this. Choose an article that interests you and start your reading by looking through the list of sources. Consider the following questions:

» *What does it tell you about the article?*

» *How current is the research?*

» *How reliable are the sources? (They could be research papers from peer reviewed journals or dubious websites.)*

» *Is the material from a primary source or has the writer already reviewed a range of secondary sources?*

Take the time to follow up some of the sources to check how reliable and trustworthy they are.

Further reading

Rose, J (2006) *Independent Review of the Teaching of Reading.* London: DfES.

This review examines the research into the teaching of reading in the early years. Although not fully implemented by the government that commissioned it, it does discuss some pertinent material and advocates a phonics based approach to reading. This is a chance to read it, or re-read it from the perspective of time, and to look at the legacy that it may or may not have left.

References

Armbruster, B B, Lehr, F, and Osborn, J (2001) *Put Reading First: The Research Building Blocks for Teaching Children to Read: Kindergarten through Grade.* Washington: CIERA.

BBC (2001) *Educashunal Lunacie or Wisdom.* www.news.bbc.co.uk/1/hi/uk/1523708.stm (accessed 17.06.15).

Brooks, G (2013) *What Works for Children and Young People with Literacy Difficulties: The Effectiveness of Intervention Schemes.* Sheffield: Dyslexia – SpL Trust.

Bullock, A (1975) *A Language for Life.* London: DES/HMSO.

Cambourne, B (1988) *The Whole Story.* Warwick: Scholastic Publishing.

Clark, M (1976) *Young Fluent Readers.* London: Heinemann Educational Books.

Cunningham, A and Stanovich, K (1997) Early Reading Acquisition and Its Relation to Reading Experience and Ability 10 Years Later. *Developmental Psychology*, 33 (6): 934–945.

Department for Education (2014) *National Curriculum in England: English Programmes of Study.* www.gov.uk/government/publications/national-curriculum-in-england-english-programmes-of-study (accessed 20.12.14).

Department for Education and Employment (1998) *The National Literacy Strategy.* London: DFEE.

Department for Education and Skills (2007) *Letters and Sounds: Principles and Practice of High Quality Phonics.* Norwich: Crown.

Doman, G and Doman, J (2006) *How to Teach Your Baby to Read* (3rd ed). New York: Square One.

Dr Seuss (1978) *I Can Read with My Eyes Shut!* London: Harper Collins.

Ehri, L C (1995) Phases of Development in Learning to Read Words by Sight. *Journal of Research in Reading*, 18 (2) 116–125.

Ford, H in collaboration with Crowther, S (1922) *My Life and Work.* New York: Garden City.

Gough, P and Tunmer, W (1986) Decoding Reading and Reading Disability. *Remedial Special Education*, 7: 6–10.

Harris, J and Jacobson, M (1982) *Basic Reading Vocabularies.* New York: Macmillan.

Moseley, D V (1990) Suggestions for Helping Children with Spelling Problems. In Pumphrey, P and Elliott, C (eds) *Children's Difficulties in Reading, Spelling and Writing.* London: Falmer Press.

National Literacy Trust (2014) *Adult Literacy.* www.literacytrust.org.uk/adult_literacy/illiterate_adults_in_england (accessed 10.12.14).

Nutbrown, C (2006) *Key Concepts in Early Childhood Education and Care.* London: Sage.

Oakhill J and Garnham, A (1988) *Becoming a Skilled Reader.* Oxford: Basil Blackwell.

Oxford University Press (2014) *Oxford Reading Tree.* www.global.oup.care/education/?region=uk (accessed 22.12.14).

Parvin, T (2014) This Is How We Teach Reading in Our School. In Bower, V, *Developing Early Literacy 0–8: From Theory to Practice.* London: Sage.

Rayner, K, White, S, Johnson, R and Liversedge, P (2006) Raeding Wrods with Jubmled Lettres: There Is a Cost. *Psychological Science*, 17: 192–193.

Rose, J (2006) *Independent Review of the Teaching of Reading.* London: DfES.

Santrock J W (2001) *Child Development.* New York: McGraw-Hill.

Shah, A (2012) The Relationship between Elderly Suicide Rates and Different Components of Education: A Cross-national Study. *Journal of Injury and Violent Research*, 4 (2) (July): 52–57.

Smith, F (1985) *Reading* (2nd ed). Cambridge: Cambridge University Press.

Stainthorp, R and Stuart, M (2008) *The Simple View of Reading and Evidence Based Practice.* www.ucet.ac.uk/downloads/1511.pdf (accessed 03.12.14).

UNESCO (2000) *Education For All.* www.unesco.org/publishing (accessed 13.07.15).

United Kingdom Literacy Association (UKLA) (2010) *Teaching Reading: What the Evidence Says.* Leicester: UKLA.

United Nations General Assembly (2013) *Implementation of the International Plan of Action for the Literacy Decade.* A/68/201 26.07.2013. www.un.org/en/ga/third/68/documents.ist.shtml (accessed 28.11.2014).

Warren, H and Paxton, W (2014) *Read On Get On: How Reading Can Help Children Escape Poverty.* London: Save the Children Fund.

Warren, H, Brooks, R and Paxton, W (2014) *Reading England's Future: Mapping How Well the Poorest Children Read.* London: Save the Children Fund.

Welsh Assembly Government (2012) *National Literacy Programme.* Cardiff: Crown.

Whitehead, M (2010) *Language and Literacy in the Early Years 0–7* (4th ed). London: Sage.

Willingham, D (2015) *Raising Kids Who Read: What Parents and Teachers Can Do.* USA: Jossey-Bass.

5 Scribblers to scribes

And as imagination bodies forth
The forms of things unknown, the poet's pen
Turns them to shapes and gives to airy nothing
A local habitation and a name.

(William Shakespeare,
A Midsummer Night's Dream, Act 5 Scene 1)

Introduction

Writing has the potential to transform our ability to reflect, think, organise, criticise and evalu-ate ourselves and our society. This skill, almost more than any other, has the power to change our democracy, political sphere and moral and cultural codes. This chapter will examine the journey that children make, both physically and cognitively, from mark making and scribbling to conventional writing.

Origins of writing

The ability to make marks on materials has been around since pre-historic times, and it is unlikely that we will ever know when these first appeared, as the materials have long since disappeared. Jolley (2010) suggests that there is physical evidence of coloured pigments being used up to 400,000 years ago. With that period of time having elapsed it is probably not possible to ever know the purpose of these, whether simply decorative or a symbolic method of communication. You may well have seen pictures of the cave drawings extant today, the oldest of which have been found on the island of Sulawesi in Indonesia but also in France, Spain and Romania. If you believe that writing is a method to convey meaning, then perhaps the first writing systems in the form of ancient cave drawings can be seen as 'pic-ture writing' or 'ideographic writing'. The problem with trying to interpret the meaning behind these is that without being part of the writer's culture, it is hard to understand their purpose, which could well be communication, but could also be part of religious or ceremonial rituals, therefore ambiguity and uncertainty can occur. In this type of communication (if that is what it was), the pictures were probably drawn to represent objects or concepts. Ideographic writing can still be seen today on road signs, exit signs or toilet signs.

Figure 5.1 *Examples of modern day ideographic 'writing'.*

Writing and speech

The great leap in the development of true writing from ideographic writing probably occurred when written symbols were finally used to represent spoken words. It is likely that this leap was made simultaneously in a number of different locations across the globe, but Ellis (1993) proposes that it probably originated in what is now Southern Iraq between 4000 and 3000 BC, and was one-word, one-symbol marks, such as the modern Chinese writing system. This is at variance with the alphabetic system of English, Welsh and other modern foreign languages used today, where each symbol (or combinations of symbols) represents a particular sound taken from the spoken language. This method of writing required a move away from pictures, which *look* like the word they are intended to represent, to a more abstract collection of symbols. Around 1000 BC, the ancient Greeks devised separate symbols for consonants and vowel sounds and according to Ellis (1993), all modern alphabets are descended from this:

> to someone brought up with an alphabetic writing system using letters to represent sounds may seem like a simple and obvious way to capture speech in a visible form, but when thinking about reading and writing it is worth bearing in mind the fact that, as far as we know the alphabetic principle has been invented just once in human history...by the Greeks around 1,000BC.

(Ellis, 1993, p 4)

Interestingly Ellis (1993) tells us that this very early symbolic writing was initially used not for any form of creative writing or enjoyment of the experience, but rather for administrative recording, transactions and gathering taxes and dues. The advantage to the move away from pictorial representation to symbolic representation was that not all words have a pictorial equivalent; for example, consider how you would represent the words 'tomorrow' or 'today'.

The 'stuff of life'

Looking at this book, and indeed most other texts concerning language and literacy, it would appear that the process of learning language has a linear model. That is, we start with receptive language, progress to expressive language, to reading and finally to writing. In reality this is probably not the case, and each apparently distinctive area morphs into the other, overlapping and intertwining in a multifarious network of developing neural pathways, reliant upon so many other areas of development. Attempting to depict that in a written medium is a difficult task, and the manner in which we read and comprehend dictates that linear pathway. In truth it is probable that no one area comes before the other, and in the way in which we are all unique, so is our ability to learn and develop language at different ages and stages, using different methods. I have thought long and hard for a model to help you to understand this and finally realised that the double helix of the double stranded molecules of DNA, or the 'stuff of life', is ideal and emphasises the vital importance of language to the unique make-up of Homo sapiens today. This model shows how the strands of reading and writing development, while running in parallel, also twist, turn and in places converge, back and forth, in a bidirectional relationship.

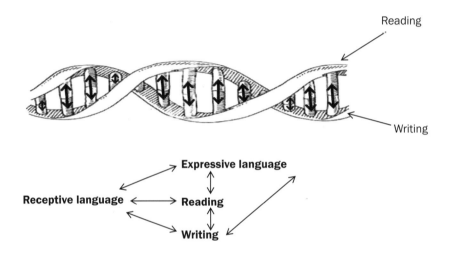

Figure 5.2 *The interrelationships of reading and writing.*

Reading like a writer

Siegler (1998) believes that writing parallels children's skills of reading, although he admits that it is more difficult to acquire. You need to have not only advanced fine motor skills to be able to hold a pen/pencil/brush, but also a sound understanding of the rules of grammar, syntax, spelling and punctuation. Siegler (1998) also suggests that there is less immediate feedback to writing, compared with expressive language and reading aloud. Smith (2007) regards this slightly differently, with what he refers to as a more asymmetric relationship between reading and writing, or I would suggest, 'chicken and egg'. Smith (2007) believes that you can learn to read without being able to write, but you cannot learn to write without being able to read. Smith (2007) describes two different types of reading, first reading like a reader and second, reading like a writer.

> *When you read like a reader you identify with characters in the story. When you read like a writer, you identify with the author and learn about writing, and that's a whole different kettle of fish.*

(Smith, 2007, p 41)

Development of writing

Although it is not helpful to put the developmental stages of writing into age constrained boxes, it is useful to look at this development in a chronological fashion, and the chart in Table 5.1 attempts to portray that.

Table 5.1 *Developmental table for writing.*

Developmental stages of writing	
Learns to hold and manipulate a mark making implement.	Develops fine motor skills first in a palmer grip and eventually a pincer grip.
Understands that they can be in control of the marks that they make.	Develops an awareness of intention.
Understands that the marks they make could have meaning.	Not yet using conventional letter shapes.
Models some conventional letter shapes with discrete 'letters' and spaces.	Often starts by copying own name, or initial letter, and may title their own art works.
Attempts to use conventional letters to convey meaning.	Understands that writing is a transcriptional code which others can interpret.
Phonetically produced words appear.	Sometimes still uses ideographic writing between the words...for example, a circle for the word moon.
Chooses to use storytelling conventions and language to write.	Writing becomes meaningful.
Composes simple sentences usually with phonetically plausible spelling...for example, sed for said and shuger for sugar.	Material produced is readable, both by the composer and others.
Begins to punctuate usually grammatically correct sentences.	Perhaps starting with a capital letter and ending with a full stop.

Mark making

One view of mark making is that of Jolley (2010), who suggests that when children first start to make marks they are not trying to be representational or symbolic in their 'drawings', rather they scribble for the sheer joy of making marks and the kinaesthetic and emotional experience that this brings. Jolley (2010) believes that rather than having intentional representation to start with, the child's attention is drawn to the scribble by adults suggesting possible intention: 'Have you drawn a dog?' or even 'What is it?' In this case the adult is making the assumption that it *is* representational. This eventually focuses the child's attention on this aspect of their marks, and they begin to start their mark making with an intention to represent something in a symbolic fashion. Jolley (2010) is sceptical about the association between writing and drawing and suggests that they are separate areas of development, but when you examine children's early writing attempts they frequently appear to emerge from the drawing. For example, they will often put shapes that resemble letters into their drawings, and at times will use drawings to represent letters such as a circle shape for the word 'moon', which is, after all, what it looks like. Whitehead (1999) also casts doubt upon whether scribble comes from drawing and suggests that

> Scribble is spiky and often in lines (linear) and even written with the speed and flourish of 'real' writers.
>
> (Whitehead, 1999, p 58)

Whether the marks come before the intentions or not, long before children start to write they start to symbolise, that is, they use one thing to mean another. Consider the toddler waving a banana in the air and making a brmmming noise, pretending that the banana is an aeroplane; the 'high five' gesture to indicate pleasure; or the drawing of an elephant following a visit to the zoo. Through these symbols the toddler is communicating meaning to others whether intentionally or not. As they mature the range of communication methods expands and they may use sculpture, modelling, drawing, roleplay, painting etc. Gradually letter forms appear and 'words' become meaningful marks, even when these are pretend words and letters. Vygotsky (1978) believed that such representational play was the cornerstone of early writing, and as the child is allowed to play and freely make marks, the play and the drawings gradually assume meaning.

Bruce (2005) describes the whole act of mark making or scribbling as representational, and children as 'symbol users'. These marks can be highly personal, creative and imaginative or they can follow more conventional signs of the culture. Bruce (2005) emphasises the importance of adults valuing both types of mark making activities for the self-esteem of the child, and for the continuing development of their representational mark making. One way in which adults can demonstrate the value that they place on the children's marks is by listening to what they have to say about them, and what the marks mean to them. Unfortunately the whole term 'scribbling' has negative connotations in the minds of many adults, which is why I prefer to use the terms 'mark making' and 'emergent writing'. Scribbling is often dismissed as nonsense, and you will hear adults tell their children to *'stop scribbling and write properly'*, so in the child's eyes, the activity is not valued. Even in the adult world you will talk about *'scribbling a note'* meaning that it does not have much value or permanence.

So far you have read about writing as being a single entity, but what makes writing so hard for children is that it is not a single thing. Writing requires numerous skills and cognitive processes to be in place before it can be achieved, even at a basic level. The act of writing is also slow and time consuming, compared to spoken language, so children will tend to use it more selectively.

Critical questions

With a colleague consider the following.

» *Look at the picture by Lewis, aged three years, five months. What do you think you can learn about Lewis' stage of development from studying this?*

» *Can you guess what Lewis feels is the value of having recorded this?*

» *What kind of setting/environment do you think would encourage this type of communication?*

» *What do you think this child understands about writing at this stage?*

Comment

Lewis is at a pre-schematic stage, when there are connections between the circles and lines that make up the drawing. There is a clear attempt to communicate an idea. In this case he has gone beyond the basic 'tadpole' shape or 'head-feet' symbol. Interestingly in this case he has omitted the arms and this is common at this stage (Jolley, 2010). It could be that his preoccupation is still with the face, which is quite detailed, including ears.

Fine motor development

Before children can start to write, draw, paint or scribble, they need to have pretty advanced fine motor skills to enable them to control the tool with which they are going to make marks. As you are so used to being able to do this, it is hard to understand how difficult this task really is. Even reaching and grasping an object requires immense concentration, and the sophisticated development of appropriate neural pathways. If you are to begin writing you have to understand your own position and location in relation to the mark making tool, and spatial perception is necessary to locate the tool's distance away from the body and for the eyes to focus and converge to complete the action successfully. However, just being able to grasp an object is not enough; you have to be able to manipulate that mark making tool in the hand. To assume the classic palmer grasp, which most young children adopt, is not good enough to allow them to manipulate the mark making tool with enough accuracy to be able to write or draw successfully. Most children master the pincer grip by about 12 months of age, allowing the thumb and forefinger to move together. This allows the child to hold the writing implement in a more horizontal position and adopt the classic tripod grasp of the mature writer.

Figure 5.3 *Holding a mark making implement.*

However, before you can write effectively you also need to develop strength in your arms, wrist and hand. Even now with your advanced fine motor skills you will know the feeling of strain in your muscles when writing for a prolonged period of time, for example in an examination situation. To be a skilled writer, you need not only to be able to co-ordinate the muscles of the hand, arm, wrist, shoulders, neck and eyes, but also to be able to control the pressure exerted on the pencil to the paper. I am sure that you have frequently seen young, inexperienced writers exerting too much pressure and pushing the pencil right through the paper. So not only do they need to learn to hold the implement, but also how and where to place the paper, and the pressure to apply, which will vary according to the tool that is used, for example, a pen a pencil or a paint brush.

Visual acuity

Visual acuity is the ability to detect visual detail and shape and is a measure of your central vision. Newborn babies have very poor visual acuity, and it is likely that they see the world as fuzzy and blurred. At this stage they also have difficulty tracking with their eyes, following a moving object and scanning a shape. Their eye movements are not smooth, but come as a series of jerky movements (Salapatek, 1975). However, Fanz (1961) showed that two-day-old babies could distinguish between important patterns and appeared to have preferences for complex patterns such as stripes, bullseye or chequered, as their eyes focused upon these for longer periods than upon plain discs or squares. Fanz (1961) also conducted an early 'face recognition study' with babies from a few days old. He showed that their interest in even a basic face configuration was greater than a scrambled face or a non-face-like pattern.

Figure 5.4 *Face recognition studies.*

This appears to concur with Slater's (2002) hypothesis, that you are born with some elements of visual acuity, but these need to be honed and developed rapidly within the first year, through experience and learning.

Visual discrimination

Visual discrimination includes aspects of perceptual constancy, that is, how you perceive an object even if it is moved to a different angle. Visual discrimination is your ability to discriminate *between* shapes/objects. Smith, Cowie and Blades (2003) give the example of a car moving away from you. The image on the retina appears smaller the further it moves away, but you do not think that the car has actually reduced in size. You are aware that the size of the object remains the same despite the distance, and this is sometimes described as 'size constancy'. Shape constancy refers to your ability to understand that a shape also remains the same, even when viewed from a different angle.

Clearly, for children to be able to start conventional writing, their visual acuity and visual discrimination need to be very sophisticated if they are to distinguish between the fine changes to shapes, which produce the alphabetic letters that we use in writing. Not only must they have good visual acuity and discrimination, but their levels of sound discrimination also need to be well developed to separate one word from another within the continuous sound of speech. In the early stages this might be as simple as understanding concepts of up, down, forward and backwards. However, visual discrimination also means an awareness of a range of concepts such as shape, size and even colour, and this requires an ability to distinguish things that are the same, similar and different. Such concepts can be encouraged with the use of simple games such as jig-saws, Kim's game, tessellations etc.

Handwriting

Handwriting is a complex visual/perceptual motor skill, unique to each of us, and some say that even our personalities can be assessed through the individuality of the style. Signing an official document puts your own seal upon that document, which can be as important to your life as signing away all your worldly goods, getting married, buying a house etc. High-profile jobs have even been won and lost on the analysis of penmanship. Most people can recognise their own genuine signature at a glance, and handwriting experts make a career from identifying people by the individual quirkiness of their handwriting.

We do not all need to be able to write in an identical fashion for it to be legible, hence the ability of most pharmacists to read the scrawl of the doctor on a prescription. However, less writing by hand is done today than in the past century as computers and typography take over, with their uniform presentation and consistency of typeface. Certainly the copperplate calligraphy taught in schools in the past is rarely in evidence today. An elderly lady who lived close to me used to write me notes in the neatest and most perfectly presented script, despite being almost blind and with very shaky hands. This was common practice in her generation, who were religiously taught penmanship in school and spent many hours practising, with teachers who would rap their knuckles with a ruler if it was not 'perfect'! In a study of 2000 British adults, commissioned in 2012, by the online stationers Docmail (Chemin, 2014), one in three admitted to not having handwritten anything *properly* for more than six months; one in seven of those surveyed were ashamed of their handwriting, and almost 17 per cent thought that handwriting did not need to be taught in schools any more. Today very little time is made available in schools to practise handwriting, and as the Docmail survey showed, some would say that it was an outdated medium which is no longer required, as we have computers, tablets and mobile phones, which can produce script faster and more consistently, than writing by hand.

Bruce (2005) warns that concentrating upon the graphic shapes of the letters could inhibit a child's creativity and enjoyment of the whole writing process:

> thinking about early writing has over-emphasized the graphic shapes (the figurative aspects) and under-emphasized the constructive aspects (the rules of composition). Handwriting, letter formation and speed have tended to be the main focus of adults helping young children to learn to write.
>
> (Bruce, 2005, p 140)

Damaged disposition hypothesis

Katz (2011) warns that forcing children into formal conventions too soon can result in what she calls the 'damaged disposition hypothesis', which she claims can actively deter children from experimenting and voluntarily taking a risk with new learning. This is the sort of risk taking that I have discussed in Chapter 3 of this book, in relation to expressive language development, and also applies to the creativity of written language development. It could be argued that the level of risk incurred in writing is even greater than in oral language, because when writing you are committing your thoughts and feelings to eternity, or at least as long as that particular written medium exists. A 'mistake' written down can be passed to so many other people, and may be there for many years to come, to be laughed at or ridiculed. Put into these terms it can be seen how important confidence, self-esteem and motivation are to the writing process.

At first a mark making tool can be an unwieldy instrument in the hands of the immature child, as s/he tries to keep up with the speed of their thought processes and commit them to paper, and this can be frustrating. Clay (1975) suggests that children find it easier initially to write using capital letters, as their limited fine motor abilities make it easier to produce them, as they find straight and horizontal lines easier to make. These straight lines are more common to capital letters than curved lines which make up most of the lower case letters. This appears to be in contrast to the practice in most schools and nurseries, which try to introduce children to lower case letters first, and more and more start with 'joined up' letters or at least flicks to join letters later.

Handedness

One aspect of handwriting that you do need to consider is that of handedness. This refers to us usually having a preference for using one hand or side of the body, over the other. Most children exhibit such a preference by approximately two years of age. According to Bruce (2005) most people have a right hand side preference, but up to 10 per cent of people have a left hand preference, while only 1 per cent can be said to be truly ambidextrous, that is, having no side preference. Scientists have long disputed the reasons for the lateralisation of our brains, and even some genetic evidence that has emerged is highly controversial. It does appear that handedness is related in some way to differentiated brain function between the hemispheres, but the evolutionary advantage of this is unclear. However, left handed children do live in a right handed world, and schools and nurseries are largely set up for right handed children with little concept of what it can be like to experience writing for a left handed child. An online survey conducted in 2006 by the Left Handed Children Organisation identified some of the difficulties that these children had when learning to write, such as smudging, aching hand and back, clashing elbows and even obstructive teachers. Left handed equipment is available to purchase but is often more expensive, and the survey showed that only 18 per cent of children were given a pen with a left handed grip, only 44 per cent had left handed scissors available and shockingly 18 per cent said that the teacher did not notice that they were left handed. While this organisation admits that this is not a 'scientific study', it does indicate some of the problems experienced by these children. Other difficulties mentioned were an increase in the numbers of children doing mirror writing, writing words back to front and smudged, untidy work. The one thing that we do know is that left handed children should *never* be forced to write/draw with their right hand, in the way that adults have been in the past.

Spelling

Smith (2007) perhaps controversially claimed that you cannot write and worry about spelling at the same time. He asserts that the problem with conventional spelling, particularly with an opaque language like English, is that it '*gets in the way*' of the creativity of writing. Controversially, Smith (2007) also claims that trying to write phonetically produces the worst spellers.

> *Listen to me carefully; say circle slowly – ser-cuh-luh. Can't you hear the i and the le? The worst spellers are those hoo rite fonetikly.*
>
> (Smith, 2007, p 44)

However, far from being a phonetic nightmare, when closely examined, even English is surprisingly regular in most of its spelling, and there are comparatively few words that sound the same and are spelt differently, for example *write*, *rite* and *right*. What we are seeing, according to Czerniewska (1992), is a conflict between reading and writing, and a battle with different accents, resulting in an attempt to remain neutral while still reflecting the way in which people talk. Research by Ferreiro and Teberosky (1983) showed that children find monosyllabic words such as 'goat' and 'frog' harder to write and spell than polysyllabic words such as 'elephant' and 'hippopotamus', regardless of whether they were phonetically regular or not. Interestingly the very youngest children preferred words with three or more letters, often rejecting the idea that words such as 'it', 'a', 'I' and 'on' were in fact proper words at all!

Clearly conventional spelling *is* an important part of writing, to enable meaning to be communicated, but could it be that in the early stages of learning to write it becomes all-consuming, and could potentially inhibit the child's willingness to be a risk taker in their creativity? This could deter the child from writing freely by making them unduly anxious. In other words perhaps we have become obsessed with deviations in spelling, at the expense of the content, and fail to notice all the other words in a child's script that have been spelt correctly. As I indicated before, spelling is an important element of writing, not only for clarity of meaning, but also for social and cultural reasons. Spelling is often used as a critcrion for educated or non-educated assumptions about people, and is often used by governments as a means of assessing the success or failure of the education system that they are funding.

Interestingly, children's idea of what writing is about often focuses upon spelling. Czerniewska (1992) asked children what was difficult about writing, and many of the respondents mentioned 'getting spellings right'. When asked what was important about writing, the answers concentrated upon correct spelling and neat handwriting.

Grammar, syntax and punctuation

Do you think about the rules of grammar when you talk? I suspect not.

Are you more likely to think about the rules of grammar when you write? Probably not.

Few of us are able to discuss conventional grammatical rules, for example the difference between an infinitive, participle, a gerund or even a split infinitive. However, most writers know instinctively when a sentence is grammatically correct; after all, learning grammar is about organising your writing. Children quickly learn the grammatical code of their mother tongue, without the need to learn formal grammatical structures.

If you listen to someone speaking, it is often in an informal manner, not usually planned, often in incomplete sentences, interspersed with errrs and ummms, pauses and repetitions. If you ask a child to take this as a model of writing you would find this unacceptable. Equally if you speak what is written it sounds stilted and too formal; writing requires the child to use more complex grammatical structures than they have been used to in their expressive language. This implies that there is a dichotomy between speech and writing. Ellis (1993) points out that if you consider the difference between the way we write a letter to a friend and a formal essay, or between a chat to that friend and a formal lecture, you see that writing and speech *do* morph together and overlap. However, for the child learning to write they need to master that strangely formal style of writing and written conventions. You might describe this as language, as opposed to conversational language. Ellis (1993) states that *'to write is to think'* and perhaps this is the difference between writing and other aspects of language. Before committing pen to paper the writer has to think through how they will transmit their thought patterns into communicable language, using the right words and the right structures to express their ideas in a way not done as formally in speech.

Children are able to make marks before they have any understanding of conventional grammar, punctuation or spelling. This is a point at which they can just enjoy the kinaesthetic experience of mark making. However, at some point they do need to understand how to divide up their writing into manageable sections, to enhance meaning and communication. At its most basic this usually starts with them putting a full stop at the end of a piece of writing, to indicate that they have finished, but this understanding of the importance of writing in discrete sentences is a great breakthrough in their understanding of the structure of writing.

Finding their own voice

The difference between reading and writing is probably similar to the difference between speaking and listening, which is receiving and expressing ideas, and what I will call the three Cs:

*   **c**reativity: generating ideas;

*   **c**omposition: making decisions about content;

*   **c**onfidence: building self-esteem.

The creative aspect of writing is, in the end, probably the most important; the chance to let children develop their thoughts, imaginations and emotions. However, to enable conventional writing to commence, the child will need liberal amounts of each of the three Cs. It is probable that one of the difficulties that children experience with writing is that adults try to overmanage it, and focus upon the physical skills at the expense of the three Cs, in particular that element of creativity. Accepting the child's own writing, the emergent writing, does not come easily to many adults, and worryingly Ferreiro and Teberosky (1983) found that many school children saw the act of writing as simply tracing and copying what an adult had already written.

> *The distance between copy writing and children's spontaneous writing is as great as between copy drawing and children's spontaneous drawing.*
> (Ferreiro and Teberosky, 1983, p 278)

Judging by the number of books advertised today to help children with their handwriting, and suggested work sheets on the web, which focus upon copying and tracing, this could well still be their response. Clearly to bridge that gap needs sensitive support from knowledgeable adults.

Cigman (2014) shows that by the time most children start school, they already have a pretty full understanding of what writing is about. They are likely to have observed adults and peers writing, whether that is a memo, a list, a recipe or an essay. The child has observed the posture of the writer, the timing of a writer, the facial expressions of a writer, and will start to emulate this mature behaviour in their play as can be seen in the case study in this chapter. Of course this process of emulation can take place only if they are provided with an environment where there are plenty of mark making materials around with which to practise. The waitress taking an order in the café and scribing this in her notebook will be copied by the child when given access to pens, notebooks, aprons and hats. In this way even the youngest children can equate meaning to the marks that they make.

CASE STUDY

Uzma and Toni

I entered the nursery to see Uzma (two years, five months of age) sitting in a corner with an upturned bucket on a broom handle over her head. She had a magazine on her lap and was pretending to read. Uzma was pretending to be at the 'hairdressers', and was now sitting under the hairdryer, something that she appeared to be familiar with. Toni was at a desk with an open notebook and a selection of pens and pencils. She picked up the mobile phone which was on the desk and started to talk into it. She explained to the 'customer' on the end of the phone that she was fully booked on Thursday, but on Friday she could have her hair cut. She scribbled on the notebook and put the phone down.

Critical questions

This is a perfect play scenario, whereby the children were given a reason to read and write, emulate adult behaviour and understand a purpose for reading and writing.

» *How could this scenario be extended to increase the potential for reading and writing in the hairdressers?*

» *Would adult intervention into this play have extended it further?*

» *Does it matter that what Toni 'writes' does not look like conventional letters/ numbers?*

A reason to write

Creating an environment where 'print is for pleasure' is clearly the starting point for encouraging young children to write and draw. This means providing inspirational opportunities for them to play with print materials which capture imaginations. The National Writing Project (1990) emphasised that children need a reason to write, and believed that in the early stages they should not be constrained by concerns of spelling and handwriting, but be encouraged to take a risk.

> *Children often judge the success of their writing by its neatness, spelling and punctuation rather than the message it conveys.*
>
> (National Writing Project, 1990, p 19)

Despite emphasis in the Early Years Foundation Stage (DfE, 2014) and the Welsh Assembly Government, Early Years Foundation Phase (Yr Adran Plant, Addysg, Dysgu Oes a Sgiliau, 2008), upon play as the principle means of learning in the early years, Cigman's writing project (2014) showed that most writing in settings was adult led and directed. Children saw it as a task to *do* before they were allowed to play, which appears to be counter to the following statements from the most recent government documentation.

> *Each area of learning and development must be implemented through planned purposeful play and through a mix of adult-led and child-initiated activity. Play is essential for children's development, building their confidence as they learn to explore, to think about problems, and relate to others. Children learn by leading their own play, and by taking part in play which is guided by adults.*
>
> (DfE, 2014, p 9)

> *enable children to enjoy experimenting with written communication.*
>
> (DfCELL and S, Welsh Assembly Government, 2008, p 21b)

Worryingly far from children enjoying written communication, the National Writing Project (1990) showed that they frequently expressed a dislike of the process, seeing it as purely school based. When asked about why they were writing, the following comments were made.

> *Because the teacher told me to.*

> *To do my work.*

> *So that I didn't get told off.*

It is probable that children need to express their ideas, feelings and emotions orally before they start to write, and that the more able they are orally, the more easily they will transfer these oral skills to pen and paper. A child with lots of positive life experiences is therefore likely to have a wider and more varied vocabulary to draw upon, to enable them to express their thoughts and to help them to organise their ideas. Writing is a new and powerful form of thinking for children, which adds permanence to their thoughts and experiences, which they did not have before.

Cigman (2014) emphasised the need for writing to be meaningful to the child, to be part of their play, offering them opportunities to express their own voice which adults demonstrate, through their actions, that they value. This does not necessarily mean that the child has to struggle alone with writing, but adults contribute by helping to transcribe their thoughts in a meaningful and supportive manner. Bruner (1978) refers to this as the 'scaffolding' of learning, leading to independence, and Vygotsky talks about the Zone of Proximal Development (ZPD),

> *the distance between the actual developmental level as determined by independent problem solving and the level of potential development as determined through problem solving under adult guidance, or in collaboration with more capable peers.*
>
> (Vygotsky, 1978, p 86)

Chapter reflections

The discussion in this chapter focused upon the origins and nature of writing development. It would appear to suggest that you need to separate the various areas that make up the writing experience, the composition from the presentation, spelling from handwriting and punctuation etc. The research into this area appears to reject the traditional notion that transcription, copying what the adult has written, and a focus upon conventional spelling is the way that children learn to write and become writers. This way of teaching writing does not provide the child with a purpose for their hard work. Usually there is an audience for our written work, and children need to understand who that audience might be, so that their work can be set into context. They need to be able to adapt their material to a variety of audiences in the way that a mature writer will: the difference between the way we write a memo to ourselves, letter to the Council, love letter, official report etc. This offers a purpose to the process, thereby establishing an attitude to writing that enables them to see themselves as writers, even if their spelling or handwriting is poor.

This chapter also discussed how historically the purpose of writing has changed society both politically and culturally, with the ability to make permanent our beliefs, lifestyles and cultures. The advent of writing has lessened our dependency upon word-of-mouth accounts which can change and vary like 'Chinese Whispers'. This has resulted in an immense accumulation of written material and knowledge which cannot possibly all be read, but does this mean that it should not be written?

In the next chapter you will read about some differences in children and the way in which they learn, which may make it more difficult for them to become fully literate, and can result in underachievement in their school life and beyond.

DEVELOPING CRITICAL THINKING

So often I hear students say 'I don't know where to start!' Sitting looking at a blank sheet of paper, knowing that you have to fill it with 2000–3000 words, is indeed a daunting task, if those words are not to be purely narrative and descriptive. Planning is the vital component of writing a critically analytical piece of academic text, so before you come to that blank sheet of paper you need to know already what you are going to write about.

The idea of writing so many words is daunting in itself, and you need to break this down in your own mind into manageable 'chunks'. No writer sits down to write a whole book in one go, rather it is broken into chapters and even these chapters are further broken down to paragraphs. *Never* start your writing from the introduction; many students make this error, and they end up introducing things that they have not gone on to write about. Leave your introduction to the last, and that way you can review your writing and offer a clear introduction to what you *have* done. However, remember that you need to allocate words for this introduction. You will also need to allocate words for your conclusion which is a vital part of your writing. So many scripts that I read have very brief conclusions, probably because the student has written the assignment and run out of words, without taking into account the importance of this section. Imagine a thriller novel or romance with no final chapter to round it off; having read the whole book and engaged with the text you now want to know who murdered whom, or who fell in love with whom. That last chapter is probably the most important chapter in the book; how many of you have turned to the last chapter before even starting to read the book? The same goes for the conclusion of your assignments; this is the place to draw together the important elements of the academic arguments that you have created, and take an evidence based stance.

If you have allocated, for example, 300 words for an introduction and 300 words for a conclusion, your 2000 word assignment is now reduced to 1200, which perhaps is not so daunting. If you plan on dealing with three different aspects of the topic within the script this now gives you only 400 words for each topic.

'Help!' I hear you say, 'I am going to run out of words!'

Clearly this is a very simplistic way of looking at writing, and one topic area will probably need expanding further than another, but I am sure that you can see the principle of this way of approaching academic writing by putting your ideas into manageable portions.

Your writing needs to be carefully thought through; without planning your opportunities to think critically will be reduced. There are many ways to plan a piece of written work and different ways work for different people. However, if this is something that you have not tried before I would suggest that once you have got an assignment title you do some reading to give yourself some background to the title.

Critical thinking activity

For a forthcoming assignment or essay:

» *Get a large piece of paper that you can spread out on the floor or the table. Put your essay title in the centre of the paper and let your mind run riot. Write down everything that you can think of to do with this title in a concept map, and I really do mean everything...cover the paper! Some things will be big and some will be small, but they are your initial ideas, and no one else need ever see it, so you do not have to hold back at all.*

» *Fold up your paper and put it away for the night...sleep on it. Your brain will be in overdrive with all these ideas 'pinging' around in it, so there is no point in trying to interpret what you have written now.*

» *The next day look at and evaluate your ideas. Almost certainly you will now look and see things which are quite ridiculous, and you can put a line through. There will also be lots of things there that you think are important to what you need to write.*

» *It is important to remember that you cannot write everything there is to know about a subject in the average assignment, so choose from your concept map three or four items, and no more, that you can prioritise to write about. There may be some that are at the heart of the assignment, but remember to be practical as well, and if you cannot obtain enough information about an aspect, for whatever reason, then perhaps these need to be ruled out. Your tutor understands that you cannot write everything about a subject and will consider the topics that you have chosen; these may well be different from other students writing the same assignment, but need not be lesser. Once you have selected your topic areas screw up the large piece of paper and throw it away, so that you are not tempted to look back at it and try to include too much.*

» Now develop a further concept map around your topic areas as shown in Figure 5.5.

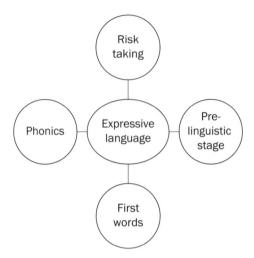

Figure 5.5 *Example of an assignment concept map.*

» Select your first topic to work with, and put this into the centre of another concept map. Start now to look for evidence in your reading to back up your thoughts, and to see a range of contrasting ideas with which to create your 'arguments'. It may help to put a line through the middle and put contrasting explanations, evidence or research perspectives on each side of the line.

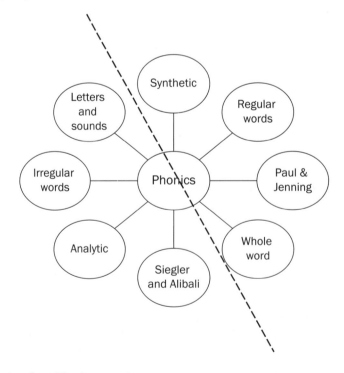

Figure 5.6 *Example of a critical concept map.*

» *You now know what one paragraph of the main body of your work is going to be about, and alternative perspectives which you can develop logically within that. You will need to do this with each of your selected topics. It is not necessary to start with any particular topic so it might be good to start with the one that you feel most confident with, or have the most research material for.*

Further reading

Cigman, J (2014) *Supporting Boys' Writing in the Early Years*. Oxford: Routledge.

This is a really readable text which is firmly based in practice. It contains a series of case studies involving children writing, which offer a relevance and significance to the text. While Cigman has looked particularly at the difficulties that boys have with writing, the work is much wider than that and she backs up all that she says with a critical reflection on both conventional 'wisdom' and up-to-date research. This book is based on the findings of the author's own research, 'Boys' Writing Project', and its findings challenge the reader to re-think some common practices when teaching writing.

References

Alexander, P (ed) (1951) *The Complete Works of Shakespeare*. London: Collins.

Bruce, T (2005) *Early Childhood Education* (3rd ed). London: Hodder and Arnold.

Bruner, J S (1978) The Role of Dialogue in Language Acquisition. In Sinclair, A, Jarvelle, R J and Levelt, W (eds) *The Child's Concept of Language*. New York: Springer-Verlag.

Chemin, A (2014) Handwriting vs Typing: Is the Pen still Mightier than the Key Board? *The Guardian*: Tuesday 16.12.2014.

Cigman, J (2014) *Supporting Boys' Writing in the Early Years*. Oxford: Routledge.

Clay, M (1975) *What Did I Write?* London: Heinemann.

Czerniewska, P (1992) *Learning about Writing*. Oxford: Blackwell.

Department for Children, Education, Lifelong Learning and Skills (Welsh Assembly Government) (2008) *Framework for Children's Learning for 3- to 7-Year-Olds in Wales*. Cardiff: www.wales. gov.uk (accessed 21.01.15).

Department for Education (DfE) (2014) *Statutory Framework for the Early Years Foundation Stage: Setting the Standards for Learning, Development and Care for Children from Birth to Five*. www.gov.uk/governmentpublications (accessed 21.01.15).

Ellis, A W (1993) *Reading, Writing and Dyslexia: A Cognitive Analysis*. Hove: Lawrence Erlbaum Associates Ltd.

Fanz, R L (1961) The Origin of Form Perception. *Scientific American*, 204 (May): 66–72.

Ferreiro, E and Teberosky, A (1983) *Literacy before Schooling* (translated by Goodman-Castro, K). London: Heinemann.

Jolley, R (2010) *Children and Pictures*. Chichester: Wiley Blackwell.

Katz, L (2011) Current Perspectives on the Early Childhood Curriculum. In House, R (ed) *Too Much too Soon?* Stroud: Hawthorne Press.

Left Handed Children Organisation (2006) *Left Handers School Experiences Survey.* www.lefthanded-children.org (accessed 26.06.15).

National Writing Project (1990) *Responding to and Assessing Writing.* Walton on Thames: Nelson.

Salapatek, P (1975) *Infant Perception from Sensation to Cognition, Vol 1.* New York: Academic Press.

Siegler, R (1998) *Children's Thinking.* Upper Saddle River, NJ: Prentice Hall.

Slater (2002) Visual Perception in the Newborn Infant: Issues and Debates. *Intellectia,* 34: 57–76. www.intellectia.org/SiteArchives/archives/n34/34_3_slater.pdf (accessed 26.06.15).

Smith, F (2007) *Reading: FAQ.* New York: Teachers College Press.

Smith, P, Cowie, H and Blades, M (2003) *Understanding Children's Development.* Oxford: Blackwell.

Vygotsky, L (1978) *Mind in Society.* Cambridge, MA: Harvard University Press.

Whitehead, M (1999) *Supporting Language and Literacy Development in the Early Years.* Buckingham: Open University Press.

Yr Adran Plant, Addysg, Dysgu Gydol Oes a Sgiliau (Department for Children, Education, Lifelong Learning Skills) (2008) *Framework for Children's Learning for 3–7 Year Olds in Wales.* Cardiff: Llywodraeth Cynulliad Cymru (Welsh Assembly Government).

6 Specific learning difficulties

I come to school
I see all the other friends,
Who can rite and read.
But me, I'm all on my own
Not good at riteing.
Not good at reading.
I sit on my bed,
I cry I cry I cry,
But I boh't see why,
It's so hared for me.
Can't you see?

(Jodie Cosgrave, age 11,
in Andrew and Chivers, 1996)

Introduction

The focus of this chapter is upon familiarising you with an understanding of key research positions of specific learning difficulties, but in particular, children with dyslexia and dyslexia related conditions. The chapter examines the historical roots of these conditions, the relationship between them and the research progress which has been made in the past few years. In this chapter I hope to dispel some of the myths about dyslexia, and to examine the mental functions common to the condition, from the perspective of a positive interpretation, as well as the challenges of managing it. A number of practical examples of children's experience of dyslexia will help you to understand the potentially devastating and lifelong effects of these conditions, if they are not appropriately identified and supported.

What are specific learning difficulties?

Historically conditions such as dyslexia and other Specific Learning Difficulties (SpLD) have had a rather 'bumpy ride', and many families affected by these conditions have had quite a battle to get them recognised and appropriate support put in place. A possible reason for this difficulty is that there are still inconsistencies of definition. Studies from around the world demonstrate an inability to agree to a consistent designation. According to Guardiola (2001), the first reference to the concept of dyslexia occurred in 1872 with the physician R Berlin of Stuttgart, Germany, who used the term to describe the case of an adult with acquired dyslexia (a loss of reading as a consequence of damage to the brain), as opposed to developmental dyslexia which is unrelated to accident or injury. In 1895 James Hinshelwood, an ophthalmic surgeon from Glasgow, published an article in *The Lancet*. This article referred to a condition that Hinshelwood described as 'word-blindness'. This inspired Pringle Morgan (1896), a British GP, to describe the case of a 14 year-old intelligent boy who apparently could not learn to read. This article is generally regarded as the first report, or at least one of the first reports, of what was called 'congenital word-blindness'.

Hinshelwood finally defined dyslexia as a hereditary defect that affected the brain's acquisition and storage of visual memories of letters and words, which *appeared* to be more common in boys. At this time Hinshelwood was of the opinion that this was a remediable condition, but felt that it had underlying biological causes. According to Guardiola (2001) despite this early recognition of the condition, dyslexia was not officially recognised in the United Kingdom until 1970, in the Chronically Sick and Disabled Persons Act. In 1993 dyslexia was finally defined as a 'special educational need' in the Education Act (DfE) of that same year.

In 1968 the definition of developmental dyslexia preferred by the World Federation of Neurology was that dyslexia was:

> *A disorder manifested by difficulty in learning to read despite conventional instruction, adequate intelligence, and socio-cultural opportunity. It is dependent upon fundamental cognitive disabilities which are frequently of constitutional origin.*
>
> (World Federation of Neurology, 1968, p 26)

This definition implies that those who are dyslexic must have 'adequate' intelligence (this was defined by Critchley [1975] as an IQ score of 90 or more), and have experienced appropriate reading instruction. This was introduced to distinguish children with dyslexia from children whose reading was poor for their age, because of general learning difficulties and low IQ. The definition emphasised the unexpected and difficult nature of the condition. According to Snowling (2000), there are some very ill defined terms within this definition, and she takes up the point of how *much* intelligence is needed for a child to learn to read. Snowling (2000) also queries what is meant by 'socio-cultural opportunity', and this would usually refer to the relationship between the individual and their environment and could include matters such as race, gender, sexual orientation, economic status etc. This, she says, is a definition by exclusion, and only states what the child cannot do; this is very different from the more positive and updated view of Davis and Braun (2010).

> *The mental function that causes dyslexia is a gift in the truest sense of the word: a natural ability, a talent. It is something special that enhances the individual.*
>
> (Davis and Braun, 2010, p 4)

According to Ellis (1984) a child diagnosed with dyslexia tends to be the

> *bright offspring of 'good' homes attending 'good' schools.*
>
> (Ellis, 1984, p 106)

This concept is undoubtedly the origin of a very popular misconception that dyslexia is solely a 'middle-class disease', rather than the tendency for these to be the children that psychologists feel most confident to diagnose, and where they can easily exclude other obvious causes of reading failure (Ellis, 1984). At this stage, reading failure appears to be the only criteria for the diagnosis of dyslexia.

Is it only reading?

In 1981 Tansley and Panckhurst coined the term 'specific learning difficulties'. Still the concentration was upon children who exhibit severe reading difficulties, but they now acknowledge that there could be associated problems, such as spelling, writing, number work and/or expressive language. The term 'specific learning difficulty' was, at this time, frequently used synonymously with dyslexia, but in 1997 Turner described it rather as a 'subset' of difficulties, which included conditions such as ADHD and autism, with only some areas of functioning affected in each condition.

Tansley and Panckhurst (1981) define those with specific learning difficulties (SpLDs), such as dyslexia, as:

> *Children who in the absence of sensory defects or overt organic damage, have an intractable learning problem in one or more of reading, writing, spelling and mathematics and who do not respond to normal teaching.*
>
> (Tansley and Panckhurst, 1981, p 259)

By 1995 a much broader definition by Frost and Emery emerged:

> *Phonological core deficits entail difficulty making use of phonological information when processing written and oral language...problems with phonemic awareness are most prevalent and can co-exist with difficulties in storage and retrieval... Children with dyslexia have difficulty segmenting words into individual syllables or phonemes and have trouble blending speech sounds into words.*
>
> (Frost and Emery, 1995, online)

It was also at this time that the British Dyslexia Association began to recognise that difficulties might also occur with motor skills and general information processing. Doyle (1996) proposed that dyslexia was possibly not one definitive condition and he broke down the terms developmental dyslexia or cognitive dyslexia or specific developmental dyslexia (all terms commonly used interchangeably at this time) into three different subgroups.

- **Visual dyslexia:** children who take longer than non-dyslexic children to perceive letters, words or numbers when they are flashed up on a screen before them.

- **Phonological dyslexia:** children who have difficulties analysing sounds and are unable to read irregular or nonsense words.

- **Surface dyslexia:** children who recognise words by sounds, but not their written appearance. There is nothing wrong with their phonological skills, and they are able to read nonsense words.

However, Doyle's (1996) concept of dyslexia still stresses dyslexia in terms of a deficit model, but in 1997 Turner described a shift of position towards a broader and more inclusive approach, by including issues of poor motor control and difficulties with speech and balance. Turner (1997) adopts the definition given by the Dyslexia Institute in March 1996, which begins to recognise the talents of the dyslexic child.

> *Dyslexia is a specific learning difficulty that hinders the learning of literacy skills. This problem with managing verbal codes in memory is neurologically based and tends to run in families. Other symbolic systems, such as mathematics and musical notation can also be affected.*
>
> (Dyslexia Institute, 1996 cited by Turner, 1997, p 11)

This definition notes that dyslexia is not one kind of learning difficulty but often co-occurs with other disorders. Turner suggests that dyslexia can occur at any level of intellectual ability, and although it can accompany, it is not a *result* of a lack of motivation, sensory impairment or meagre socio-cultural opportunities.

> *Many dyslexic people have visual and spatial abilities which enable them to be successful in a wide range of careers.*
>
> (Dyslexia Institute, 1996, cited by Turner, 1997, p 11)

Medical or educational?

Despite the existence of these definitions, Pumfrey and Reason (1991) note that many educationalists and psychologists remain unwilling to use a concept that they considered flawed, on the evidence at the time. Friction frequently occurred between the believers and the sceptics, many of whom saw SpLDs as purely a cultural phenomenon. A bilateral tension existed at this time between whether there was a medical or educational origin for these conditions. According to Whittaker (1981):

> *We do not have a medical condition called dyslexia. We have an educational problem about how to teach more effectively.*
>
> (Whittaker, 1981, letter)

Gift or difficulty?

The shift of paradigm from disability to gift is taken up by Davis and Braun (2010), in the earlier quotation; they suggest that dyslexia can be considered a perceptual talent. They recognised that no two people with dyslexia are the same, or experience the same environmental conditions. As a consequence, Davis and Braun (2010) suggest that dyslexia cannot be definitively explained, as the symptoms are likely to be distortions of vision, hearing, balance, movement and time, but the severity and degree to which each of these affects an individual will vary.

In October 2007, the British Dyslexia Association published an updated definition of dyslexia that encompasses many of the aspects so far discussed.

Dyslexia is a specific learning difficulty that mainly affects the development of literacy and language related skills. It is likely to be present at birth and it is life-long in its effects. It is characterised by difficulties with phonological processing, rapid naming, working memory, processing speed, and the automatic development of skills that may not match up to an individual's other cognitive abilities. It tends to be resistant to conventional teaching methods, but its effect can be mitigated by appropriately specific intervention, including the application of specific intervention and supportive counselling.

(British Dyslexia Association, 2007, online)

However, it is still possible to see differences of definition in the production of a report by Sir Jim Rose (2009). Rose says that he is reluctant to offer a clear definition as he admits that it will vary so much between individuals; however, his report is founded on the following statement, which still focuses upon a deficit model.

Dyslexia is a learning difficulty that primarily affects the skills involved in accurate and fluent word reading and spelling.

- *Characteristic features of dyslexia are difficulties in phonological awareness, verbal memory and verbal processing speed.*

- *Dyslexia occurs across the range of intellectual abilities.*

- *It is best thought of as a continuum, not a distinct category, and there are no clear cut-off points.*

- *Co-occurring difficulties may be seen in aspects of language, motor co-ordination, mental calculation, concentration and personal organisation, but these are not, by themselves, markers of dyslexia.*

- *A good indication of the severity and persistence of dyslexic difficulties can be gained by examining how the individual responds or has responded to well founded intervention.*

(Rose, 2009, p 10)

The one thing that you will have noted so far is that making a clear definition or diagnosis is a difficult and bewildering task, with a theme of overlapping common features. Miles (2004) was one of the first to describe dyslexia as a 'syndrome', with characteristics that encompass clusters of both talents and difficulties, thus offering a multivariate explanation rather than trying to rely on one causal factor. It may be that Miles (2004) is right, and that we need to continue to refine our definitions as our knowledge grows.

The lack of consensus of definition means that the assessment of the prevalence of dyslexia in the community is difficult to measure. Rose (2009) estimated that in English speaking countries it is between 4 and 8 per cent of the population, but it is thought to be one of the most common learning differences. Shaywitz (2005) shows that estimates as high as 25 per cent have been made, depending upon the definition, and whether the numbers are based on the true prevalence or just the numbers of those identified and receiving support.

Difference or difficulty?

Claiming that dyslexia and other SpLD conditions are 'difficulties' implies that there is something 'wrong', and it offers a very negative view of the child. It produces a deficit model of the conditions which blames the child for not being able to do certain things. Mackay (2005) claims that transposing this to a specific learning *difference,* rather than difficulty, gives a more positive view of these conditions. Such a view celebrates the positive difference in the way that these children learn, but still acknowledges their difficulties. It may also suggest that someone with specialist knowledge and understanding is required to help the child with the condition. Mackay (2005) goes one step further and describes dyslexia as a learning preference, which clearly has better linguistic connotations. My concern with this description is that a 'preference' could imply that a child has a choice about the way in which they learn, which clearly they do not. Interestingly Sir Jim Rose (2009), who has had a significant influence on the teaching of reading in schools, still retains the definition of a 'learning difficulty'. When considering this as a learning difficulty it may make you wonder who has the difficulty: is it the child, or is it the teachers, parents, government or society? Could it be that they cannot be flexible enough in their teaching and child rearing practices, to accommodate for differences in the way in which individuals learn?

What can be agreed upon is that dyslexia is about processing language, multitasking and managing many of the complicated things that the twenty-first century demands. It is about so much more than just reading differences, and even when reading and literacy skills improve, other issues associated with dyslexia remain, such as poor short-term memory, organisation, sequencing and other physical differences. However much we might dislike the idea of labelling children at a young age, to establish any sort of help or support, they must first be identified as having a specific learning difference.

> *The existence of several definitions with different possible causations reflects the lack of an agreed, reductionist, explanation for dyslexia, but has become a resource/time consuming debate because a 'diagnosis' is essential in order to gain assistance for the child with learning problems under current guidelines.*
>
> (Poole, 2003, p 170)

According to Poole (2003) many children do not receive the support which they need because it is dependent upon a diagnosis, and until that point is reached 'battles' for scarce resources frequently take place. At this level you can see that an operational definition is important, but on a global level it will also form the basis of further vital research and policymaking. Any definition assumed must be theoretically sound and supported by research that can be objectively measured, valid and useful.

CASE STUDY

Lewis

Lewis was six years of age and the youngest of three boys. Two of them learned to read quickly and apparently effortlessly, but Lewis could not understand what all these shapes on the page really meant. In school the teacher found him 'hard work' as he had become the class 'clown', distracting other children, noisy and inattentive. Lewis spent most of the day on his own with a craft or drawing activity (which was the only thing that he appeared to be good at). The other children surged ahead, but as he found reading so difficult most of the traditional school subjects began to leave him behind. Colouring and craft kept him occupied, but really what Lewis wanted was to be able to read.

At night Lewis sneaked a torch into his bedroom and when his mother put out the light he would get out a book, and under the covers would surreptitiously try to make sense of the words in front of him. Often he ended up crying himself to sleep, having found the task just too difficult.

Critical questions

Lewis' experiences are in line with many children who have dyslexia. Now consider the following questions.

» *How do you think this made Lewis feel?*

» *What effect do you think this had on his social/emotional development?*

» *How could this have influenced his life choices and experiences?*

» *What do you think would have helped Lewis and his family at the time?*

» *How could the teacher have made Lewis' experience in the classroom more stimulating and challenging?*

Aetiology

With the controversy which exists over the definition of the range of specific learning differences, it is understandable that even more uncertainty exists about the causes and origins. The complexity of the research in this area is compounded by the generally held view that one simple definitive cause for any of the SpLDs is unlikely to exist. Frith (2002) suggests a three level causal model and proposes that all these interact to differing degrees with environmental and contextual factors needing to be taken into account:

- biological;
- cognitive;
- behavioural.

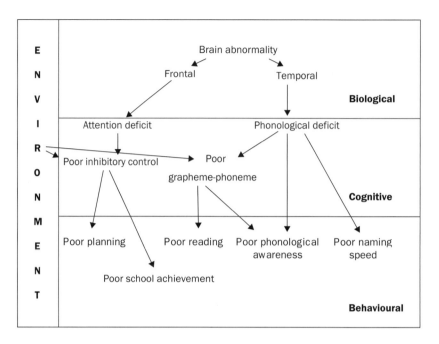

Figure 6.1 *A causal model of dyslexia with attention deficit disorder, adapted from Frith in Reid and Wearmouth (2002, p 58).*

Biological

There is strong evidence that disorders such as dyslexia and specific language impairment (SpLI) have a genetic basis, although the exact genetic factors are likely to be extremely complex. Newbury et al (2014) talk about the strong familial association that electroencephalogram (EEG) recordings of the brains of newborn babies appear to demonstrate. These show differences in patterns of response to language sounds, when one or both parents have been identified with an SpLD. Brain imaging studies reviewed by Shaywitz (2005) have shown that there are normally three areas of the brain which involve reading. These are all in the left hemisphere of the brain, the Broca's area, parietal temporal and occipital temporal.

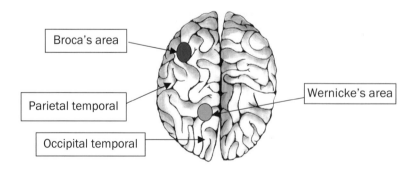

Figure 6.2 *Areas of the brain associated with reading and language development.*

The occipital-temporal region appears to be responsible for identifying patterns in whole words, and is sometimes referred to as the 'word form' area. Shaywitz (2005) claims that in skilled readers, this is the most active region, but in the dyslexic reader it is the least active. However, Galaburda et al (1985) suggest that this classic concept of language development is too simplistic, and it is probable that a complex network of regions, distributed throughout the brain, is more likely. Newbury et al (2014) undertook research which connected the origin of developmental dyslexia to a range of possible candidate genes (ROBO1; K1AA0319; DCDC2; DYX1X1 and several others). Newbury et al (2014) also claim that these are involved in the early stages of brain development and have been associated with laterality, that is, hand preference, leg, eye and ear preference. The detailed genetic research by Newbury et al (2014) links the genetic basis of dyslexia to neuronal migration in early brain development, that is, the way in which neurons in the brain move from their place of origin in the developing foetus, to their final position within the brain. This research also links dyslexia to a process known as ciliogenesis, which is the process by which small hair like structures on the cell walls, called cilia, develop and by rapid and rhythmic beating move fluids, helping the neural migration to take place appropriately. Ciliogenesis may also play a role in the brain's mid-line development, the corpus callosum, which divides and connects the two hemispheres of the brain and allows communication between the two sides.

Images of the normal human brain would generally show that the two hemispheres of the brain, as shown in Figure 6.2, were asymmetrical, but Galaburda et al (1985) showed that there was a deviation from that cerebral asymmetry in the brains of individuals with developmental dyslexia, which they concluded probably occurred in the early stages of gestation.

Images of the brains of individuals with dyslexia have clearly shown developmental anomalies within the cerebral cortex (often referred to as the 'grey matter'), in the left hemisphere of the brain, but the complexity of the research into the aetiology of dyslexia can be illustrated as in Table 6.1 from Kere (2014).

Table 6.1 *Multilayers of the research into developmental dyslexia, adapted from Kere (2014, p 241).*

Social layer	Learning
	Computer aided teaching
	Self-esteem
	Motivation
	Social experience
Neuropsychological layer	Auditory processing
	Short-term memory
	Brain activation
	Mismatch negativity
	Rapid naming

Table 6.1 (cont.)

Neurobiological layer	Plasticity
	Axon guidance
	Brain development
	Cortical ectopias
	Neuronal migration
	Biochemical networks
Molecular genetic layer	Associated genes currently under investigation:
	DYX1C1
	CYP19A1
	ROBO1
	DCDC2
	KIAA0319
	C2Orf3
Evolutionary layer	Basic developmental mechanisms
	Evolution
	Language development
	Species differences

DEVELOPING CRITICAL THINKING

When you are reading it is important that you are able to critically evaluate the content. When you are writing it is just as important that you do the same with your own work. Always read through your assignments and use some of the questions that follow to assess how they relate to *your* writing. Most importantly you need to be sure that you have presented your arguments in a well-structured and logical manner, which is consistent with and valid for your conclusions.

Read the following adapted passage, and then try to consider the critical questions at the end of the passage.

> Children whose first language is not English and who are dyslexic are doubly challenged, coping with the linguistic challenges of a second language and with the stress of their own difficulties. It is therefore particularly important that bilingual children are assessed as early as possible to enable the appropriate support, in the appropriate language, to be put into place. It is imperative that these children have the support in their first language. In the past, according to Peer and Reid (2000), multilingual children have frequently been misdiagnosed and ignored, with

their difficulties explained away by their background or poor oral language skills etc. It could be possible that this misdiagnosis is a consequence of a lack of proper consideration for their first language.

A research questionnaire was distributed to schools throughout Wales on an entirely random basis. No account was taken of whether the schools within the survey were English or Welsh medium schools. Each school was asked what allowance was made, in the testing process, for children for whom English was not their first language. Almost a third of the sample (33%) admitted that they did not take a child's first language into account at assessment. In a bilingual principality, it is surprising that such a high percentage of children do not have their first language considered.

This issue was further demonstrated at the interview stage, when each policy maker was asked what allowance was made during an assessment for dyslexia, for children for whom English was not their first language. In the interview it was made clear to each respondent that the interviewer had a particular focus upon children for whom Welsh was their first language. In this question almost 32% of the authorities said that no allowance was made, and a further 22% of the authorities made very little allowance.

The Welsh Language Scheme of the Welsh National Assembly is based on the principle contained in the Welsh Language Act 1993, and the Government of Wales Act 1998, that the Welsh and English languages should be treated on the basis of equality. It is therefore surprising that in a principality where the use of Welsh is so embedded into the everyday life of the people, there is so little apparent support for these children and their particular needs.

(Adapted from Hayes, 2007)

Critical questions

»   *Has the writer made her position clear?*

»   *What evidence is cited for the writer's position?*

»   *Has the argument been securely structured?*

»   *Has the writer managed to highlight the key points and main issues?*

»   *What, if any, inconsistencies of the arguments can you identify?*

Magnocellular explanations

With the increased sophistication of brain scanning (PET, NMR, CAT and EEG) in recent years, Bradford (2003) has detected groups of cells which lie just on the surface of the brain of the non-dyslexic child (these are the largest cells in the brain called magnocells). These cells, in the dyslexic child, are found deep within the brain and are known as 'ectopic cells' or brain warts. These clusters of cells are mainly found in the left and front of the brain, the regions most important for reading and writing. Another difference frequently seen in the brains of dyslexic children is in the magnocellular system, which is the area of the brain dealing with moving images and visual perception; according to Bradford (2003) this is smaller in the brains of dyslexic children than in non-dyslexic children. With the use of an EEG it is possible to see increased brain activity on the right side of the brain when a child with dyslexia begins to read (in an advanced reader, this increased activity is more noticeable on the left side of the brain). Bradford (2003) suggests that this unusual variation in left and right activity in dyslexic children could be an explanation for why they often find reading activities very tiring, as they are using the side of the brain not usually 'wired' for language, so they are working harder to effect reading.

Visual or perceptual disturbance?

According to Stein and Talcott (1999), magnocells are large neurons in the brain. To enable reading to be successful the visual magnocellular system needs to be working efficiently, and any weaknesses can lead to visual confusion of letter order and poor visual memory for the written word. Stein and Talcott (1999) believe that there may also be an auditory equivalent, essential for meeting the phonological demands of reading and speaking, leading to a confusion of letter sounds and weak phonology. The cerebellum, which contains the magnocells, is also thought to contribute to the control of steady eye fixations and timing for visual events when reading. This area of the brain is also thought to be responsible for 'inner speech', the term that Vygotsky (1978) coined for the silent, internalised monologue which is necessary for sounding out words. The cerebellum therefore signals any visual motion that occurs if unintentional movements lead to images moving off the retinal slip (fovea); these signals would normally bring the eyes back on target. According to this research many children who are dyslexic have poor binocular fixation (ie where both eyes are focusing upon the same object at the same time) and hence visual perceptual instability, where the letters on a page *appear* to move. Thus good magnocellular function is essential for reading.

To enable reading to take place in most European languages, the eye movements across the page will usually be in a left to right direction. Studies by Zangwill and Blakemore (1972) found that in children with reading disabilities, the eyes moved more slowly across the page, and they were more prone to making regressions. In 1993 Evans concluded that those who have difficulty with reading increased the number of fixations (discussed in Chapter 4), to inspect the written word, and this resulted in a very slow read and many more regressions. The key issue here is one of cause and effect, that is, atypical eye movements could be the result of poor reading skills or the underlying cause, and this is an area hotly debated. Visual causes of dyslexia have been the subject of considerable research particularly with reference to the dominance of one eye over another. Stein and Fowler (1985) showed that 68 per cent of dyslexic children had an unstable reference eye; however, some of the research conducted in this area has proved hard to replicate and the findings somewhat controversial.

Scotopic Sensitivity Syndrome

Perceptual disturbance as a cause for dyslexia has long been of interest to researchers, and this was exemplified by Helen Irlen (1991), who claimed to have discovered a new condition, Scotopic Sensitivity Syndrome or Irlen Syndrome. This suggested that features of photophobia (a sensitivity of the eyes to light) were common to children and adults with dyslexia, causing discomfort and resulting in an inability to see groups of words or letters at the same time.

> Scotopic Sensitivity Syndrome is not, of itself, a learning difficulty in the accepted sense. Rather, it is a complex and variable condition often found to exist as a component of dyslexia, dyscalculia, attention deficit disorder and many other learning problems.
>
> (Irlen, 1991, p 30)

However, Irlen is keen to point out that dyslexia is *not* a disorder of the eyes, but rather a perceptual processing disorder, that is, the brain alters the way in which it interprets what the eye 'sees'. Irlen (1991) claims that children with Scotopic Sensitivity Syndrome also have difficulties with concentration; she believes that between 50 and 75 per cent of children with SpLD suffer from this syndrome. These children complain that when they are reading, the visual disturbance means that they see the white background colour of the paper jumping out at them, rather than the dark type, resulting in the impression of the writing moving on the page in rivers and swirls. Irlen suggested that prescribing coloured/tinted lenses or coloured overlays to what is read could ease the problem.

Figure 6.3 *Examples of visual perceptual disturbances of Irlen Syndrome, adapted from Irlen (1998).*

Subjective reports have certainly shown that some people find coloured lenses and overlays very useful, but according to Ott (1997) conclusive proof from 'vigorous scientific studies', that tinted lenses or overlays can help poor reading performance or visual disturbances, is not yet available.

Stress and anxiety?

According to Hunter-Carsch (2001), 82 per cent of the children and young adults with dyslexia in her research stated that reading and writing difficulties had impeded their progress at school. Of the adults that she surveyed, many said that it had severely affected their vocational options and life experiences. The children in the Hunter-Carsch (2001) survey described feelings of fear, shame, anger, frustration, distress and confusion, when they attempted to read and write. This in turn builds up a picture of loneliness, aberration, humiliation, unfair treatment and inappropriate help. The following quotation is from a text written by the three times Emmy winning actress Susan Hampshire OBE, who has been a champion of dyslexia issues for many years.

> *After I had been diagnosed as being dyslexic I couldn't be helped to overcome my dyslexia, because by that time I had got myself into such a state that I had a nervous breakdown...I went catatonic and I was totally agoraphobic. I literally sat at home next to the radiator rocking backwards and forwards, for months and months...when I tried to kill myself they put a care order on me and put me away in a special unit...I was given all sorts of drugs.*
>
> (Hampshire, 1991, pp 33–39)

Reading extracts such as this allows us to see the extent to which dyslexia can affect the day-to-day life, and even the mental health, of those with the condition if they are not given the right level of support that they need. To enable that support to be put into place it is important to understand the nature and severity of the difficulties. It is vital that the policy-makers, in government positions, be aware of the most up-to-date research in the field, and construct and adapt their policies with this research in mind. This will in turn illuminate and inform good practice.

There has been much evidence over the years (Beard, 1990; Crombie, 2002) that associates delays in early reading success with emotional factors, such as anxiety and depression, but it would be unfortunate to jump to the conclusion that these may be causes rather than the results of not learning to read, because the reverse seems a more likely and plausible conclusion. Clearly learning to read and anxiety can become a vicious circle of delay: the more anxious the child becomes about their inability to read, the less likely he/she is to be able to absorb the teaching and support that is being offered.

Identification of dyslexia in the early years

The identification of dyslexia in the past has usually occurred around the age of eight years, and this is because until this point children are not *expected* to be fluent readers; in fact it is 'normal' for children in the early years to be non-readers. Talking to the parents of children with the condition I have frequently heard the comment that when they raised their concerns with some teachers they were viewed as difficult parents, and told not to worry as children develop at different ages. Clearly this is true, but if you understand that an inability to read is an effect of dyslexia and not causal, you can see that reading is only one part of the condition and therefore should only form one part of the process of identification. Perhaps these teachers need to be taking a little more notice of parents, who know so much more about the whole child, when they flag an alert.

Screening

If the new genetic research is correct, then potentially it could be possible to identify children at risk of dyslexia (and other SpLDs) from birth or even before. The overwhelming advantage of this to the children is that appropriate support can be put in place from the earliest stage, and this could avoid the concurrent lowering of self-esteem and confidence that can occur. Mass genetic testing of young babies, however, would not be either financially feasible or morally acceptable to most parents. Such screening could lead to some very disturbing ethical issues around the concept of *'perfect babies'*. The fact that we *can* do something does not necessarily mean that we should.

However, there could be manifestations in our youngest children which might indicate their greater susceptibility to the condition, before reading underachievement occurs, and if these were identified, it would enable them to be closely monitored. Catts (1991) suggests that dyslexia is a developmental disorder which presents in different ways during overall development, and this he claims allows the potential for identification in the nursery based on oral language deficits. He suggests that young children who exhibit delays in their speech and language development (in particular semantic–syntactic difficulties), often but not always, go on to experience difficulties when learning to read. Shaywitz (2005) clarifies this further by saying that signs to be aware of are children who are not saying their first words until after 15 months of age, and do not speak in phrases until after 2 years of age.

Singleton (1992) said that rather than *label* a child (which is a phrase which has very negative connotations), screening for dyslexia could avoid the child being wrongly labelled as lazy or stupid at a later stage. Conversely such early screening could lead to mis-identification of children (both through false-positive and false-negative identification), which in turn could disadvantage the child by having low expectations of their achievements, and putting in place the self-fulfilling prophecy. Children particularly at risk of this are those whose development, in all other areas, is at norm or above norm.

One of the many difficulties of assessing children at such a young age is their quite normal lack of good verbal skills, and the problem with any screening process used is whether their lack of positive response is down to the particular test, or their lack of receptive and expressive language. It is vital that any assessor is able to use a range of spoken language, non-verbal language and visual prompts to ensure that the young child is able to understand what is required of the test. A compounding factor is that shy and quiet children may not respond well to being assessed, especially if this is an unfamiliar adult, and so may be unwilling to co-operate. Another potential challenge is the relatively short attention span of very young children, and therefore any screening tests need to be adapted to play-based activities.

Any or all of these difficulties could lead to unstable screening results, and some researchers have suggested that it is perhaps unsafe to embark upon an identification of dyslexia in the early years. However, screening *could* provide indicators of children who are at greater risk, and they could be targeted for further and more detailed screening/monitoring in the future. This could provide an early warning system for children who may be at risk, and allow opportunities for more detailed and targeted observational assessment.

Early identification

If you are working in an early years setting now, what should you be looking for?

This question is not as easy as it sounds as there are so many indicators, but they do not all occur in every child, and this may depend upon the severity of the condition and the number of co-morbid conditions that lie with it. However, most researchers in the field agree that a familial link is probably the strongest indicator of all. In other words the child may have one or both parents, or perhaps a grandparent, already identified with the condition. The British Dyslexia Association (online) offers the following additional pointers to be aware of.

- Finds nursery rhymes hard to learn – *however, children who have not heard the rhymes before or those with English as a second language may be starting from a different base level.*

- Finds it hard to listen to stories and hard to sit still – *poor concentration generally.*

- Enjoys listening to stories but has no interest in the letters or words on the page – *looks at the book but never asks about words or letters.*

- Finds it hard to learn the words to songs or to recite the alphabet – *memory and sequencing issues.*

- Speech slow to develop – *poor vocabulary with limited grammar and poor pronunciation.*

- Directional difficulties – *confusion over terms such as before/after, right/left and up/down etc.*

- Often an early walker but has a limited crawling stage – *rarely crawls but may bottom shuffle and then just gets up and walks.*

- Often gets words muddled – *jamas instead of pyjamas, nana instead of banana.*

- Finds it hard to maintain a simple rhythm – *clapping, playing a drum or a triangle.*

- Finds it hard to follow a sequence of two or more instructions, but is fine if they are given individually – *'Wash this cup under the tap (1), take it to Mrs Jones (2) and tell her that we are all finished now (3).'*

- Finds it hard to remember names – *name of the practitioner or teacher, names of colours etc.*

- Finds it hard to understand concepts – *colour, shape, size etc.*

- Poor auditory discrimination – *They may appear to have difficulty with their hearing, especially if there is lots of background noise. Cannot distinguish individual phonemes, so finds it hard to distinguish between:*

    Cat and Hat

    Dog and Dot

    Pat and Pet

- Finds scissors and mark making tools difficult – *always be aware of the child who is left handed or ambidextrous.*

- Finds the fine motor skills required for getting dressed difficult – *fastening zips, threading buttons, tying shoe laces etc.*

- Finds the sequence of dressing difficult – *forgets to put his/her vest on before their shirt, puts clothes on back to front etc.*

- Poor personal organisation – *always loses things, never has a pencil when needed or outside without their coat.*

- Finds it hard to catch and/or throw a ball: *playing games with peers and adults.*

- Always falling over, bumping into things or tripping – *what used to be called the 'clumsy child'.*

- Finds it hard to skip and hop – *be aware that these are high level skills and most children find these hard until they are at least five years of age.*

- Memory retrieval problems – *cannot recall what happened earlier in the day.*

- Has 'good' and 'bad' days for no apparent reason – *don't we all!*

Considering this list I am sure that you can see any one of these indicators in *all* children that you care for, and this would be perfectly normal. The concern comes when a number of these issues cluster together in one child.

Poor phonological awareness

Probably the most studied indicator is that of phonological awareness, that is, whether the child can:

- identify rhyming words (dog, log, pog);

- blend sounds together (m-a-t put them together to form 'mat');

- provide the final sound to a word (bed – the final sound is D);

- manipulate/delete sounds in words ('rat' without the first sound is 'at').

This ability is likely to be related to their early vocabulary growth around 18 months–2.6 years. Muter (2005) suggests that although initially they acquire language in individual words, as they mature they notice how words overlap and have similar sounds and appearance. It is this knowledge that produces the vocabulary growth spurt seen at this stage, which is described in Chapter 3 of this book. Muter (2005) also draws attention to the speed at which children acquire letter knowledge and their ability to relate sounds to letters. Her research suggests that children who make faster progress with this are also those that make faster progress when learning to read. These two aspects, phonological awareness and a comprehensive knowledge of letter/sound relationships, interact, link and merge with each other to produce the skilled reader.

It must be emphasised that it is not possible to cure dyslexia or any of the other SpLDs as they are constitutional in origin, but it is likely that early identification could enable targeted intervention to take place, before the child experiences the lack of self-esteem and other social/emotional problems that frequently result in devastating failure.

Table 6.2 Importance of vocabulary to reading, adapted from Muter (2005).

Pre-school	Nursery	School
Vocabulary		
	Phonological awareness	
	Letter knowledge ──────── ►Reading	
	Phonological...letter linkage	

Testing, profiling and monitoring

It is easy to see that all pre-school children *could* be screened and it could be done straight-forwardly and cheaply by non-teaching early years practitioners. Crombie et al (2004) suggest a simple observational screening process for practitioners to use.

1. Ask the child to balance on the spar of an upturned bench or equivalent.

2. Ask them to count to five.

3. Ask them to recite a rhyme.

4. Observe a sequencing activity such as fastening buttons, ordering a short story, sorting three story cards or copying a sequence of three movements.

Crombie et al (2004) emphasised that while this will not label a child it could be an indicator for future monitoring.

The Early Years Foundation Stage profiles are a system of base line assessment of children entering school. This type of assessment probably has two aetiological strands.

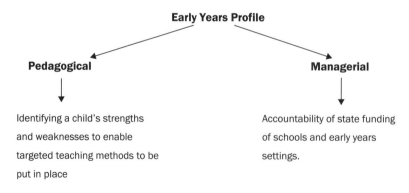

Figure 6.4 Aetiology of the Early Years Profile.

However, the EYFS profile must not be seen as a diagnostic tool, but rather a chance to obtain evidence based information about children arriving at school from diverse origins and settings and comparability to the norm. The information is, however, of value only if *used* by the schools and teachers, but subjective evidence when talking to early years practitioners has suggested that not many teachers consider the information useful. Teachers cite poor consistency between settings in their production of the profiles as a reason to disregard the information. It must also be remembered that language and literacy forms only a minimal part of the profile, so it could be said to be too general for identification purposes, and could have potential risk elements, but it could also flag up areas for more careful monitoring and observation in the future. Clearly this is an area for further well-validated research to take place.

Co-morbidity

Research by Haslum and Miles (2007) and others has repeatedly found that dyslexia rarely occurs alone, and children with identified dyslexic tendencies are frequently found to have other co-morbid conditions alongside, reacting with their dyslexia. Conditions such as Developmental Communication Disorder (hereafter referred to as DCD), ADHD, Specific Speech Disorder, Specific Language Impairment, Dyscalculia, Dysgraphia etc are commonly co-morbid conditions. An example of this can be seen in Figure 6.5.

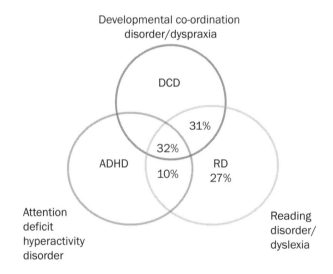

Figure 6.5 *Co-morbid conditions, adapted from Kaplan et al (1998).*

Depending upon whose work you read, there are between 70 and 80 different learning differences which appear to be related to dyslexia, including the following more commonly known ones:

•   attention deficit disorder (ADD);

•   attention deficit and hyperactivity disorder (ADHD);

- autism;

- Asperger's syndrome (pervasive developmental disorder, similar to autism but less severe);

- central auditory processing disorder (affects the way that the brain recognises and interprets sounds, particularly speech);

- dyscalculia (difficulties with number and calculation);

- dysgraphia (impairment with writing – just holding a pencil and writing on the line is difficult);

- dysmapia (difficulties making and interpreting maps and cartography);

- dysphasia (Specific Language Impairment/SLI).

So dyslexia is rarely a stand-alone condition, but these conditions frequently cluster together in a range of different combinations and vary in degree from one child to another producing a series of spectrum disorders which can range from mild to severe, and anywhere in between, along a continuum.

Mild dyslexia   Severe dyslexia

Figure 6.6 *Spectrum disorders.*

CASE STUDY

Nazia

Nazia is now at a university enjoying her degree in Early Childhood Studies, and she wants to be a teacher in Key Stage 1, but as a child no one thought that she would ever be able to achieve what she has. Nazia was described as a difficult child at school, a late talker and poor reader. When she talks about her experiences at school she recalls the frustration, embarrassment and isolation of her time. She describes how as a child she felt that she was not wanted at home because she was so 'stupid', and that at school it felt that her teachers were cruel to her because she was always getting things wrong. Nazia describes the teasing and bullying that she got from her classmates, and how they never chose her to play with them. In time she became quite disruptive at school and unwilling to co-operate with the teachers.

Nazia's parents were very supportive, although at first they did not understand what was the matter with her. She claims that without their help she could very easily have 'gone off the rails' and ended up in the criminal justice system. Nazia's self-esteem still is low, and she is always in a state of self-doubt, and she describes it as a tremendous 'relief' when before sitting her A levels she was identified with dyslexia. She now understands her condition better, and takes advantage of the support available in the university. She is determined to complete her degree and start her teaching programme.

Critical questions

» *How do you think that Nazia's experiences in early life will affect how she works with children in the early years?*

» *How valuable do you think it would have been for Nazia if her diagnosis had been earlier?*

» *What sort of support do you think would have helped Nazia's parents?*

» *In the light of your understanding of the difficulty of defining dyslexia, make a list of the behaviours that you think may have presented in Nazia before she started school. Can your list be placed in order of priority?*

Social and academic expectations

Children have a fundamental emotional need to be loved and accepted by others. This forms the basis of the development of their self-esteem and feelings of self-empowerment; however, with no sense of belonging it may be hard to show socially acceptable modes of behaviour. According to research by Heiervang et al (2001), children who continue to read inaccurately and have trouble with spelling and handwriting risk becoming frustrated by their own inabilities. In my experience these children are often labelled 'slow' and 'thick' by the bullies and the uninitiated, and can become moody and depressed. Research by Newman (1999) suggested that by the time they leave school their self-image and worth can have disappeared off the bottom of the scale. These children could well be heading for prison or worse (Newman, 1999).

Even before they start school many children with dyslexic tendencies will have experienced difficulties and can be identified as the child who *cannot* do things. Children who cannot join in and play effectively can become marginalised in their play. Some children will react to this by becoming isolated, while others vent their frustrations by showing aggressive behaviour, and this might result in bullying, ridicule and social exclusion. The same difficulties can affect the child's experiences out of school, such as cubs/beavers/brownies/rainbows/after-school clubs etc. Here competitive games and the ability to read and write are often key components of the core activities. All of these issues mean that the social and academic expectations in the child's environment can result in high levels of stress and anxiety, which may result in psychosomatic symptoms such as stomach aches, headaches etc. Unless these signs are recognised and action taken, there is always the danger of a child becoming a school refuser or at least disenchanted with academic work. All this adds up to a child who is very unhappy.

Dyslexia friendly initiative

The idea of a dyslexia friendly school originated in a school in Flintshire, with an inspirational teacher called Neil Mackay. He saw that the type of specialist teaching being put in place in many of the specialist dyslexia units was in fact just good teaching, and that all children with their individual learning differences could benefit from this. He saw that a whole-school approach was going to benefit all the children, and that dyslexia was the responsibility of all teachers and should not be 'hived off' to special education. As a result of this new thinking, and in co-operation with the British Dyslexia Association, a Dyslexia Friendly kite mark was born. Mackay (2005) recognised that the cornerstone of such an initiative has to be ongoing staff training, and ideally every member of staff in a school or nursery (both teaching and non-teaching staff) needs to be trained and supported. It is vital for the success of this initiative that any staff, in contact with the child, are appropriately trained and aware. This approach allows for all staff to respond suitably to the needs of the children within their care, without having to wait for the child to fail for a substantial period and having a label, before doing anything about it. This approach makes it a truly inclusive environment for all the children and needs to be at the forefront of every school's curriculum and pedagogy.

However, the current approach, by the government, to the teaching of language and literacy would appear to fly in the face of this inclusivity, with an insistence upon a very structured, synthetic phonics approach to learning to read. You might question whether a single approach will work with all children, all of the time. Winebrenner (1996) suggests that no one programme, or single approach, can take into account the individual learning patterns and multiple intelligences (Gardner 1993) of all the children in a school. No one method can seek to value individual talents and specialisms of the children or indeed the teachers who work with these children.

The Dyslexia Friendly Schools initiative carries with it some excellent ideas for integrating children with dyslexia into mainstream classrooms, with suitably qualified staff and leadership, appropriate resources of time and management, and effective partnerships with parents and pupils. However, it is clear from my earlier research into schools in Wales (Hayes, 2007) that within some schools this policy is not working in the way in which it was intended. Despite this, many of the schools, within the research sample, did claim that they were working within a Dyslexia Friendly framework. The comforting phraseology of being 'friendly' could be working against the children with dyslexia, by preventing them accessing the specialist intervention that they require, as staff console themselves with the idea that by being 'friendly' and empathetic to the children, they are doing the best that they can to enable their pupils to fulfil their potential. My research into schools in Wales (2007) indicated that the schools claiming to be Dyslexia Friendly were struggling to meet the stringent requirements of the quality mark process and found it hard to find time, with all the new government initiatives, to screen the children. They also reported upon the training which Mackay (2005) identified as so essential to this method of working, and showed that most schools had no staff with additional qualifications in dyslexia, and most had not even had an inset day on the subject.

Children are traditionally taught in groups and classes, which makes it extremely difficult for teachers and schools to cater for individual differences of the children. In order to be responsive to their needs, policies of exclusion (children in special needs schools, separate from the mainstream), integration (children in mainstream schools taught alongside mainstream) and inclusion (children taught within mainstream) have all been put forward. You might question whether it is a practical suggestion for every school to have a policy for every eventuality. If they do have a policy for dyslexia should they also have one for attention deficit disorder, dyspraxia, autism etc, or is one which addresses all specific learning difficulties enough? Considering the prevalence of dyslexia in the population, perhaps there is a case for suggesting that this condition should have a policy formulated to deal specifically with the needs of children with this condition. However, any policy decided upon must be a working document that is used constantly, regularly reviewed, and revised in the light of new research.

Chapter reflections

From what you have read in this chapter it makes sense to assume that the earlier dyslexic tendencies are identified, the sooner appropriate intervention can be put in place and the more likely it is that the sense of failure associated with SpLDs can be avoided. It is important to understand that this is not about labelling, but about monitoring and intervention. It may not be possible to identify children who are dyslexic before going into school, but it is possible to identify children who are at risk. Early screening in the nursery may enable the child's school to be better informed and allow them to be adequately prepared to put that appropriate monitoring and intervention in place.

You have seen in this chapter that the brains of those with dyslexia look and function differently from those of skilled readers. It is unlikely that one gene is responsible for this, rather an interaction between multiple genes pre-disposing to dyslexia and SpLDs, but not defining them. Importantly the epigenesis of inherited factors and environmental circumstances may make a child more susceptible to the conditions.

DEVELOPING CRITICAL THINKING

Reflection is an important area of critical thinking. At its simplest this just means thinking about something, replaying it in your mind and considering different ways in which this could have unfolded. When you are reading you need to reflect on what you read and consider some of the following.

* Is the information just the author's opinion?
* Has the author backed up the information with unbiased evidence in research?
* Has the author offered a balanced view of the evidence that they have reviewed?

Consider how you could make *your* reading more active and purposeful.

Critical thinking activity

Reflect upon the elements of critical thinking so far discussed in this book. As you read on you will find these themes discussed in more detail.

Evaluation	Reflection
Finding evidence	Reading
Creating arguments	Structuring and planning

»   *Look back over the book and write one short sentence to describe each of these.*

»   *With these areas in mind, reflect upon your own academic writing and think of four things that you like about the way that you write and four things that you would like to improve.*

Things that I like about the way that I write	Things that I would like to improve
1.	1.
2.	2.
3.	3.
4.	4.

Further reading

Davis, R D and Braun, E M (2010) *The Gift of Dyslexia, Revised and Expanded: Why Some of the Smartest People Can't Read...and How They Can Learn.* New York: Perigee Trade.

This is an updated and expanded version of a classic text which has helped to reshape a whole vision of what dyslexia is, and how it feels to have this condition. Ronald Davis is himself dyslexic and he sets out to produce a text which is not only founded in up-to-date research, but also offers practical step-by-step ideas for you to support children with this condition. The author attempts to portray dyslexia in a positive light, moving from a negative and deficit model to one which builds upon the strengths of the condition and the unique learning style associated with it. This book deals with a range of interconnected conditions such as dyscalculia, dysgraphia, ADD and ADHD but dyslexia is at its heart. It concentrates upon aspects of orientation and attention focus that the authors believe are essential to supporting fellow dyslexics.

References

Andrew, S and Chivers, M (eds) (1996) *The Inner Hurt.* Peterborough: Poetrynow.

Beard, R (1990) *Developing Reading 3–13* (2nd ed). London: Hodder and Stoughton.

Bradford, J (2003) *What Causes Dyslexia?* www.worldofdyslexia.com (accessed 28.02.15). Dyslexia on Line Magazine.

British Dyslexia Association (2007) Definition. www.bdadyslexia.org.uk/dyslexic/definitions (accessed 21.06.15).

Catts, H (1991) *Early Identification of Dyslexia: Evidence from a Follow Up Study of Speech-Language Impaired Children.* Annals of Dyslexia, Vol 41. University of Kansas: Orton Dyslexia Society.

Critchley, M (1975) Specific Developmental Dyslexia. In Lenneberg, E H and Lenneberg, E (eds) *Foundations of Language Development.* New York: Academic Press.

Crombie, M (2002) *Dealing with Diversity in the Primary Classroom: A Challenge for the Class Teacher.* In Reid, G and Wearmouth, J (eds) *Dyslexia and Literacy.* Chichester: Wiley.

Davis, R D and Braun, E M (2010) *The Gift of Dyslexia, Revised and Expanded: Why Some of the Smartest People Can't Read...and How They Can Learn.* New York: Perigee Trade.

Department for Education (DfE) (1993) *Education Act.* London: HMSO.

Doyle, J (1996) *Dyslexia: An Introductory Guide.* London: Whurr.

Ellis, A W (1984) *Reading, Writing and Dyslexia.* London: Open University Press.

Evans, B (1993) Dyslexia, Eye Movements, Controversial Optometric Therapies and Transient Visual Systems. *Optometry Today*, 33: 17–19.

Frith, U (2002) Resolving the Paradoxes of Dyslexia. In Reid, G and Wearmouth, J, *Dyslexia and Literacy: Theory and Practice.* Chichester: John Wiley and Sons Ltd.

Frost, J A and Emery, M J (1995) *Academic Interventions for Children with Dyslexia Who Have Phonological Core Deficits.* www.ericdigests.org/1996-1/academic.htm (accessed 21.06.15).

Galaburda, A M, Sherman, G F, Rosen, G D, Aboitiz, F, Geschwind, N (1985) Developmental Dyslexia: Four Consecutive Patients with Cortical Anomalies. *Annals of Neurology*, 18 (2): 222–233.

Gardner, H (1993) *Frames of Mind: The Theory of Multiple Intelligences.* London: Fontana.

Guardiola, J G (2001) Evolution of Research on Dyslexia. *Psychologia*, 32 (1): 3–30.

Hampshire, S (1991) *Every Letter Counts: Winning in Life Despite Dyslexia.* London: Corgi.

Haslum, M and Miles T (2007) Motor Performance and Dyslexia in a National Cohort of 10 Year Old Children. *Dyslexia*, 13 (4) (November): 257–275.

Hayes, C A (2007) *Policy and Prevalence of Dyslexia in Wales.* Unpublished research. University of Liverpool.

Heiervang, E, Lund, A, Stevenson, J and Hugdhal, K (2001) Behaviour Problems in Children with Dyslexia. *Nordic Journal of Psychiatry*, 55 (4): 251–256.

Hinshelwood, J (1895) Word-Blindness and Visual Memory. *The Lancet*, 2: 1564–1570.

Hunter-Carsch, M (2001) *Dyslexia: A Psychosocial Perspective.* London: Whurr.

Irlen, H (1991) *Reading by Colours.* New York: Perigee.

Irlen Institute (1998) *Sample Distortions* www.irlen.com/ (accessed 16.10.15).

Kaplan, B, Wilson, B, Dewey, D and Crawford, S (1998) DCD May Not Be a Discrete Disorder. *Human Movement Science*, 17: 471–490.

Kere, J (2014) The Molecular Genetics and Neurobiology of Developmental Dyslexia as Model of a Complex Phenotype. *Biochemical and Biophysical Research Communications*, 425: 236–243.

Mackay, N (2005) *Removing Dyslexia as a Barrier to Achievement.* Wakefield: SEN Marketing.

Miles, T (2004) Some Problems in Determining the Prevalence of Dyslexia. *Electronic Journal of Research in Educational Psychology*, 2 (2): 5–12.

Muter, V (2005) *Language, Phonology and Beginning to Read.* In Tresman, S and Cooke, A (eds), *The Dyslexia Handbook.* Bracknell: British Dyslexia Association.

Newbury, F, Monaco, A P and Paracchini, S (2014) *Reading and Language Disorders: The Importance of Both Quantity and Quality. Genes,* 5: 285–309.

Newman, D (1999) When Words Dance. *Guardian Weekend.* 24.04.99. London.

Ott, P (1997) *How to Detect and Manage Dyslexia.* Oxford: Heinemann.

Peer L and Reid G (2000) *Multilingualism, Literacy and Dyslexia: A Challenge for Educators.* London: David Fulton.

Poole, J (2003) Dyslexia: A Wider View. The Contribution of an Ecological Paradigm to Current Issues. *Educational Research,* 45 (2): 167–180.

Pringle Morgan, W (1896) A Case for Congenital Word Blindness. *British Medical Journal,* 2 (1): 1378–1379.

Pumfrey, P D and Reason, R (1991) *Specific Learning Difficulties: Dyslexia Challenges and Responses.* London: Routledge.

Reid, G and Wearmouth, J (eds) (2002) *Dyslexia and Literacy: Theory and Practice.* Chichester: John Wiley and Sons Ltd.

Rose, J (2009) *Identifying and Teaching Children and Young People with Dyslexia and Literacy Difficulties.* London: DCSF-Crown.

Shaywitz, S (2005) *Overcoming Dyslexia.* New York: Vintage Books.

Singleton, C H (1992) Current Research on the Early Identification of Dyslexia. *Dyslexia Contact,* 11: 13–17.

Snowling, M (2000) *Dyslexia.* Oxford: Blackwell.

Stein, J and Fowler, L (1985) Effect of Monocular Occlusion on Visuomotor Perception and Reading in Dyslexic Children. *The Lancet,* 13.07.85: 69–73.

Stein, J and Talcott, J (1999) Impaired Neuronal Timing in Developmental Dyslexia: The Magnocellular Hypothesis. *Dyslexia,* 5: 59–77.

Tansley, P and Panckhurst, J (1981) *Children with Specific Learning Difficulties: A Critical Review.* Windsor: NFER-Nelson.

Turner, M (1997) *Psychological Assessment of Dyslexia.* London: Whurr.

Vygotsky, L S (1978). *Mind in Society: The Development of Higher Psychological Processes.* Cambridge, MA: Harvard University Press.

Whittaker, M E (1981) Letter. *The Times Educational Supplement. The Times,* UK. 13.11.81.

Winebrenner, S (1996) *Teaching Kids with Learning Difficulties in the Regular Classroom.* Minneapolis: Free Spirit.

World Federation for Neurology (1968) *Report of Research Group on Dyslexia and World Illiteracy.* Dallas: WFN.

Zangwill, O L and Blakemore, C (1972) Dyslexics' Reversal of Eye Movements during Reading. *Neuropsychologia,* 10 (3): 371–373.

7 Gender influences

Girls are bundles of joy and gifts from heaven.
Boys pick their noses in front of 7-eleven!
Girls are made of sugar and spice and everything nice.
Boys are made of boogers, cooties and head lice.
Girls smell sweet like cut flowers.
Boys smell like doodie and never take showers.
Not all boys are useless!
Some boys have unique talents and contribute great things to society.
Some can actually read! (picture books, of course).

(Goldman, 2005, *Boys Are Stupid, Throw Rocks at Them!*)

Introduction

Is it a boy or a girl?

This is frequently the first excited question that a baby hears when s/he emerges at birth. Even with today's advanced technology, the sex of a newborn baby is often kept a well-guarded secret until after the birth. In modern human society there does seem to be an obsession with gender and the young baby. So exactly how different are boys and girls, or for that matter men and women? This chapter looks more closely at some of the gender barriers discussed in Chapter 6, and some attempt will be made to analyse why there is unequal performance in boys and girls and to consider some of the myths that surround this area of research.

Where are we now?

This is a strangely contested question, especially when you deviate from examining the physical difference (which you can clearly see), to differences of the mind (which are not so easy to see). Some would challenge whether there are any innate differences of the mind, referring to 'pseudoscience' and 'neurosexism'; they would claim that if such differences exist they are simply a product of stereotyping and social conditioning. Cameron (2008) suggests that this whole area has the potential to be politically highly sensitive, and because it has been such a 'hot potato', the role of genetics has at times been ignored. She claims that some writers have had to:

> present themselves as latter-day Galileos, braving the wrath of the political correctness lobby by daring to challenge the feminist orthodoxy which denies that men and women are by nature profoundly different.
>
> (Cameron, 2008, p 2)

There is certainly no reliable evidence that men are more intelligent than women (despite what some may like to tell us!), but it does not take much research to see that women are under-represented in certain occupations, particularly those involving science, maths, engineering and technology. On the contrary, they are over represented in occupations requiring empathy and advanced language and communication skills, such as teaching, childcare, social work and psychology etc. Emmeline Pankhurst and the suffragettes fought long and hard to ensure that society accepted the equality of women, with equal rights and opportunities. Perhaps this is why we are repelled by the idea that males and females could be different, think differently and behave differently, regarding this as discrimination and stereotypical.

Exploding the myths

There are so many myths and fabrications that talk about the gender gap that they have almost formed part of our accepted thinking in early years, to the point where they are not really questioned and reflected upon any more. Often there is no reliable evidence to substantiate these ideas, and the following section will try briefly to separate the fact from the fantasy.

Myth number 1: boys never achieve as well as girls in language and literacy tasks

WRONG! This is not correct and many boys achieve as highly as, and often more highly than, girls. The Department for Children, Schools and Families (DCSF) (2009) showed that social class and ethnicity were more significant markers for achievement in language and literacy tasks than gender. However, it is likely that the interplay between these factors is probably more indicative of poor achievement than any one of these alone.

Myth number 2: all girls achieve better than boys across the curriculum areas

WRONG! This is also not correct. While there is some evidence (National Literacy Trust, 2012) that statistically boys do less well at communication, literacy and language based tasks, in other areas of the curriculum, such as maths, science and technology, males and females are broadly similar.

Myth number 3: boys are not appropriately catered for in our schools and early years settings due to an over feminisation of the curriculum

UNLIKELY! It is certainly true that in the early years and Key Stage 1 there is a preponderance of female practitioners and teachers. However, there is no reliable research evidence that this affects genders either positively or negatively. I often hear the plea for more male early years practitioners, and I would certainly not oppose the drive to get more males involved in early years, as common sense probably tells you that they bring a different aspect to practice. However, I find no definitive evidence of this improving male achievement or literacy and language rates. So despite the many calls for more males in early years, the strength of the effect may not be as profound as you may think. I cite the example of both World War I and II, when most active and fit young men were drafted away from home, often for many months and even years. Young children at this time were cared for both at home and in schools and nurseries, almost exclusively by women, but I have read of no evidence that this gender imbalance was detrimental to their rates of learning or potential for academic success. I am not suggesting that we do not try to recruit more males to early years, but hoping to resolve the gender gap by supplying more males is not, I believe, a feasible solution.

While teachers and practitioners need to be constantly vigilant and reflective of their pedagogy, and the way in which they present the curriculum to avoid gender stereotyping, there is little evidence that providing a 'boy-friendly' curriculum is effective (whatever that might mean). Potentially this could reflect the practitioner's own gender expectations, stereotyping expected male behaviour and preferences. DCSF (2009) claim that having *'high expectations'* of *all* children is what increases achievement, not inclining to one gender or the other. This sentiment is echoed by Whitmire (2010) who suggests that what boys respond to is 'good teaching', not male teachers.

Myth number 4: males and females have innately different learning styles

VERY CONTROVERSIAL. The whole concept of 'learning styles' is hotly contested. The phrase 'learning style' really means that different people have different ways to learn the same thing. The theory goes that you would learn better if the teaching was targeted to your particular learning style. However, I find no credible evidence that learning styles exist in this way, and certainly nothing that indicates a gender split.

> *Research has questioned the validity of notions of discrete learning styles, and studies have also failed to find conclusive links between gender and learning style.*
>
> (DCSF, 2009, online)

A quick scan of the available literature on learning styles shows that there are literally thousands of papers written about this, but it also shows that reliable and valid, peer reviewed research is in very short supply. What you will find is a wealth of commercial companies willing to sell you their latest, expensive version of the idea. Each has different names for the so-called learning styles, and the number can range from 2 to over 70! Jarrett (2015) amusingly suggests:

if we view each learning style as dichotomous (e.g. visual vs. verbal) that means that there are 2 to the power of 71 combinations of learning styles – more than the number of people alive on the earth!

(Jarrett, 2015, p 208)

What is generally agreed by researchers is that we all learn differently and have different talents, abilities, interests, experiences and backgrounds. Each of us is an individual and probably we all learn in different ways, but this also highlights the impossibility of targeting practice to a particular learning style for every member of your group or class. You might even question whether this is desirable or not; surely we all need to have a range of ways of learning in our arsenal, to enable us to learn things as diverse as maths, changing a light bulb, philosophy, the creative arts etc. If we are not particularly adept at one, perhaps we should be trying to practise this and improve.

Myth number 5: assessments have a gender bias

CONTROVERSIAL. The one thing that researchers do appear to agree upon is that girls develop and mature more quickly than boys. This could have an influence upon testing and assessment which is often not accounted for, with both males and females assessed on similar scales at similar ages at similar times. The implication of this is that potentially some males will receive a false-positive assessment for language and literacy delay. It is very rare to find standardised psychological or literacy tests which compensate for cognitive gender differences.

Myth number 6: all boys prefer non-fiction to read

WRONG! Much has been written about boys preferring non-fiction materials over fiction. Levy (2011) challenges this idea and believes that boys' *perceived* preference for non-fiction is more to do with a lack of confidence in people's reaction to their choice of fiction. Boys could be concerned that the material that they choose is seen as 'babyish', rather than a text that is more about content and information which might not be classed in that light. Non-fiction can also be dipped into and out of more easily than fiction, and the style of reading non-fiction is different from the requirement for sustained reading of continuous fiction text.

The gender gap

Despite the myths mentioned earlier, concerning the differential of potential and ability for males and females, the actual statistical gender gap in educational attainment is well documented. The report by Formby (2014) for the National Literacy Trust suggests a 15 per cent gap between boys and girls in reaching expected literacy attainment in the Early Years Foundation Stage. Interestingly this gap is not restricted to the UK or even to English speaking countries, and evidence from the Programme of International Student Assessment (PISA) (2003) found similar discrepancies between male and female achievement in 32 different countries. An interesting argument was developed by Smith and Elley (1998), whose research looked at the gender gap in reading internationally. They noted that among the top ten countries for literacy achievement for both genders, only one, New Zealand, starts formal teaching of reading at the age of five years (as in England and Wales). In all the other countries, formal reading instruction does not start until seven years of age. In countries where children start at five years, there are large gender gaps in literacy development by the age of nine years. It is perhaps feasible to think that boys are not mature enough to learn to read at five years; they cannot achieve and therefore develop negative attitudes. Smith and Elley (1998) query whether we are spending our scarce resources on trying to bridge a gap, which may not occur if reading instruction started later.

Motivational rates and behaviour

Cigman (2014), while acknowledging that boys are as able as girls, suggests that, probably because of differences in maturational rates between males and females, they may learn at a different pace. For this reason she suggests that they may need to be taught separately. Clearly this is a controversial stance, particularly in this day of almost total co-education in primary schools and early years settings. Cigman (2014) emphasises the need for you to understand, not only typical child development, but also individual development rates, learned from close observation of the children in your care. An anecdote usually attributed to the philosopher and theologian Ignacio Estrada springs to mind here: 'If *a child can't learn the way we teach, maybe we should teach the way they learn.*' Cigman (2014) suggested that boys do not thrive within the passive learning methodology common to most early years settings and schools (sitting still, inactive listening, table-bound), as they are often unwilling or unable to accept this regime.

> *Practitioners taking part in the boys' writing project consistently described their boys as reluctant writers when asked to write by an adult, particularly if the writing was at a table. When writing opportunities moved to the places where boys chose to play and were included in the boys' play, they became keen and motivated writers.*
>
> (Cigman, 2014, p 9)

In Cigman's (2014) research project, early years boys were variously described by practitioners with the following labels:

- strong-willed;
- boisterous;
- competitive;
- in perpetual motion;
- an unguided missile!

Maclure and Jones (2009) showed that once a child was classified as 'difficult' or unwilling to conform, this was a label that was very hard to repudiate, and it could be that practitioners and teachers find this more boisterous behaviour just too inconvenient in the setting. However, the following more positive labels were also applied to boys by the practitioners in Cigman's research:

- enjoys discovery;
- likes to describe how things work;

- likes to list things;
- likes to classify things;
- is bold;
- is curious;
- is excited;
- is confident;
- is strong.

This second list is surely extremely positive, and these characteristics are ones which most practitioners would say they were striving to achieve with their children. These features need to be built upon and perhaps adapted to, if boys *and* girls are to achieve equally.

CASE STUDY

Boys at play

Attending a local early years setting (with an outstanding Ofsted report), I adopted the role of observer for the morning. In that short time it was clear that the boys were more active than the girls, preferring activities involving technology or construction over the book area or the domestic corner. Most of the boys' play observed was of a rough and tumble nature, and they appeared to require more space than the girls. The boys were moving constantly, and in the free flow circumstance, they appeared to prefer the outside area to the inside activities, even if those activities were the same. During the morning's observation none of the boys came voluntarily to a table to sit and draw or write, but would come reluctantly if *required* to do so by the nursery staff.

Clearly this is a very subjective snapshot of what goes on in early years, and is possibly not representative, but does agree with subjective comments heard from practitioners in other settings including the practitioners in Cigman's research; this appears to be the pattern of experiences for boys in many early years settings.

Critical questions

» *Observe the children in your own setting and consider whether you agree with what you have read. Does it apply to ALL the boys in your setting?*

» *Discuss with a colleague how you could incorporate more language based activities naturally into the activities that the boys appear to enjoy.*

» *Reflect on the design and layout of your setting. Do the literacy and language based activities stand out as exciting and interesting? For example, is your reading area small and uninviting, tucked out of the way at the back of the room or does it take 'centre stage', large, attractively presented and frequently reviewed?*

Gender and SpLD

It is frequently reported that difficulties with learning to read are generally more common in boys than girls. It is certainly true that there are more boys than girls receiving support with reading, possibly as much as four to six times as many. However, Shaywitz (2005) was keen to challenge the assumption that boys are inherently less able at reading than the girls. She believes that because most of the research studies are conducted on children who have already been identified with reading difficulty, there is a possibility that there may be bias in the identification process. Her research identified a representative sample of children of all abilities, *and* a sample of those already identified as poor readers for comparison. This rigorous, longitudinal study showed that school based identification procedures identified three to four times more male children with difficulties than female. However, the open sample showed no significant difference in the prevalence of reading difficulties between males and females.

> *In general when each child in a school or school district is individually tested, researchers report as many reading-disabled girls as boys.*
>
> (Shaywitz, 2005, p 32)

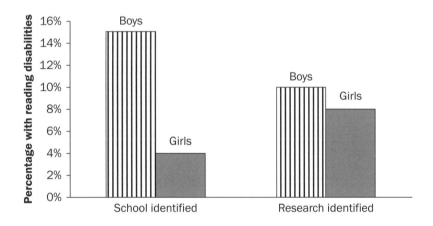

Figure 7.1 *Prevalence of reading disabilities in boys and girls, adapted from Shaywitz (2005).*

Teacher assessments

Shaywitz (2005) claims that there are significant differences between different teacher assessments of boys and girls, with classroom behaviour taking a significant role.

> *As a result, boys who are a bit rambunctious – although still within the normal range for the behavior of boys – may be perceived as having a behavior problem and referred for further evaluation.*
>
> (Shaywitz, 2005, p 33)

She believes that the girls who may be quieter than the boys and less physically active, but are nevertheless failing to read, are often overlooked and may never get the intensive support that they need. Although this research was conducted in America, the hypothesis put forward by Shaywitz may well have resonance here in England and Wales, but it is hard to assess and quantify, and Thomson (1990) says:

> It would depend very much on individual subculture norms, expectations and attitudes to the behavior of the sexes.

> (Thomson, 1990, p 26)

Brain imaging differences

Shaywitz (2005) went on to conduct a series of brain imaging studies that showed a difference between brain activation patterns in males and females during a language based activity.

> Men activated the left inferior frontal gyrus, while women activated the right as well as the left.

> (Shaywitz, 2005, p 77)

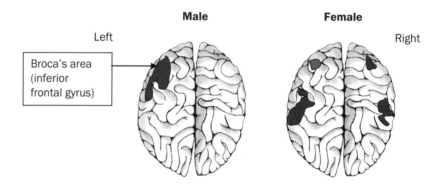

Figure 7.2 *Example of sex differences of brain activation during a language based activity, adapted from (Shaywitz, 2005).*

Using fMRI scans (functional Magnetic Resonance Imaging), Burman (2010) examined the gender differences in brain activity between boys and girls when reading. He concluded that although differences were small there was greater activity in girls than in the boys in the:

- inferior frontal gyrus;

- superior temporal gyrus (just above the external ear);

- fusiform gyrus (sometimes called the occipito-temporal gyrus).

These are all areas closely associated with language based tasks. Burman (2010), unlike Shaywitz, showed that boys and girls used both sides of the brain for these language tasks, but in boys he confirmed that there was more activity in the left side than in the right. Interestingly girls appeared to rely more on auditory/listening areas of the brain, while boys were dominated more by visual areas of the brain. Burman (2010) suggests that the reason for this is the girls are generally more developmentally advanced than boys, which would account for the process of 'catch up' which takes place in boys as they mature.

Research in America by Wannamaker (2008) also showed that boys were less likely than girls to read anything and were more susceptible to being diagnosed with conditions such as ADHD and ADD. Boys were also more likely to commit suicide than girls, to commit violent crimes, turn to drugs and alcohol, and to end up in the criminal justice system. Boys in the American study were more likely to end up in a remedial class and less likely to sit higher level qualifications. This was even referred to in 2005 by Laura Bush, the then First Lady of America, in an American television programme 'NewsWeek', as a 'boy crisis'.

Born to be a man?

As the foetal nerve cells in the brain develop they are influenced by the production and levels of the hormone testosterone. The production of testosterone programmes the brain before birth and causes the sexual differentiation of the brain. This programming process is also influenced by the production of the hormones oestrogen, progesterone, oxytocin, vasopressin, cortisol, dopamine and serotonin. The levels of each of these have been shown to influence the structure and operation of the brain, which in turn affects behaviour as shown in the list.

* **Cortisol**: probably responsible for the relief of stress and anxiety.
* **Dopamine**: this is a neurochemical which stimulates the pleasure areas of the brain.
* **Oestrogen**: found in much higher levels in females than males, and appears to influence the preference for avoiding conflict and maintaining harmony.
* **Oxytocin:** often attributed to the 'nest making' behaviour in girls, and to nurturing and bonding. It is also possible that oxytocin impedes memory and learning.
* **Progesterone**: while primarily a reproductive hormone, there is some evidence that it contributes to mood formation and aggressive behaviours.
* **Serotonin**: females have approximately 30 per cent more serotonin than males and it provides a sense of calm and control.
* **Testosterone**: found in much higher levels in males than females, is the sex drive hormone and can be responsible for aggression, competition and poor concentration.
* **Vasopressin:** an interactive hormone, and depending upon whether it interacts more with testosterone or oestrogen, it can support nurturing or aggressive behaviours.

Research into the exact nature of these hormones and their effects on the brain is still very incomplete, presenting a confused picture. New research is emerging all the time examining not only hormone levels, but also the timing of their production, and effects on development and maturation. However, despite these physiological differences there is still no real *proof* that they are innate, and the production of hormone levels, for example, could still be the result of social and environmental pressures, as the plasticity of the brain is so malleable and adaptable. It could be that Whitmire (2010) was right with his statement:

> *The world has gotten more verbal; boys haven't. (p 29)*

Size matters

Hormones are not the only difference between male and female brains. In most cases male brains are larger than those of females (that does not mean more intelligent!). On the whole males tend to be larger all over than females, taller, more heavily built etc. Male brains also appear to have more of what researchers call 'grey matter' than females, and females have more 'white matter', so called because of their appearance. Grey matter is made up of the cell bodies of neurones in the brain, and white matter connects the different regions of that grey matter. Females also usually have a larger hippocampus or memory centre than males.

Clearly these are subjects of great complexity and far beyond the scope of this book, especially as new and exciting discoveries about the working of the brain are being made almost daily. However, this whistle stop tour through these areas is enough to show that there are physiological differences in the brain of the newborn baby, which are likely to influence their ability to develop language at different rates, and possibly in different ways.

Boyd and Bee (2014) suggest there is one other physiological and maturational difference between genders that could be contributing to males being less advanced than females in writing. The bones in the wrist and the hand are fewer at birth than in an adult and these bones develop in girls at approximately four years and two months but in boys they are not developed until five years and six months. It is possible that this differential could affect fine motor skills and in turn boys' ability and motivation to want to write. This, Boyd and Bee (2014) say, is particularly noticeable when developing cursive writing, which boys appear to find harder than girls.

Environmental issues

Clearly there are biological differences between males and female but social/environmental differences probably also play a part. Adults react differently towards boys than girls, thereby providing the children with different childhood experiences, expectations and environments. From the moment of birth adults talk differently to boys and girls, using more emotional language to girls and more action type language to boys. Owens (2008) reports gender differences in the language interactions between children of different genders as well as the adults. He claims that adults frequently use longer sentences, with more complex sentence structures, when talking to two year-old girls than boys. This research also showed a greater willingness for adults to listen to girls than to boys, which resulted in more repetition and turn taking. However, Owens (2008) also suggested that it was possible that certain cultural practices may favour boys over girls and the importance paid to their education in general.

There is clearly some evidence that the differences between the genders in communication, language and literacy are environmental and socio-economically constructed. A report by Warren (2014), written for Save the Children, showed some disturbing figures in which white British males in low income families were likely to be among the poorest readers by the age of 11 years, and this included children for whom English was not their first language. Overall the number of girls in England, reading well by the age of 11 years, is, according to this report, 78 per cent compared to 72 per cent of the boys. Internationally there is also a gap between males' and females' reading levels but in England this gap appears to be one of the greatest. Save the Children (2014) report that only Romania, Norway, New Zealand and Australia have greater gaps between male and female literacy levels.

Social construction

If you accept that the gender gap in language and literacy is socially constructed, this implies that boys could be taught and guided to do things in a different way, when you learn to target the teaching appropriately to eliminate the gap. If, however, you see the gender gap as biological and unchangeable, the idea that 'boys will be boys', it follows that we are penalising boys for their rough and tumble play, play fighting, shooting and super hero production, which seems to be discriminatory and unworkable. This brings into question whether today's schools and nurseries, with an emphasis upon sitting still and passive learning, are better suited to girls than boys.

Moseley (1972) examined the motivation of males to acquire language and showed that peer pressure played a vital role, as they were more influenced by the approval of their peers than their parents, teachers or other adults. In other words they did not see it as 'cool' to read! In so many areas girls mature more quickly than boys, but no more so than in verbal skills. Girls' spoken language develops more quickly than boys' in verbal encoding and short-term memory (Thomson, 1990); on average a 20-month-old girl has twice the vocabulary of a 20-month-old boy (Burman, 2010). This could be linked to hemisphere function, and in particular to the link between the left hemisphere of the brain and language development. Interestingly, according to Thomson (1990), the right hemisphere of the brain is responsible for visuospatial function, and boys tend to be better at visuospatial tasks, so perhaps this disparity between the two hemispheres could be linked in some way to the higher incidence of language and literacy related difficulties in boys.

Reading for pleasure

Research by the National Literacy Trust (2012) reports an important difference between males and females when reading for pleasure. This report, with a sample of 17,089 children, demonstrated the following in the 8–11 years age groups:

* 73 per cent of girls reported that they enjoyed reading;
* 59 per cent of boys reported that they enjoyed reading;
* 24 per cent of boys read for pleasure less than once a week;
* 13 per cent of girls read for pleasure less than once a week;

- 17 per cent of boys said that they *never* read outside the classroom;
- 8 per cent of girls said that they *never* read outside the classroom;
- 51 per cent of boys said that reading was 'cool';
- 62 per cent of girls said that reading was 'cool';
- boys were twice as likely to read comics as girls;
- girls were more likely to read a range of genres;
- girls were more likely than boys to visit a library;
- 8 per cent of boys claim that they NEVER write outside school;
- 4 per cent of girls claim that they NEVER write outside school.

Clark and Douglas (2011) reported that 3 per cent of children surveyed for their research had no books at home, and boys, Asian children and those on free school meals were twice as likely to be in homes with no books. The correlation between books in the home and reading attainment was striking with only 10 per cent of children classed as 'poor readers' living in homes with over 500 books. Approximately 34 per cent in the sample were 'poor readers' living in homes with no books. The number of good readers in this survey increased exponentially with the number of books in the home.

Critical questions

Book Start is a programme in Wales which aims to provide every 7–9-month-old baby and 18–24-month-old toddler with a free pack of books in both English and Welsh. These books are distributed through the Health Visitor system, along with helpful advice to parents about reading and playing with their babies and toddlers.

» *Considering the results of the research by Clark and Douglas (2011) seen earlier, could there be other explanations for such a stark correlation between the number of books in the home and the level of reading attainment?*

» *If this research is correct, would improving reading levels in this country be as simple as providing every child with books to keep in the home?*

» *What reasons might there be for homes and families to have no books?*

Clark and Poulton (2011) also showed that owning books was an important motivator for children to read for pleasure, and showed a positive correlation between the number of books in the home and attainment. Of course this may be a chicken and egg relationship, as it is likely that children who are given lots of books are also likely to be from homes where the families are literate and value books and reading, thereby providing constant positive role models for children to follow. Such homes enable boys and girls to regularly see adults reading and thereby develop 'the reading habit'. This enables them to practise their skills in a supportive environment. Clark and Poulton (2011) suggest that these families were also more likely to use a public library.

The OECD (2010) report on the PISA results emphasised the importance of reading for pleasure, not only for the children's reading success but also for their general knowledge, grammar, text comprehension, vocabulary and self-esteem. However, the report showed that boys still read less than girls. In all 32 participating countries, boys showed different reading habits from girls, preferring to read newspapers and comics over fiction and magazines.

Boy-friendly literature

McCabe (2011) conducted a series of extensive research studies into over 6000 children's books and showed that children's literature was overwhelmingly dominated by male characters in the central roles. As can be seen in the chart in Figure 7.3, even animal characters were mostly male.

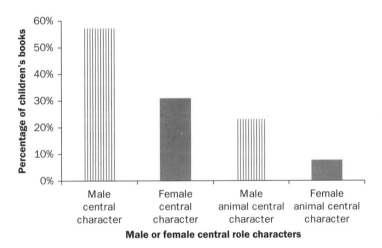

Figure 7.3 *Percentages of male and female character roles in children's literature, adapted from McCabe (2011).*

It is possible to surmise that these messages contribute to what it means to be male and female and indicate that females are less visible and therefore less important than males. The study showed that mothers when reading to their children about gender neutral characters, for example the fox in the Gingerbread Man, tended to refer to them as males, thereby unintentionally increasing further the female underrepresentation.

On the contrary, following an examination of books in his local library, Whitmire (2010) suggests that most books written for children are targeted at girls, and for this he blames the publishers. He believes that publishers target books to groups that read, as this makes commercial sense. It follows then that if boys are less inclined to read, fewer books are going to be targeted at boys. Perhaps more controversially, Whitmire (2010) claims that in the publishing world there is a preponderance of women who work in the business, and they promote the books that *they* like. He takes this one step further, and claims that as most teachers and practitioners in early years are women they incline towards less 'boy-friendly' books (whatever they may be!), insinuating that boys have fewer books to choose from. This creates the vicious circle and chicken and egg situation that you see in Figure 7.4.

Figure 7.4 *Cycle of availability of reading material.*

Early Years Foundation Stage Profiles

Some sort of gender gap does seem to be emerging at a very early age, and according to the DfE (October 2014) Early Years Foundation Stage Profile Statistical First Release (SFR 2013/2014) the children achieving a 'good' level overall was:

*   69 per cent female;

*   52 per cent male;

*   furthermore, girls outperformed boys on ALL of the 17 early learning goals (ELGs).

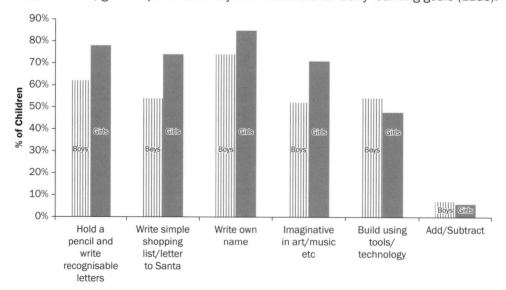

Figure 7.5 *Figures from DCSF (2009) to show how many five year-olds reached specific learning goals.*

This gender gap still remains five years later as the chart in Figure 7.6 shows.

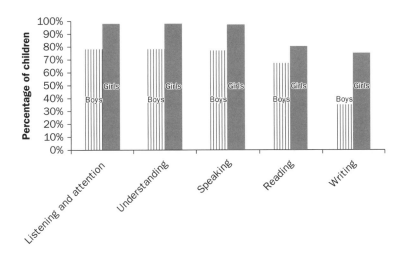

Figure 7.6 *Gender gap in language, communication and literacy, adapted from DfE (2014).*

Contributory pedagogy

Research conducted by the National Literacy Trust (2012) for an All Party Parliamentary literacy group showed that only one in four boys read outside of class each day. They claim that grouping children according to their ability to read could be detrimental to their self-esteem, which this research suggests is particularly damaging for boys, who appear to react badly against their low status in class. Boys seem to resent reading 'easy books' in a way that girls do not. Boys in this research also show resistance to asking for help and attempt to disguise their difficulties to avoid further lowering their status. This means that boys are not practising their reading skills in the way that girls do, which is essential to improve their already weaker competencies. If this is correct it surely has a profound impact upon the way in which practitioners and teachers manage literacy and language skills in the setting. The National Literacy Trust (2012) appears to be claiming that how you handle issues of self-esteem and social development is key to closing the literacy and language gap between girls and boys.

Challenges for practitioners

No matter how young children are when they arrive in nursery, they already know a great deal about their expectations of men and women. These expectations are usually reinforced by practitioners who respond to children in gender specific ways. For example, verbal inter-actions have been shown to be more frequent between practitioners and boys, as boys are often more *visible* in the room with more attention seeking behaviours than girls. However, these interactions tend to be more instructional and have more closed questions, rather than those inviting verbal response and initiating conversation, which might be aimed at girls. This type of interaction does not allow children to practise and extend their verbal skills, and practitioners need to be aware of how and when they talk to the children in their care.

Reflecting upon the day-to-day experience of each child in a group should be a daily ritual, thereby ensuring that each child has an equality of opportunity in the setting. You may be surprised when you do this to find that each child during the day will experience the setting in a very different way.

The difficulty for practitioners attempting to encourage children to engage with stories and to read for pleasure is that it is likely that the more the child reads and looks at stories (and practises their skills), the better they get at it and the more they enjoy what they read. In this way they come to understand how this new skill can unlock a huge area of interest and potential for satisfaction and delight. This in turn means that poor readers are less likely to read or engage with books, less likely to find it easy to do, and less likely to enjoy the experience. This becomes self-perpetuating and a cyclical process that is so hard to break out of. Breaking into this sequence is a major challenge for you as a practitioner or teacher.

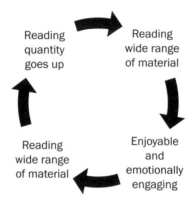

Figure 7.7 *Readers engaging with text.*

The OECD (2010) showed that enjoying the experience of looking at books, stories and reading was the key element for reading success and exceeded socio-economic status, gender, ethnicity and culture in promoting reading. The OECD (2010) showed a significant link between positive attitudes to books and stories and reading success. Creating such positive attitudes to books and stories does not come overnight, and once a child has entrenched negative attitudes to reading they can be hard to change. McKenna, Ellesworth and Kear (1995) showed that if a child did not enjoy books and stories early on, they were unlikely to do so as they got older. This emphasises the importance of the earliest years of a child's life to their eventual academic success and enjoyment of reading and language, and to the importance of the role of parents and the home learning environment. Reading to babies (under one year of age) and looking at pictures may seem at first to be a futile task, but the opportunity to create a feeling of warmth, closeness, excitement and fun in a literacy based activity is likely to set the tone for that baby's future success in reading, and potentially life skills, career and relationships.

New literacies

New literacies are all the screen-based reading opportunities that children encounter, such as instant messaging, blogs, websites, social networking, email, digital storytelling, online discussions, gaming software, avatars, virtual worlds, 'smart' toys etc. Children today live in such a media rich digital environment and reading from technology is now so embedded within their lives that they are bound to interact with these at a very early age.

According to Formby (2014) there are gender differences in the engagement with this type of text. Formby's research indicates that more boys than girls use technology for educational activities, and go on to read stories and articles for longer than they would do from a traditional print book. Boys were also shown to be more likely to read a story online when shared with an adult, yet more parents of girls than boys say that they are likely to support them in their online reading.

Formby (2014) highlighted a YouGov survey of over 1000 parents of 3–5 year-olds, and over 500 early years practitioners where only 41 per cent of practitioners said that children in their settings had access to touch screen technology, and 59.7 per cent believed that it was beneficial to their progress. However, it may be of some concern that almost a quarter of the practitioners (23.7 per cent) said that they did not see a role for touch screen technology in their setting. One reason for this could be, as Aubrey and Dahl (2008) showed, that many practitioners were not confident enough in their own abilities with technology to be able to use them effectively to enhance learning. They highlighted a significant technology skills shortage in early years settings, which appeared wider in the non-maintained than the maintained sector.

Whitmire (2010) reports an American study which appears to show that when reading from a screen you are using different reading skills and techniques than when reading from a hard copy. He describes this as the **F** pattern.

> *At the top users read all the way across, but as they proceed their descent quickens and horizontal sight contracts, with a slow down around the middle of the page. Near the bottom, eyes move almost vertically, the lower-right corner of the page largely ignored.*
>
> (Whitmire, 2010, p 73)

He claims that when reading online, eye tracking experiments have shown that you jump about looking for key words and unusual variations. Many schools and nurseries have made huge investments in technology, which Whitmire claims offers very poor return in learning, despite schools trying to 'out-technologise' each other. He argues that through the use of online reading you are not enhancing their learning in the way that you may believe, but in fact diminishing children's literacy skills for reading challenging texts, which require slow and considered steady focus. Taylor (2012) found that the percentage of children reading stories with an e-reader had doubled since 2010 to 46 per cent and had become the fastest growing publishing sector in 2011. His research showed that children, particularly boys, wanted to engage with the e-reader more than a print book; however, they distracted from the story and often prevented the children from remembering the narrative.

Research into the benefits of reading online is indeed rather limited and at times contradictory; however, the OECD (Organisation for Economic Co-operation and Development) (2010) did find a positive relationship between proficient readers and those reading extensively online, but once again you need to question whether the more proficient readers are drawn to online reading more than less proficient readers. In other words it is not necessarily the straightforward cause and effect that it may at first seem.

Chapter reflections

It must be remembered that despite the apparent gender differences that have been reviewed in this chapter, there is probably less difference between genders than there is within gender. The DfE (2012) says that the gender gap in literacy and language development is not a 'mystery', but attributes the difference to differences of attitudes and behaviours in males and females. The fact that there is a statistical gender gap in communication, language and literacy is undeniable; the real issue is why. This government report falls very much on the environmental side and suggests that higher levels of motivation to read are needed in boys, which could be achieved through 'effective learning strategies'. This places the burden of bridging the gender divide on the pedagogy and understanding of teachers, practitioners and parents. Clearly those working with young children need to reflect on strategies to foster gender equitable environments, if literacy rates in the country are to rise, but this does not account for the potential for innate issues which may also be contributory.

The review of the research in this chapter shows that in every measure of language and literacy ability there is considerable overlap between males and females. Girls can be as good or better at spatial visualisation, and boys can be as good or better at verbal and language related tasks. Even where the difference does exist it is very small and is only evidenced in large statistical samples. So knowing the gender of your baby should not influence your expectations of their life and abilities.

DEVELOPING CRITICAL THINKING

Structuring your work is essential as it is so easy to wander off the point and lose track of the question. A clear structure will allow you to create shape to your work and focus your writing. You have already seen, in Chapter 5 of this book, how important it is to plan your assignments, but structuring using the following component parts is just as central to critical thinking:

*   introduction;
*   main text;
*   conclusion;
*   references.

Having a structure to your work is like building with Lego; it needs to have a firm base, be logically constructed, and each piece needs to fit snuggly alongside each other.

Your *introduction* needs to 'set the scene', letting the reader know what to expect and creating interest. It may be that you need some definitions of the language that you intend to use, to guide the reader through, particularly if this is technical or specialist language. So often I read students' work with an introduction that promises so much but fails to deliver. Students who start their assignments by writing the introduction first often say what they are *hoping* to write:

This assignment will examine the issues of X, Y and Z.

However, for whatever reason (perhaps they changed their mind as the writing progressed, or perhaps they just ran out of words), when the reader examines the text they see that *X* is there *Y* is there but *Z* is missing, sometimes replaced by *W*!

The way to avoid this mistake is to write your introduction last; that way you will introduce what you have actually written, rather than what you thought you would write.

The introduction is the first thing that someone reads in your work, so it needs to be well written, engage the reader and encourage them to read on. This is the point to make the reader 'sit up and take note' to acknowledge that this is a document worth them giving up their valuable time to read. This is not the place to reiterate the question or the title, but for you to 'set out your stall', to say what you are going to write about, and most importantly, why. This is the place to define the scope of your work, and to offer the reader order and structure to their reading, by setting the overall tone of the piece.

Your *main text* is likely to consist of three or four paragraphs developing one point at a time, creating an argument, offering alternative views or opinions and presenting your case; these are your evidence paragraphs. There need to be smooth links between one paragraph and the next, to allow consistency and flow to your work.

Your *conclusion* brings together all the ideas from the main text and there should be no new material in this section. However, it should not simply be a repetition of your introduction. This is the consummation of your writing and you need to revisit the original question to ensure that it has been answered appropriately.

References ensure that the reader knows which ideas are yours and which belong to other people. Having a rigorous reference list offers a level of credence to your work, as the reader can see that you have consulted other published works widely and with discretion. When reading an academic piece it is helpful to know where the ideas come from, and the reference list enables the reader to obtain the texts for themselves and read further.

Critical thinking activity

» *In the table that follows list five reasons why maintaining a clear structure to your work is important; the first one has been done for you.*

	Maintaining structure to your work is important because
1	It maintains focus and clarity.
2	
3	
4	
5	

Now find three different pieces of writing: a magazine article; an academic paper; and a novel. Read the introductory paragraph of each of these, and considering the issues discussed, answer the following questions. It may be helpful to do this with a colleague to compare ideas.

» *How do the three paragraphs compare and contrast in their length, complexity and structure?*

» *Which paragraphs did you feel you most engaged with and why?*

» *Which introduction made you want to read more and why?*

» *How did the writer create this feeling?*

» *These are three entirely different pieces of writing, each with a different purpose and potential audience. Can you identify what that purpose and audience might be?*

» *Does the purpose of the writing dictate the way in which the introduction is written?*

Further reading

National Literacy Trust (2012) *Boys Reading Commission.* www.literacytrust.org.uk (accessed 15.06.15).

The National Literacy Trust sponsors many research projects related to language, literacy and communication, often in collaboration with the Department for Education. They produce a wealth of useful material online and free to download, which is up to date and often peer reviewed. This particular report is from the All Party Parliamentary Literacy Commission and offers some in-depth analysis of issues related to the reading gap between boys and girls. While the report recognises that this is a highly complex issue, it does make some suggestions as to why the gap exists and provides certain key recommendations for taking on the challenge of closing the divide. The report looks at a range of research evidence from schools, early years settings, home environments and experts in the field.

References

Aubrey, C and Dahl, S (2008) *A Review of Evidence on the Use of ICT in the Early Years Foundation Stage.* Coventry: University of Warwick. www.becta.org.uk (accessed 18.06.15).

Boyd, D and Bee, H (2014) *The Developing Child* (13th ed). Essex: Pearson.

Burman, D D (2010) *Gender Differences in Language Abilities: Evidence from Brain Imaging.* www.education.com/reference/article/Ref_Gender_Differences/ (accessed 13.06.15).

Cameron, D (2008) *The Myth of Mars and Venus: Do Men and Women Really Speak Different Languages?* Oxford: Oxford University Press.

Cigman, J (2014) *Supporting Boys' Writing in the Early Years.* Oxford: Routledge.

Clark, C (2014) *Children and Young People's Reading in 2013: Findings from the 2013 National Literacy Trust Survey.* London: National Literacy Trust.

Clark, C and Douglas, J (2011) *Young People's Reading and Writing: An In-Depth Study Focusing on Enjoyment, Behaviour, Attitudes and Attainment.* London: National Literacy Trust.

Clark, C and Poulton, L (2011) *Book Ownership and Its Relation to Reading Enjoyment, Attitudes, Behaviour and Attainment.* London: National Literacy Trust.

Department for Children, Schools and Families (DCSF) (2009) *Gender and Education...Mythbusters.* www.teachernet.gov.uk/publications (accessed 13.06.15).

Department for Education (DfE) (2012) *Research Evidence on Reading for Pleasure.* www.gov.uk/government/publications (accessed 05.06.15).

Department for Education (DfE) (2014) *Statistical First Release: Early Years Foundation Stage Profile Results in England 2013–14 16th Oct 2014.* London: DfE. www.gov.uk/government/publications (accessed 01.07.15).

Formby, S (2014) *Children's Early Literacy Practices at Home and in Early Years Settings: Second Annual Survey of Parents and Practitioners.* London: National Literacy Trust/Pearson.

Goldman, T H (2005) *Boys Are Stupid, Throw Rocks at Them!* New York: Workman.

Jarratt, C (2015) *Great Myths of the Brain.* Chichester: Wiley-Blackwell.

Levy, R (2011) *Young Children Reading: At Home and at School.* London: Sage.

Maclure, M and Jones, L (2009) *Classroom Behaviour: Why It's Hard to Be Good.* www.esrc.ac.uk/news-and-events/press-releases/2821/classroom-behaviour-why-it's-hard-to-be-good.aspx (accessed 13.06.15).

McCabe, J (2011) Gender in Twentieth Century Children's Books: Patterns of Disparity in Titles and Central Characters. *Gender in Society*, 25 (April): 197–226.

McKenna, M C, Ellsworth, R A and Kear, D J (1995) Children's Attitudes towards Reading: A National Survey. *Reading Research Quarterly*, 30: 934–956.

Moseley, D V (1972) Children Who Find Reading and Spelling Difficult. In Brennan, W K (ed) *Aspects of Remedial Education*. London: Longman.

National Literacy Trust (2012) *Boys' Reading Commission.* www.literacytrust.org.uk (accessed 15.06.15).

OECD (2010) *PISA 2009 Results Executive Summary.* www.oecd.org/pisa/pisaproducts/46619703.pdf (accessed 13.06.15).

Owens, R E (2008) *Language Development: An Introduction* (7th ed). Boston: Pearson.

Programme of International Student Assessment (PISA) (2003) *Literacy Skills for the World of Tomorrow: Further Results from PISA 2000.* Paris: OECD/UNESCO.

Shaywitz, S (2005) *Overcoming Dyslexia.* New York: Vintage Books.

Smith, J and Elley, W (1998) *How Children Learn to Write.* London: Richard C Owen.

Taylor, J (2012) *Raising Generation Tech: Preparing Your Child for a Media-Fueled World.* Chicago: Source Books Inc.

Thomson, M (1990) *Developmental Dyslexia* (3rd ed). London: Whurr.

Wannamaker, A (2008) *Boys in Children's Literature and Popular Culture: Masculinity, Abjection and the Fictional Child.* New York: Routledge.

Warren, H (2014) *Reading England's Future: Mapping How Well the Poorest Children Read.* London: Save the Children.

Whitmire, R (2010) *Why Boys Fail.* New York: AMA.

8 Living with language: the literate environment

'Hey, Ms. McMillan, you have three McDonald's in your name.' This observation, made by 4 year-old Jadin as his prekindergarten teacher wrote her name, reflects young children's familiarity with popular logos and commercial print that they see every day.'

(McMahon Giles and Wellhousen Tunks, 2010, p 23)

Introduction

This chapter examines the influence of a positive literate and language rich environment to children's learning and prospects and discusses purposive opportunities for children to 'meet' language through the home learning environment. It will consider what is meant by a language rich environment and how children respond in a holistic manner, making links with their existing knowledge and their subject understanding. The chapter will reflect on this holistic learning and show how although it needs to be compartmentalised, it also needs to be generalised, to enable the accommodation and assimilation of the experiences to make a difference to their language and literacy development.

Living in a reading society

In Britain today there are over 70,000 people who can truly be classed as illiterate, and 5.2 million who are classed as functionally illiterate, with literacy levels below that expected of an 11 year-old (Clark, 2015). All these people are living in a 'reading society', where everyone assumes that if you are of a certain age you can read. No one in the bank, or the job centre or the benefits office asks *'can you read'?*; instead the forms are passed out and there is an *expectation* that this very complex, uniquely human and advanced skill has been achieved.

CASE STUDY

Delwyn

Delwyn is so excited, he has finally secured a job having been out of work for two years; unemployment in his area of North Wales is very high. The effect on his self-esteem and his whole demeanour since securing employment has been immense. He has been given all the details of when and where to start, and all that his employer now needs is a bank account number into which to pay his wages. Delwyn has never had a bank account before, so this is why he is walking into the bank today. He is nervous and very anxious as he has never been good with paperwork. He approaches the counter and explains what he wants. The teller smiles politely and gives him a form to fill in; she even offers him a pen. Delwyn looks at the form and at what appears to be line after line of gobbledegook. His heart is now pounding but he cannot pluck up the courage to explain that he cannot read. He makes an excuse and leaves the form on the counter as he hurries out of the bank. This is a familiar scenario for many like Delwyn; it could mean that Delwyn cannot accept the offer of work.

Consider for a moment what it really means to live in a reading society if you cannot read. If you are reading this you may find it hard to empathise, but language and print are all around you. Look for a moment around the room that you are sitting in and note the number of words that you see, perhaps the newspaper on the table, writing on the gas fire, on the lamp, the clock, the mat that you put your coffee on, washing instructions on the sofa, a box of tissues, your mug, a can of pop, ingredients on the sweet wrapper etc. Words are all around you and for those of you who call yourself 'readers', they are so common that most of the time you fail to notice them. If you are literate you can take for granted the skills that enable you to exist in that literate society. However, imagine sitting where you are now and wondering what all these words mean; they must be important, otherwise why would they be there? Imagine how disempowering this would be, and how the feelings of inadequacy and ineptitude would seep into your whole being and affect every aspect of your life, happiness, relationships, employment, financial stability and even mental health. Living in a reading society, when you are not a part of that *'reading club'* as Smith (1985) puts it, must be frightening and a living nightmare.

Some years ago I worked with the Adult Literacy and Basic Skills Unit (ALBSU) and was amazed to hear the stories of the adults who participated. Many told me that their wives/ husbands/partners were not aware of the fact that they could not read! They were so good at concealing the truth with excuses and avoidance behaviours, to escape the extreme social stigma.

Environmental print

Environmental print is the print all around us; it is what you see in the room that you are sitting in right now; what you see in the street, at the shops, in work etc. Environmental print is what you see on adverts and signs and is designed to have both print and contextual cues (the word McDonald's beside the golden arches, the meerkats on Compare the Market adverts) to draw and hold your attention. Neumann, Acosta and Neumann (2013) describe environmental print as:

> Functional, ubiquitous and salient and provides children with their earliest experiences of print.
>
> (Neumann, Acosta and Neumann, 2013, p 1)

Neumann, Acosta and Neumann (2013) divide environmental print into three categories:

1. child based logos: Barbie, Lego, Brio, Meccano etc;

2. community based logos: road signs, McDonald's, KFC, Tesco etc;

3. household based logos: Cheerios, Coca-Cola, Pepsi, Fairy etc.

Environmental print saturates the environment, on junk mail, bill boards, road signs, television, T-shirts, food labels, house signs...it is everywhere! So that by the time children go to nursery or school they already have an extensive knowledge of what print looks like, its functionality and in some cases, its meaning. Smith's (1985) idea that you learn to read by reading suggests that reading begins the moment a child becomes aware of this print.

This has prompted some educationalists such as Prior (2009) to suggest that practitioners and teachers can use this exposure to increase literacy in the setting.

> By intentionally including environmental print activities in their classrooms teachers can provide opportunities for children to connect their prior knowledge to literacy experiences in school. Experiences with familiar print assist children with word recognition and provide a sense of ownership when they recognise logos and product labels that they see every day.
>
> (Prior, 2009, p 11)

One word of warning regarding the use of environmental print and logos. It could be that some parents and children might interpret this as practitioners and teachers promoting certain products, and at a time when there is so much publicity about healthy eating and obesity, the use of environmental print such as the McDonald's sign, Coca-Cola or Walkers crisps may not be appropriate. Some families may also object to their children being further exposed to logos relating to Barbie, Teenage Mutant Hero Turtles or Disney. So if environmental logos are to be used to engage children with meaningful print they need to be selected with extreme care.

Meaningful print

The concept of providing an artificial print environment really depends upon children engaging with adults and encouraging questions about that print, such as:

> What is that letter?

> What does it say?

> Is that curly shape (S) the same one as is in my name (Sarah)?

This is only going to happen if it is genuine print for genuine reasons. In my role as an Ofsted inspector, I went to many settings where the children were surrounded by print for print's sake. For example, the word 'window' beautifully printed on the window and 'door' on the door etc, but you have to question why. Even young children know what a window is, and what a door is for. Print needs to have a purpose and that purpose is communication with an audience. Print needs to reflect real circumstances for the child, for example:

- 'what is for lunch today?' with the menu written up;

- names and titles on pictures for people to see and understand;

- labels to help with tidying up;

- photographs of events in the setting that the children have participated in, with explanations beside;

- names on coat pegs and trays for children to find the right one.

This would be meaningful print, encouraging the child to question and wonder. One way to test whether your print is meaningful is to consider whether you or the children refer to it on a regular basis, or whether it is just a bit dog-eared and gathering dust on the wall.

From the moment you are born you are surrounded with words, both verbal and written, and one of the first things that happens is a growing understanding that these sounds have meaning. You have already read in Chapter 2 of the need to separate individual words from a string of sounds, but understanding that these sounds can be written down and replicated is a further vital early step to literacy. This stage of representation or symbolisation is important to the learning process, as is being able to distinguish between letters and words as opposed to lines and patterns. The first indication that a child is seeing these symbols as meaningful is when he/she asks:

What does that say?

However, making that first step will come only if the child is surrounded by print which is potentially meaningful to them. Simply swamping a child with words is not enough; they have to be words that the child wants or needs to know about, the words need to *matter* to the child. If you grow up with too many words around you (whatever 'too many' may be), they can easily be ignored like wallpaper. Only when the word is 'real' to the child will they ask that all important question.

A literate environment

A literate environment goes beyond the idea of simply surrounding the child with print. A literate environment means one that *engages* a child with words, expressive language, receptive language, written and read. Clearly this starts from the moment of birth, or as you read in Chapter 2, even before birth. This requires you to immerse and involve children with meaningful and complex language, with adults prepared to give the time for thinking and responding. A literate environment means stories, both told and read, poems, rhymes, songs, music, drama, dance etc. However, a literate environment also involves offering a child a visible, literate role model which involves adults who talk together, discuss, question, describe, write letters, lists and recipes. A literate role model involves adults who read, not only to and with the child, but as adults for pleasure and information. This literate environment is also the child's introduction to their cultural life and national diversity.

Poverty and the reading society

This concept of a reading society is, in evolutionary terms, a very new one. Many societies around the world still have no writing systems, and even in Britain the idea that everyone *should* be able to read and write is very modern. The concept of universal literacy in Britain really did not exist before the twentieth century.

> *The universal ability to read and write is a measure of social, educational and economic progress in modern nations, while for individuals, being literate makes all the difference to their chances of social acceptability, worthwhile employment, extended opportunities and material success. These hugely important issues explain not just the power of literacy but the pain and pressure it puts on young children and their families and communities.*
>
> (Whitehead, 2009, p 49)

In this quote Whitehead talks of the *'pain and pressure'* of learning to read and it is clear that in some cases this pain and pressure is immense and all-consuming. In the nineteenth century literacy was largely the preserve of the church and was probably connected to moral and religious status, as opposed to economic and intellectual status as it is today. Certainly literacy in today's society has assumed a very high status, and without it people are often considered to be stupid, intellectually inferior, lazy or unworthy. However, Czerniewska (1992) reports that in this country we do not value *all* reading. She suggests that there is a hierarchy of reading so that reading from a book, whether fiction or non-fiction, is valued in our schools and nurseries, but 'real' reading, that is, reading from the words that surround us, is insufficiently valued by teachers and practitioners. Children are expected to read specifically designed reading materials, and as a consequence 'school literacy' is often seen by children as different from that found in their homes and immediate environment.

Field (2010) claimed that an impoverished environment was responsible for lower academic success for children in the poorest homes. Field went so far as to say that living in financial poverty pre-set a child to fail. He claimed that if children start school in what he calls a *'linguistically deprived'* state they are already on course for failure. Interestingly early years children who were assessed in research by Shaffer and McNich (1995), as in a low socio-economic group and academically at risk, were able to recognise significantly fewer print logos than children they called academically advantaged. However, Whitehead (2009) points out that environmental print is 'free'; it engulfs us from the moment we open our eyes in the morning. Therefore, material poverty should not in theory be an inhibiting factor, which it may be in the purchase of books and expensive literacy aids:

> *There is no necessity to buy special early writing and reading exercise books or expensive software which promises to teach pre-school children all about the alphabet, phonics and spelling. These materials will not allow the children to ask their own questions about print and invent their own experimental systems for*

writing, and they may instil a belief that there is only one right answer to every question and wrong answers must be avoided.

(Whitehead, 2009, p 55)

However, perhaps it is not as simple as a direct causal relationship between poverty and academic failure. Goouch (2014) states that the number of books, stories and rhymes in the home is not automatically related to income, and there are low income families with a rich home language environment, despite having fewer printed books available to them. She also suggests that it is not as simple as a numbers game, because a home might have many books and print resources available, but if they are not used, or babies are not spoken to or encouraged to engage with language, family income is irrelevant. If poverty was directly causal to literacy achievement this would have a simple solution that would be the darling of the politicians such as Field (2010): give the *poor* more books! Unfortunately, what on the surface appears simple has very complex, underlying difficulties.

Family support

Creating environments which support language learning requires knowledge and understanding on the part of those caring for young children, starting from the moment they are born. Whitehead (2009) claims that what children need are knowledgeable adults to encourage a fun and playful engagement with the language around them, and to encourage them to investigate, question and predict as a *'word detective'*.

Nutbrown and Hannon (2011) devised what they called the ORIM framework to assess how families could support their child's literacy development.

* **O**pportunities: families can provide books, DVDs, rhymes, stories, writing materials etc.

* **R**ecognition: families can provide praise, encouragement and value their early attempts at literacy.

* **I**ntervention: families can scaffold their learning, making print meaningful by pointing out environmental print.

* **M**odels: families can act as role models by allowing children to see them interacting with print.

This emphasises the importance of sound antenatal education for parents, which goes beyond informing them of potential birth traumas and how to deal with the physical and emotional effects of the birth process. The birth of a baby is arguably the most life changing experience that anyone undertakes, and yet there is almost no training for how to nurture this baby beyond the physical aspects of feeding, changing and clothing. For some reason modern society relies on this being an innate and natural process, and perhaps this is not always the case. Interestingly the rise in the importance of literacy has coincided with the decline of the extended family, where older, more experienced members of society are able to contribute to the upbringing of the child. Often in today's society families and parents feel unsupported and unsure of what they need to be doing (Newburn et al, 2011). However, we cannot lay all the responsibility for raising children upon parents, when Powell and Goouch (2012) found

Table 8.1 ORIM framework, adapted from Nutbrown and Hannon (2011).

		Strands of early literacy			
		Environmental print	Books	Writing	Oral language
	Opportunities				
Families can provide	Recognition				
	Interaction				
	Models				

that in England in 2012 almost half of all babies were cared for in formal daycare settings. This indicates that we need to see this more as a partnership than a devolved relationship. Once in a cared for setting the young children will experience the Early Years Foundation Stage framework (DfE, 2014) or the Welsh Foundation Phase (Yr Adran Plant, Addysg, Dysgu Gydol Oes Sgiliau, 2008), with more formalised and artificially created environments.

Play

Play in all its guises, and however it is defined, is essential to human life and health, both physical and mental (Palmer, 2014). Many books have been devoted to attempting to define play and extol its virtues, but what we do know about play is that if children are deprived of the opportunity to play they become mentally and physically unwell.

> 'The opposite of play–if redefined in terms which stress its reinforcing optimism and excitement–is not work but depression.
>
> (Sutton-Smith, 1999 p 239)

The activity of play occupies the majority of a child's waking hours, and in this context it becomes highly significant to the child and their development. Play is not only a means to occupy their time but, without their overt understanding, they are learning about the world around them. Engaging with print and language through their play supports that learning. This could be flicking through the pages of a catalogue, filling in an appointments book in the 'hairdressers', reading the menu for lunch, reading the train timetable at the pretend railway station, talking to the puppets, listening and responding to the toy telephone, making warning signs for cars on the road playmat or writing a Mother's Day card. Sutton-Smith (1997) showed that lack of opportunities for play could lead to a rise in anxiety, depression, poor self-control and low self-esteem, leading at its extreme to increased thoughts of suicide.

> Not only are children developing the neurological foundations that will enable problem solving, language and creativity, they are also learning while they are playing. They are learning how to relate to others, how to calibrate their muscles

and how to think in abstract terms. Through their play children learn how to learn. What is acquired through play is not specific information, but a general mind set towards solving problems, that includes both abstraction and combinatorial flexibility, where children string bits of behavior together to form novel solutions to problems requiring the restructuring of thought or action...A child who is not being stimulated by being played with, and who has few opportunities to explore his or her surroundings, may fail to link up fully those neural connections and pathways which will be needed for later learning.

(Sutton-Smith, 1997, p 35)

The Early Years Foundation Stage (DfE, 2014) and the Welsh Foundation Phase framework (Yr Adran Plant, Addysg, Dysgu Gydol Oes Sgiliau, 2008) both acknowledge the central role of play to children's learning:

Each area of learning and development must be implemented through planned, purposeful play and through a mix of adult-led and child-initiated activity. Play is essential for children's development, building their confidence as they learn to explore, to think about problems, and relate to others. Children learn by leading their own play, and by taking part in play which is guided by adults.

(DfE, 2014, p 9: 1.8)

Play is not only crucial to the way children become self-aware and the way in which they learn the rules of social behaviour; it is also fundamental to intellectual development.

(Yr Adran Plant, Addysg, Dysgu Gydol Oes Sgiliau, 2008, p 6)

Creating an environment where play and language collide is a skilful process which practitioners and teachers need to explore and one which enables the child to sample the 'real' world of language in a non-threatening and empowering manner. By skilfully creating areas for role play together, children and adults can mirror the 'real' world. Palmer (2014) suggests that this leads them to develop social skills and imagination and to the use and practice of technical and specialist vocabulary. Play enables them to develop confidence in a whole range of literacy skills, and all this within a contextualised environment reflecting the 'real' world outside the nursery setting/classroom. This co-construction of an enabling environment ensures naturally occurring and evolving situations to read, write, speak, listen, problem solve and risk take, in a stress-free and language rich environment.

The enabling environment

However valuable books and stories are to children, comparatively the time spent each day engaged with books is likely to be very small, even in homes and nurseries with the most passionate adult readers. Compare this to the time spent surrounded by environmental print, and then the role of books may be less than you like to think. This is by no means intended to lessen the impact of children being regularly engaged with books and stories, but you need to understand their place and see that there are many other opportunities for children to engage with print.

CASE STUDY

John

The children in John's nursery had a particular favourite book, *Can't You Sleep Little Bear?* by Martin Waddell (1988). This book always engendered lots of discussion from the children about going to bed and when they could not sleep. Lots of them said that they too were afraid of the dark, and they talked about how they dealt with their fears. After the story John and the children set up a bed with lots of cushions and brightly coloured covers, and used the teddies to rock to sleep. The next day the children chose a range of materials to build a 'bear cave' around the bed. They asked how they could make it dark, and lots of their suggestions were tried out.

John recorded himself reading the book and put this into the 'cave' for the children to listen to again and again. The children were frequently seen sitting in the 'cave', on the bed 'reading' to the teddies. John provided a range of torches in different sizes, including coloured and flashing lights; he noticed that the boys in particular would sneak into the 'cave' and sit to read by the light of the torch.

The 'cave' flowed out into an area with writing materials allowing the children to record some of their experiences.

Critical questions

The next time that you are at work, before the children arrive, kneel down in the centre of the room and consider the room from a child's eye level.

» *What print can you see?*

» *Where is the most print? Probably in a story/book area.*

» *Is the literacy area small, insignificant and tucked out of the way, or is it a central feature of your room? What does this say to the children?*

» *What other facilities for literacy are in there?*

» *Can children readily access lots of clean, attractive books with a good range of subject matter and genre?*

» *Can they sit, like readers, in a comfy chair or lie down comfortably on the floor?*

» *Can they access paper and mark making materials, to draw and make 'notes'?*

» *Can they access electronic books and stories?*

» *Are there props and puppets to bring the stories to life?*

Fisher et al (2014) suggest that what they call 'focused attention' is crucial to learning. They point out that children in the early years tend to be in one room for significant periods of the day, and that room is often covered in a plethora of brightly coloured displays and supposedly eye-catching materials. The research by Fisher et al (2014) suggests that the average early years room/primary classroom provides too much of a visual onslaught for the children and a form of visual overload. The children appeared to spend more time 'off task' in the visually cluttered environment than in a bare room. This rather flies in the face of the concept of environmental print being useful to literacy learning. It could be that there needs to be a compromise arrangement whereby less vivid, relevant, meaningful and quality rich displays are used where children are seen as protagonists in their own learning.

CASE STUDY

Jack

Jack has been at school for 12 weeks now and is the youngest child in his Reception class. He has already informed his mother that *'reading is too hard!'*

The greater structure of the day, compared to the nursery that he previously attended, does not seem to be suiting his best interests. He struggles with not being able to play and remain as self-directed in his choice of activities. The teacher is worried about his lack of engagement with literacy based tasks, yet his mother noted that Jack recognised the words Thomas the Tank Engine from his lunch box; he also finds letters of his name in the alphabet spaghetti that he has for tea. Despite this Jack is very unsure of his school based reading activities.

Critical questions

» *How could play be structured for Jack to promote his willingness to engage with print?*

» *How could the teacher provide a more enabling environment for Jack's particular needs?*

» *Was 'reading' spaghetti real reading? Does this have a place in the development of literacy for Jack?*

But does it work?

Research by Dickinson and Snow (1987) and Kassov (2006) concluded that the knowledge of environmental print was a poor predictor of later literacy, regardless of socio-economic status, ethnicity and geographical region.

> The evidence to date indicated that the relationship or association between environmental print awareness skills and later reading skills is very weak.
>
> (Kassov, 2006, p 6)

Nuemann et al (2013) used eye tracker technology to measure the levels of children's attention to words in the environment by comparing the fixations and letter/word knowledge. They showed that although the children could recognise the print with the contextual cues (the word McDonald's alongside the golden arches logo), once the visual cue was no longer present, and the letters were presented in black and white plain font, the children were no longer able to identify them. This means that children are not paying attention to the words and the letters, and brings into question the value of environmental print.

Masonheimer et al (1984) showed that when some of the letters in the signs were replaced with other letters, for example 'McDoxxld's', the children failed to notice the substitution. This suggests that the children are 'reading' the context rather than the individual letters and words. Similar conclusions have been reached by Levin and Ehri (2009).

Nuemann et al (2013) also showed that when adults and children shared stories the children paid attention to the print in only 2–4 per cent of occasions; instead they focused their attention on the pictures. This same research showed that there was very little evidence that children's visual attention on the storybook print correlated with their knowledge of the alphabet. However, the research did show that children focused more on the environmental print, with its large font, attractive designs and colours than on plain text. Nuemann et al (2013) suggest that this may extend their overall experience of early print knowledge.

Kassov (2006) says that environmental print is part of a hierarchy of literacy and comes in at the lowest level. Therefore children who do not engage with environmental print will not necessarily have difficulties when learning to read more formally. Robins and Treiman (2010) also see this as part of a hierarchy; they describe environmental print as *'general surface'* level learning, that is, what print looks like and how it differs from other symbols. They divide this into three sections.

1. General surface features of print: understanding the difference between the linear features of print as opposed to the non-linear features of drawing. This also allows the child to understand that alphabetic symbols do not look like the object that they represent and also linearity, iconicity and directionality.

2. Surface features of words: such as their own name as a particular, constant sequence of letters.

3. Knowledge of letters: attention to the shape of letters.

Names

One word that is very familiar to a child is their name, and frequently this is used as environmental print in settings, on clothes pegs, drawers, placemats etc. Levin and Ehri (2009) showed that unlike commercial logos, children *did* notice the difference when letters in their name were altered, and this ability was related to their letter knowledge and phonological awareness. Furthermore they also showed that children were able to read the names of their peers on their drawers, coat pegs etc. These children they called either:

•   contextual readers – according to the position of the drawer or coat peg; or

•   visuographic readers – using non-alphabetic cues, such as the overall shape or length of the name; or

•   alphabetic readers – mapping graphemes and phonemes in the names.

Zhao et al (2013) found that the age of exposure to environmental print may be influential. Younger children (3–4 year-olds) appeared to be more affected by colour cues and logo cues, while five year-olds were more affected by the font type cues. They described this as a *'critically transitional period'* when the attention to the words and word form outweighed the colour and the logo. Their conclusion was that environmental print was not effective in teaching literacy in the early years, but *could* be effective as the child matures, if it was accompanied by adult scaffolding, interaction and support. Interestingly previous research by Masonheimer et al (1984) showed no such link to age.

Writing

Environmental print is recognisable and readable but it is also writable and Tunks and Giles (2007) believe that it can help to give young children the confidence to write. They claim that:

- environmental print is a source to copy regardless of meaning;
- environmental print is a spelling resource;
- environmental print could inspire writing topics.

Tunks and Giles (2007) consider that it is irrelevant whether a child understands the words; what is important is that they create a bridge to literacy.

Pictures ⟶ Symbols ⟶ Text

This allows the child to understand that reading and writing are a part of everyone's life.

Writing is glottographic, that is, it is based on the sounds of speech, so the more that the adults around the child talk about the print and what they are writing, the more likely that the children will make that connection.

> *Look Amanda that word <u>says</u> 'STOP'...can you <u>say</u> that?*

Robins and Treiman (2010) believe that the important word here is '*say*'. By equating these two meanings of the word, children come to understand the sound and how it equates to the look of the word. Robins and Treiman (2010) also suggest that the constancy of words and letter combinations is also learned through environmental print. They give the example of the word 'dog'; pictures of dogs will vary with different breeds, sizes, colours etc, but that three letter combination always says 'dog'. This suggests that even some deeper features of language and writing (Robins and Treiman, 2010) can be achieved through environmental print.

Chapter reflections

That environmental print is 'powerful' cannot be disputed. Why else would large organisations such as McDonald's, Coca-Cola, Kellogg's and Tesco want to get their name and logo 'out there'. Advertising is big business and subliminally we are all susceptible to it. We buy certain products because we believe them to be good quality or value for money, thereby transforming the profit margins for these companies. Whether we are aware of it or not, we are all subject to the effects of environmental print, so love it or loathe it you are engaging and interacting with environmental print on a moment by moment basis throughout your life.

During the research for this book it was not possible to establish a direct causal link between a child's ability to read and environmental print. Despite the government's promotion of rich environmental print surroundings in schools and nurseries, there is limited research evidence that it does aid children's emergent literacy. It could be that children simply see the print around them as pictures and pictorial symbols, rather than extracting the meaning from the words within the logo.

Despite the arguments discussed in this chapter it is clear that at one level children do learn about reading and writing prior to any formal instruction. However, it may well be that for most children to achieve literate status they will need formal instruction to master the skills required. This interaction with language will take many forms, from verbal interaction with families and other adults, to exposure to the print around them, to the observation and modelling of skills such as writing and symbolisation.

DEVELOPING CRITICAL THINKING

The thing about critical thinking is that it challenges you and challenges texts. You *have* to be an active participant in this engagement between you and the author. This should produce a response to that text not only on an academic level, but also on a personal and emotional level.

The best critical thinkers ask the questions that no one else asks, and seek answers to the questions that everyone else asks. To be able to do this you need to be able to distinguish whether you are reading material which contains one of, or a combination of, the following.

- **Subjectivity**: the level of subjectivity in a text is the amount of material which reflects the personal opinion of the writer. This is unlikely to be backed up with credible evidence. If a piece of writing is subjective it does not require you to interpret it in any way, as this has already been done for you by the author. This is possibly the author's viewpoint only.

- **Objectivity**: this is likely to be factual or at least measurable and observable by parties other than the author. Good research is objective research, and shows that the author is prepared to consider other interpretations of the data presented, however 'obvious' it may appear on the surface.

- **Description**: This is reporting just what you can see or hear, with no attempt made to interpret the material. A description aims to give you a mental image of what the author has observed.

Critical thinking activity

» Read the following three passages and say whether they are subjective, objective or descriptive.

Passage	Category
1. Having secured parental permission in their study, interview protocols were drawn up so that all members of the interviewing team would offer a clear explanation to the children about the interview, ensuring that the children understood that they did not have to participate if they did not wish to. The researchers also stressed to the children that the interview could be stopped at any time. What is more, the interview schedule was piloted with a number of children who were asked to comment on how they felt when being interviewed. (Levy, 2011, p 19)	Objective? Descriptive? Subjective?
2. They [displays] should be for the children; to help them to learn, to feel comfortable at school, and to value their work. They should not be used as a public way of demonstrating what a good job you are doing. The children don't care how well you can mount their work – they just care that it's on the wall in the first place. (Jarmin, 2015, p 36)	Objective? Descriptive? Subjective?
3. We suggest that better knowledge was an important factor contributing to children's ability to read and spell classmates' names. However, another possible interpretation is that learning to read and spell classmates' names taught children their letters. We regard this explanation as less likely. In the classrooms we studied, teachers only provided instruction in children's own names, not classmates' names, so it is unclear how personal names might explain growth in letter knowledge...However, it is more likely that other sources such as alphabet books or Sesame Street or letters on refrigerators at home explained higher levels of letter knowledge. This issue awaits further research. (Levin and Ehri, 2009, p 27)	Objective? Descriptive? Subjective?

» Now work with a colleague to see whether you agree and why.

Further reading

Marsh J and Hallet, E (eds) (2008) *Desirable Literacies*. London: Sage.

This superbly edited book combines a sound theoretical stance to the development of literacy with practical ideas to help you to guide your children towards all aspects of language and literacy competence. The authors of each chapter are all committed to the early years and have a wide range and depth of experience in the field. There is recognition of the ever changing notion of what literacy means and it tackles topics as diverse as culture and media, computer literacy, play, drama, assessment and many others. This is a book that you can dip into and out of regularly, and is a must have for the book shelf of all early years practitioners and teachers.

References

Clark, C (2015) *Children's and Young People's Reading in 2014: Findings from the 2014 National Literacy Trust's Annual Survey*. London: National Literacy Trust.

Czerniewska, P (1992) *Learning about Writing*. Oxford: Blackwell.

Department for Education (DfE) (2014) *Statutory Framework for the Early Years Foundation Stage: Setting the Standards for Learning, Development and Care for Children from Birth to Five*. London: Crown.

Dickinson, D K and Snow, C E (1987) Interrelationships among Pre-reading and Oral Language Skills in Kindergartners from Two Social Classes. *Early Childhood Research Quarterly*, 2: 1–25.

Field, F (2010) *The Foundation Years: Preventing Poor Children Becoming Poor Adults*. London: Cabinet Office.

Fisher, A V, Goodwin, K E and Seltman, A (2014) Visual Environmental, Attention Allocation and Learning in Young Children: When Too Much of a Good Thing May Be Bad. *Psychological Science*, 25 (7): 13, 62–70.

Goouch, K (2014) Baby Rooms. In Bower, V (ed) *Developing Early Literacy 0–8: From Theory to Practice*. London: Sage.

Jarmin, L (2015) *How to Create Class Displays that Pay Off. TES* 27th March: 36–37.

Kassov, D (2006) *Environmental Print Awareness in Young Children*. Washington: Talaris Research Institute.

Levin, I and Ehri, L (2009) Young Children's Ability to Read and Spell Their Own and Classmates' Names: The Role of Letter Knowledge. *Scientific Studies of Reading*, 13: 1–25.

Levy, R (2011) *Young Children Reading: At Home and at School*. London: Sage.

Marsh, J and Hallet, E (2008) (eds) *Desirable Literacies*. London: Sage.

Masonheimer, P, Drum, P and Ehri, L (1984) Does Environmental Print Identification Lead Children into Word Reading? *Journal of Reading Behaviour*, 16 (4): 257–274.

McMahon Giles, R and Wellhousen Tunks, K (2010) Children Write Their World: Environmental Print as a Teaching Tool. *Dimensions of Early Childhood*, 38 (3): 23.

Neumann, M, Acosta, C and Neumann, D (2013) Young Children's Virtual Attention to Environmental Print as Measured by Eye Tracker Analysis. *Reading Research Quarterly*, 20 (10): 1–11.

Newburn, M, Muller, C and Taylor, S (2011) *Preparing for Birth and Parenthood: Report on First-Time Mothers and Fathers Attending NCT Antenatal Courses*. London: NCT.

Nutbrown, C and Hannon, P (2011) *ORIM: A Framework for Literacy*. www.real-online.group.shef.ac.uk/docs/ORIM%20A%20Framework%20for%20Practice.pdf (accessed 12.07.15).

Palmer, J (2014) Role Play Areas for Early Years Foundation Stage, Key Stage 1 and Beyond. In Bower, V, *Developing Early Literacy 0–8*. London: Sage.

Powell, S and Goouch, S (2012) Whose Hand Rocks the Cradle? Parallel Discourses in the Baby Room. *Early Years: An International Journal of Research and Development*, 32 (2): 113–128.

Prior, J (2009) Environmental Print: Real-World Early Reading. *Dimensions of Early Childhood*, 37 (1): 9–14.

Robins, S and Treiman, R (2010) Learning about Writing Informally. In Aram, D and Korat, O (eds) *Literacy Development and Enhancement across Orthographies and Cultures*. New York: Literacy Studies 101.

Shaffer, G and McNich, G (1995) Parents' Perceptions of Young Children's Print Awareness of Environmental Print. In Linek, W and Sturtevant, E (eds) *Generations of Literacy: Seventeenth Yearbook of the College Reading Association*. Harrisonburg: College Reading Association.

Smith, F (1985) *Reading* (2nd ed). Cambridge: Cambridge University Press.

Sutton-Smith, B (1997) *The Ambiguity of Play*. Cambridge, MA: Harvard University Press.

Sutton-Smith, B (1999) Evolving a Consilience of Play Definitions: Playfully. *Play and Culture Studies*, 2: 239–256.

Tunks, K and Giles, R (2007) *Write Now! Publishing with Young Authors*. Portsmouth: Heinemann.

Waddell, M (1988) *Can't You Sleep Little Bear?* London: Walker Books.

Whitehead, M (2009) *Supporting Language and Literacy Development in the Early Years*. Buckingham: Open University Press.

Yr Adran Plant, Addysg, Dysgu Gydol Oes Sgiliau (2008) *Foundation Phase Framework for Children's Learning for 3–7 Year Olds in Wales*. Cardiff: Welsh Assembly Government.

Zhao, J, Zhao, P, Weng, X and Li, S (2014) Do Pre-school Children Learn to Read Words from Environmental Print? *PLOS ONE*, 9 (1). www.ncbi.nlm.nih.gov/pmc/articles/pmc3899066/ (accessed 06.07.15).

9 Books and stories

So please, oh PLEASE, we beg, we pray,
go throw your TV set away,
and in its place you can install,
a lovely bookshelf on the wall.

Roald Dahl
(*Charlie and the Chocolate Factory*, 1964)

Introduction

There has probably never been a human society in which people did not tell stories. Many are not written down, but the best are preserved in oral format and handed down from generation to generation, to explain the unexplainable aspects of life and determining social roles within society. These form our cultural heritage of myths, legends and fairy tales. This chapter examines how books and stories provide the link between the oral tradition and the symbolic conventions which children experience; how they offer opportunities to focus their listening skills, extend their vocabulary and engage with differing social roles and emotional literacy. Stories provide opportunities for speaking and writing and creativity, thereby offering a rich source of activity for holistic development. Through story children construct and interpret the language of the writer or the storyteller and set this within their current understanding and experience.

Cultural heritage

If you examine the well-known and well-loved stories of Hans Christian Andersen (died in 1875), such as *The Ugly Duckling, The Snow Queen* and *The Little Mermaid* and the brothers Jacob and Wilhelm Grimm (died 1863 and 1859 respectively) with the timeless classics of Cinderella, Snow White and Hansel and Gretel, you can see how these portray the workings of society at the time, both culturally and psychologically. It is likely that such a foundation and purpose of stories is still in evidence today, if you consider the ethical and moral implications of stories such as *The Enormous Crocodile* by Roald Dahl (1978), where the wicked crocodile gets his comeuppance in the end, and the trickery of the Gruffalo (Donaldson and Scheffler, 1999).

Whenever people have come together they have exchanged stories, personal narratives, chronicles and anecdotes in an effort to make sense of the world around them. Such stories provide a framework in which human behaviour can be made sense of by both children and adults. Stories offer an opportunity to talk about characters, plots, pictures and illustrations and how these may relate to our own life experiences. Wells (2009) talks about stories being *triggers* for language, allowing children to respond in their own way, by bringing their personal experiences to bear on the text, as a bilateral experience between the text and the child. However, stories also provide opportunities to examine the text's grammar, syntax, semantics, pragmatics and a range of other linguistic structures which can provide a valuable preparation for reading.

Relationship with the text

Potentially books and stories can offer a child enjoyment, pleasure, relaxation, increase developing vocabulary and can elicit strong emotional responses to personal development and self-understanding. By introducing new people, new locations, periods of history, and as yet undiscovered situations, books and stories can extend a child's experience of life. This is achieved with a strong bond between the author and the reader, or recipient of the story, through the words on the page, in a triangular relationship, which goes beyond the bilateral experience suggested by Wells (2009). This offers the child a different perspective of another person's consciousness, a chance to delve into someone else's thoughts and feelings.

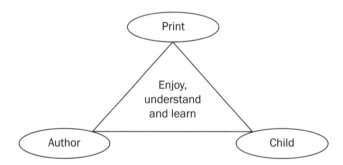

Figure 9.1 *A triangular relationship with books.*

Whitehead (2010) claims that it is this first experience of linguistic structures and assumptions about text that has the potential to shape a child's feelings toward literacy for the rest of their life.

Rhyme probably provides the start and fun of reading, with traditional nursery rhymes, songs and modern jingles that you share with a baby. Listen to a baby in a cot 'talking' to him/herself, making noises and delighting in sound and what it can do. S/he is playing with the language, and from there it is a short step to the nonsense language of rhymes such as 'Hey

Diddle Diddle' and 'Humpty Dumpty' (Meek, 1982). These lead the child into a realm of fantasy where animals talk and spoons and plates run away or jump over the moon, yet they are grounded within a world where these things do not happen and cannot happen. Children see this as funny and we all love to laugh. Jokes and riddles are important to a child; they are like mini stories, with a beginning, middle and end, which is fun. So, many children's stories are based on that intention to play with words and have fun, to provoke laughter, books such as that by Dr Seuss, *Green Eggs and Ham* or Lewis Carroll's 'Jabberwocky'.

The centrality of literature

In the past the place of the storyteller in society was an exalted one and even today with computers, television, film, DVDs, the prominence of the story is rarely questioned. Wray and Medwell (1991) suggest that stories are one way of allowing children to break free from an egocentric view of the world and to see life from differing perspectives.

> *'This broadens their perceptions of the world and helps them decentre.'*
> (Wray and Medwell, 1991, p 46)

Research by Wray and Medwell (1991) and later by Clark and Rumbold (2006) ascribes many advantages of stories to children and their development:

- decentring, becoming less egocentric;

- stimulating imagination, offering opportunities for creativity, originality and resourcefulness;

- encouraging predictive thinking and offering opportunities to hypothesise future happenings: *'I wonder what would happen if...?'*;

- allowing children to develop as people: form attitudes, opinions, beliefs and decision-making skills;

- enabling children to explore problems in a *safe* context, once removed from reality;

- allowing children to see others do things that they would never quite dare to, as in Max in *Where the Wild Things Are* (Sendak, 1963);

- developing language and vocabulary, with better comprehension and grammar;

- familiarising children with the language of books and the difference between written and spoken language;

- introducing children to things outside their experience, thereby introducing the concept of abstract ideas, as in *Green Eggs and Ham* (Dr Seuss, 1957);

- stimulating other learning by helping to develop a positive attitude to reading;

- offering opportunities for shared experiences between children and adults, and children and peers;

- demonstrating a better understanding of different cultures and communities;

- increasing their general knowledge and confidence generally;

- encouraging reading – children who hear stories are more likely to read for pleasure as adults;
- improving their reading and writing ability: those who read more are better readers;
- above all providing fun and pleasure, appealing to the heart and the emotions.

However, Cooter (1991) showed that although story is used extensively in pre-school settings and is seen as valuable to language development, it is not as valued in the primary classroom. Teachers often regard story as a dispensable extra, and an activity done only when there is 'time' for it. This suggests that in schools, story time is seen more as a leisure/relaxation activity, than making a serious contribution to language development and literacy.

Choosing books

Browne (2009) suggests that simply learning to read is not enough for a literate society, but it is the *active* use of reading that is important. For this reason books become a vital resource to any nursery or school setting and their selection and inclusion needs to be considered carefully. It is their choice and selection that has the potential to turn a child who can read into a 'reader'. In a research overview by Clark and Rumbold (2006) one factor shown to encourage children to read was the choice of books available to them, and whether they had chosen books themselves to match their own interests and requirements. This has clear implications for practitioners, teachers and parents when selecting books for children. This study also emphasised the importance of children owning books; children with books of their own were shown to be almost twice as likely to read on a daily basis as children with limited access to books. It stands to reason that a book by the bedside is going to be looked at more frequently than one in the library.

Books are usually classified into two main types, fiction and non-fiction, but in children's literature there can be some blurring of the edges, with books containing a factual message worked into a fictional format.

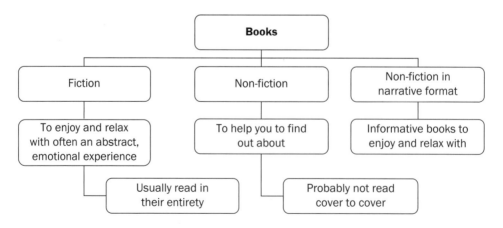

Figure 9.2 *Classification of book types.*

Browne (2009) suggests that every setting should have at least a hundred books available to the children, and these should be regularly reviewed and changed. Although I would not want to impose an arbitrary number, there does need to be a wide range and reasonable quantity within that range, as only then can you begin to capture and reflect the interests and imagination of the children. Browne (2009) cites a number of classifications and genres of books that she feels are essential for every setting:

- books with pictures but no words;

- caption and concept books, such as an alphabet or number book;

- picture books where the pictures depict the limited text, enabling very young children to 'read' the book within the context of the picture, such as *Rosie's Walk* (Hutchins, 1968);

- books with longer text: a more substantial read such as *Charlie and the Chocolate Factory* (Dahl, 1964);

- picture books for experienced readers with increasing amounts of text within the context of a picture or photograph, such as *The Stinky Cheese Man and Other Fairly Stupid Tales* by Scieszka and Smith (1993);

- books for sensitive situations dealing with life – these might be designed to help children come to terms with issues such as death, going to school for the first time, visits to the dentist etc, such as *Little Bear's Grandad* (Gray and Cabban, 2000);

- information books that are written in a narrative format such as *Stone Age Boy* (Kitamura, 2008) or as a reference type book such as *See Inside Planet Earth* by Daynes and Allen (2008);

- narrative texts – perhaps instruction manuals for a construction toy or diaries;

- non-narrative texts such as dictionaries, thesaurus, encyclopedias, atlases;

- home-made books.

Different genres

There is clearly a range of opinion, even among the so-called experts, about the most appropriate reading materials for children. The great essayist Charles Lamb (1880) distinguishes between 'books' and 'no books'. He wanted to banish anything but imaginative literature, poems, plays and novels, but Lamb's fanciful distinction is not altogether different from practice in some settings today. I assume that no school or nursery would go as far as Lamb, to exclude books on travel, biography, history, geography etc, but such books are often not thought of as literature in the same way as fiction. On the contrary, stories, poems and literary genre such as comics, magazines and newspapers are often looked upon by educationalists as 'lower class' writing, unlike non-fiction and academic books. However, comic strips, for example, could be seen as a very successful way to tell stories in a highly visual format. The short, sharp message of the comic strip can have considerable advantages for children learning to read, allowing them to visualise the content before reaching a more intense level of abstraction and symbolisation. Much-loved and well-read authors, such as Roger Hargreaves, have capitalised upon this in his *Mr Men and Little Miss* series of books. Perhaps this ability to interest children and hold their attention is an important first step to literacy.

The language of the comic strip attempts to bridge the gap between the formal language of the written word and the less formal spoken language. Whether or not you approve of the idiom and vernacular used in a comic strip, it is certainly a much read medium, attested to by the longevity of the comic in society, which probably started in the late nineteenth century. The first copy of the Beano, which was originally bought in July 1938 for 2d (equivalent to just over 1p today), was recently sold at auction for £3499! This medium continues to be a popular source of literature for children and adults in the form of graphic novels such as Runton's (2004) 'Owl: the way home and the bittersweet summer' and Japanese manga such as the 'Skip Beat!' series by Yoshiki Nakamura. These texts are fast paced with word–picture correlation which appeals to many readers, young and old.

What children like

Wray and Medwell (1991) believed that to capture a child's imagination and to hook them into reading, you need to explore what it is that the *child* enjoys about books and reading. This research asked the children what *they* liked about their reading, and depicted a number of elements that can help when you choose books and stories.

*   Children appeared to prefer plots which produced suspense – the 'page turner'.
*   Children disliked long descriptive passages.
*   Children enjoyed strong, action plots.
*   They enjoyed characters that they could identify with, or those they would like to be.
*   They enjoyed characters that have more power and control over events than 'real' children.
*   They enjoyed stories with clear distinctions between the 'goodies' and the 'baddies' – stories with a moral reality.

Remember that children, like adults, read for fun. So if the book does not interest them or they find it boring, they will not engage with the print. Children constantly presented with 'boring' books are unlikely to enjoy the experience and will not read, making a vicious circle of not reading and poor literacy skills.

So what is a 'good' book?

Whatever the answer is to this question it is going to be highly subjective. For you a good book might be a romance, for me a murder mystery; for one it might be Shakespeare, for another Barbara Cartland. Perhaps a 'good book' can be described as one that you enjoy, a rollicking good read, and therefore you read it to the end. A 'good book' is one that makes you want to read more, the next page, next chapter, next book. According to Chris Kloet (editor-at-large for publishers Walker Books), there are approximately 10,000 new children's books published each year with a further 35,000 in print at any one time, so that puts the task of choosing a 'good' book into context. It would only seem right that you select the 'best' literature for children to experience, whatever that may be, but how do you assess quality, and whose quality is it? It may be possible to fill your literacy area with so-called quality literature which none of the children wants to engage with. A 'good book' is clearly not a 'good book' if the children do not read it. Before they read it they need to pick it up, so regardless of the content it needs to have visible 'kerb appeal', in other words it needs to be attractive to the age group it is targeted at. Above all it needs to be clean, bright and well presented.

The language contained within a book needs to be accessible to the reader or listener, words they are familiar with, and when they are unfamiliar their meaning is clear through the context or the illustrations. An example of this would be *Where the Wild Things Are* (Sendak, 1963) which uses the phrase 'they gnashed their terrible teeth'. I would suspect that very few children have come across the term 'gnashed', yet I have not had a single child, to whom I have read that book, who did not understand what the author intended. Such a word, in context, can become a part of their lexicon, stretching their understanding of the world and enlivening their enjoyment of the text.

A 'good book' is one in which the text and the illustrations match, thereby supporting the child in their efforts to make sense of the text. Such illustrations need to be clear, attractive and relevant. The illustrations and the text combined can promote positive images and attitudes about life. Although not every book has to be a moral tale, it is important when selecting books that the equality and diversity of the community in which the child lives are reflected in a positive and supportive manner, promoting balanced, non-stereotypical images for the mind.

Enid Blyton

The late children's author Enid Blyton, whose books I remember devouring as a child, from *Noddy* to the *Famous Five*, *Secret Seven* and the *Faraway Tree*, is an example of an author who is loved by children worldwide, but not always considered quality literature. Enid Blyton sold 600 million of her books, translated into over 90 different languages, but in the 1930s–1950s her work was banned from many libraries, and the BBC refused to broadcast her work because they regarded it as second rate, unchallenging and lacking in literary merit. Amazingly more of her books have been banned from public libraries than any other author in history! However, her books are still popular with young children today, despite all the criticism of poor quality; surely someone who has sold so many books must finally be taken seriously? Meek (1982), while accepting that Blyton's books can be undemanding and divorced from the real world, acknowledges that children love her work, and suggests that children learn a lot from her books that is important for literacy and their development as readers. For example, they learn:

• to recognise the villains and heroes;

• satisfactory endings;

• episodes;

• chapters/paragraphs and some form of literacy structure;

- cliffhangers;

- climax;

- moral issues of right and wrong.

Meek (1982) suggests that children love Enid Blyton because her stories make them feel safe with the use of familiar words and phrases. How many of you have taken a 'trashy' novel on holiday with you, where the speed of reading, banal plots and easy text become an escape from reality? We probably all know the difference between the books we *like* to read and the books we *ought* to read.

Meek (1982) believes that magic and fantasy are an integral part of early years, with play and 'let's pretend' occupying such a large part of their lives.

> At this stage the inner world of imagination and outer world of the here and now are the same universe for the child; both are equally real, and both need to be ordered. Stories make this possible, especially fairy stories, because the characters...Snow White, Jack and the Beanstalk and the rest...are busy changing the world by acting in it. This is also what children do. If we want to give our children reading matter that will initiate them into the kinds of <u>meanings</u> that reading makes possible as the extension of 'let's pretend', they must have fairy stories. (Meek, 1982, p 138)

Most importantly, and often forgotten in books like this, is that the books that you choose for children need to be ones that *you* enjoy reading. Only then will you be able to transmit the passion, enjoyment and enthusiasm for the text, and hook the children into an appetite for reading themselves. This implies that practitioners need to have read a wide range of literature themselves, in order to introduce and share engaging books with children.

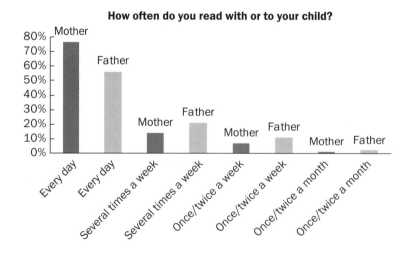

Figure 9.3 Reading with children.

Critical questions

Consider Figure 9.3 adapted from research conducted for Save the Children (2014) with a sample of 1000 English families.

» *What does this tell you about the 'health' of story reading with the children in the survey?*

» *What does this tell you about the 'health' of story reading with children in England?*

» *What other information would it be helpful to know about the sample, and the way in which the research was conducted?*

Comment

Some of the issues you should have considered.

1. Was there a large enough sample?

2. Was this a representative sample or self-selecting?

3. Were mothers and fathers equally represented? Does this matter?

4. Were differing socio-economic backgrounds, educational backgrounds or cultures accounted for?

5. Do you think that parents would answer the question honestly?

6. How old were the children?

7. Were all parents in the sample literate?

Examples of poorly used statistics can be found regularly in newspapers and magazines, with editors using unsubstantiated and sensational headlines to grab your attention.

Consider the following examples of headline grabbers that are a poor use of statistics and reflect on why that might be.

'*Taller children are better readers*.'

Consider this.

• Taller children are likely to be older children and therefore more experienced at reading.

'*Increased SATS results show that teachers are less rigorous in their testing procedures*.'

Consider this.

• Could children be getting better at SATS based activities?

• Could parents be more aware of the importance of SATS and encourage children more?

- Could the tests be getting easier?

- Could the government's need to see improvements, for political purposes, be driving their levels of difficulty?

  '10 per cent of children have no books in their home.'

Consider this.

- Does this refer to *all* books or only books specifically for children?

- Can the number of books in a home be correlated with an aspect of their development?

- Do they have no books because they read avidly online with e-books and tablets?

'Spellbinders'

Telling stories to young children is a real art, and although I believe that anyone can learn to tell stories well, there are those of you that I refer to as 'spellbinders'. I have had the pleasure and honour of watching some, weaving their plots and capturing the attention of every child in the room, children sitting so still with their mouths dropped open, hanging on every word, desperate to know what comes next. Telling a good story is a very physical activity, as well as an intellectual communication, drawing into the deception all who are around; a good story is a performance. The advantage of storytelling, as opposed to story reading, is that the story can go off in any direction that the teller and the audience might want. This enables the story to be adapted at a moment's notice to include the children, their lives and their families, but also in response to their interests and enthusiasms. A storyteller is not hidebound by the words on the page so rather than developing a topic from a book, the storyteller can adapt the story to meet the topic. A good storyteller has nothing between themselves and the audience, no book and no pictures to distract from their skilful use of eye contact, intonation, volume, emotional tones, gestures, facial expressions and body language. This can make the teller feel naked and vulnerable, but also offers them power to create, imagine, develop and escape from the language and creative intentions of another author. Without a book the children have been shown (Isbell et al, 2004) to focus more upon the teller, and this two way interaction makes this a more personal experience for each child in the group.

Isbell et al (2004) suggest that storytelling differs from story reading in that the children are more likely to join in with repetitive phrases and refrains ('*Fee Fi Fo Fum*' in *Jack and the Beanstalk*; or '*Run, run as fast as you can, you can't catch me I'm a gingerbread man*'). The children are also more likely to participate and co-operate in suggesting variations to the story, thereby promoting visual imagination and creativity. Isbell et al (2004) also showed that the storytellers in the research used more gesture, repetitive phrases and sounds than story readers.

> *stories provide a conceptual framework for thinking, which allows children to shape experiences into a whole they can understand. Stories allow them to mentally map*

experiences and see pictures in their heads; telling traditional stories provides children with a model of language and thought that they can imitate.

(Isbell et al, 2004, p 159)

Tancock (2014) goes so far as to say that the telling of traditional stories is at the 'moral heart' of our cultural tradition, helping children to come to terms with themselves and their psychological and emotional development.

Telling a good story

So often inexperienced practitioners and teachers rush through a story without giving time to enable them to '*weave their magic*' (McDonald, 2014, p 157). McDonald believes that when you are reading a well-illustrated picture book, children instinctively attempt to make meaning from the pictures, and only when this is done will it encourage them to want to find out more. Clearly interpreting the pictures and engaging with the colours, shapes and images takes time, and a 'spellbinder' knows this and allows for a slower pace, with time for discussion. Pictures, colours, font size and design can all help to engage the child's imagination. An example of this can be found in Dr Seuss, *I Can Read with My Eyes Shut*, where the font colour changes to match the colours '*I can read <u>red</u>. I can read <u>blue</u>. I can read pickle colour too*'. Later when he reads upside down the words are placed in a circle and the page needs to be turned around to read it. '*I can read in a circle and upside down.*' Another example would be the delightfully illustrated book by Dick Bruna, *Miffy and the Gallery,* which is written in rhyme to give the text pace and intonation; this is a style used by many other children's authors.

Public libraries

At a time of budgetary constraint, where public libraries are closing and children in their homes have limited access to books, the need for libraries has probably never been greater. However, according to the Chartered Institute for Public Finance and Accounting (CIPFA, 2013) 349 public libraries have closed since 2009. A study by Clark and Hawkins (2011) showed that almost half of all children have never used a public library, and these same children were also more likely to say that they read books only in school.

Of course early years children cannot access libraries alone, so are dependent upon families understanding their importance and taking them along. Interestingly in the research by Clark and Hawkins (2011), one of the main reasons why young people said that they did not go to their public library was that their family did not go, so there was no role model of library borrowing to emulate. The study showed that children who do use the library are almost twice as likely to read outside school, to report that they enjoy reading and to be better readers. Once again you cannot make direct comparisons, and it is not as simple as just making *all* children go to the library. An analysis of these figures would probably show many other issues in families who do not use the library, which are more causal to this relationship. For example, perhaps these families have lower levels of literacy, or perhaps they are working families with no time, or they live too far from a public library; clearly this is an area which requires further research.

CASE STUDY

Jenna

Jenna is an experienced childcare practitioner who recently moved to a new nursery. She told the staff that she loved to tell stories to children, so on her first day the staff gathered all the children into a circle and they sat down and awaited her story.

Oh what a disaster, and on her first day too! The children fidgeted on the chairs and most did not listen or take in very much about the story, some wandered off and clearly were not interested.

Figure 9.4 *Example of children in a circle where the storyteller cannot engage eye contact with all the children.*

Jenna was really cross with herself that she had not had the courage to set up the story area in the way that she normally would. The next day she gathered the children to the carpet, gave them cushions to sit on, lie on or just cuddle in their arms and arranged them all within her line of eyesight.

Figure 9.5 *Example of all the children in clear line of sight engaging with the story.*

Now she was able to draw the children into the story with eye contact, gesture and facial expression. Children who were starting to lose concentration she brought back to the story by incorporating them into the tale. The children loved it and they all stayed with Jenna for a full 15 minutes. The staff were amazed at what a difference there had been with such a small change to the organisation of story time.

Critical questions

» *Why do you think the change in the way that the children were seated made such a difference to their engagement?*

» *Ask a trusted colleague to observe you reading/telling a story and try to identify ways to improve your technique.*

» *With their permission observe your colleague reading/telling a story and watch the reactions of the children to their practices.*

More than just reading

I love books but I sometimes wonder where that love of books originated. Whether there was one moment in my childhood when books began to have meaning for me; if there was I cannot recall it. What I am aware of is that books are a whole sensory experience, not just appealing to the intellect and academic mind, but to a whole being. I love the smell of books, particularly old and 'undiscovered' books; the pages emit an aroma of age and antiquity. Even new and as yet unread books have a redolence of freshness, a pristine fragrance. Watch a baby with a book and their first instinct is to explore it with their mouths, tasting the paper or card, relishing the flavour of the print. As children mature they will use books to stand on to be taller, build with, carry around, section off areas, tessellate and play peek-a-boo with; the book becomes an object to be enjoyed irrespective of its content. Handling a book means feeling the smooth, shiny pages, the breeze created by flicking the pages and the close-cut corners and edges. So a book is to appeal to all the senses, and can be smelt, tasted, touched as well as listened to and read.

Publishers make the most of this sensory nature of books by making them in different shapes, having holes in them (Carle, 2002: *The Very Hungry Caterpillar*) or interactive, pop ups and push outs (Campbell, 1985: *Dear Zoo*, or Ahlberg and Ahlberg, 1999: *The Jolly Postman*). They hope that this will encourage little fingers to explore their structure and line. Quite quickly children will learn that books are special and invoke a special reaction in adults which ensures attention, warmth and emotional comfort as they cuddle up and share the experience together.

Wells (2009) claims that the number of hours that a child is read to, in the early years, is the best predictor of later literary success; of course it may not just be the act of reading, but the literary environment that a child is initiated into in such homes that results in this achievement. The PISA (2009) scores also show that reading stories is positively correlated with later reading attainment levels, with increased inferential and comprehension abilities, better letter/symbol recognition and more positive attitudes in general to reading.

It is not the bookish home, nor necessarily the middle-class family (except in so far as they are usually aware of what is at stake), not high intelligence, good eye movements, right-handedness, not even extensive vocabulary that makes the successful beginner [reader]. The supportive adult, who shows him what a book is and how print works, who helps him to discover reading and expects him to be successful makes all the difference. Together, adult and child learn about reading.

(Meek, 1982, p 31)

Listening

Mellon (2000) talks about a child's need for silence as a foundation to active listening, allowing the child to give their undivided attention.

Silence is the kindest, and the most powerful starting point for stories. Creating silence is different from waiting for children to be quiet. It is an active, radiant power. In the atmosphere of silence our hearts centre into gentle rhythms, our senses open, the very pores of our skin relax.

(Mellon, 2000, p 18)

Books and stories give children opportunities to actively listen, to practise skills of listening either singly (one-to-one), or corporate listening in a group story session. Both of these require different skills of concentration, proximity to the storyteller/reader and listening to different storytellers/readers. Through books and stories children are also introduced to listening to many different authors; some may be very familiar to them, with familiar styles which they get used to, but some will be new and unfamiliar encouraging them to listen to a unique voice, unpredictable and surprising.

Ellis (1997) believes that books and stories are the best way to promote active listening, as the child is participating with the process of interpreting the language of the author, creating the story with the author as it proceeds.

Literary text teaches us to be readers because it urges us to turn the page and make the meaning the author intended.

(Whitehead, 2010, p 135)

Of course listening to stories does not have to be just an indoor activity, and a new project by the Exploration Society (ESOC) blends Bear Grylls type survival experience with stories, bringing the books to life in the outdoors. In Gypsy caravans and bluebell woods last year hundreds of children took part in activities centred on Donaldson and Scheffler's book *The Gruffalo* (Dickinson, 2015). Interestingly these projects led some of the children to writing about their adventures and the stories they read, promoting spelling, punctuation and grammar in a forest school type approach.

Writing

Stories are not just for reading or telling; they are also for inventing and creating, which children appear able to do more naturally and easily than many adults. Stories can progress from an oral/listening tradition to encourage writing, where children can record their creativity either directly to paper/screen, or by allowing adults to transcribe them. In such a written format the children can see themselves as authors, as they read, tell and share their stories. It is really important that children understand that authors are real people, that books have been written and illustrated by real people, and not just materialised from nowhere. This is one reason why it is helpful to start each book by looking at the cover and discussing the writer, putting it into context. This offers opportunities to discuss favourite authors and differing styles of writing and illustration.

The language of books is very different from everyday spoken language, or even the sort of language that children use when they start writing. However, the stylised manner of stories does enable children to be introduced to a range of language genres that are not necessarily common in their everyday environment. Stories have structure and frameworks, beginnings, middles and endings. There are often traditional openings and endings to stories such as 'Once upon a time...' or '...and they all lived happily ever after'. Whitehead (2010) showed that such stylised language provides a bridge between colloquial spoken English to formal Standard English that will be needed for writing. This produces a complete package and story cycle as shown in Figure 9.6, developing all areas of language development through listening, speaking, reading and writing.

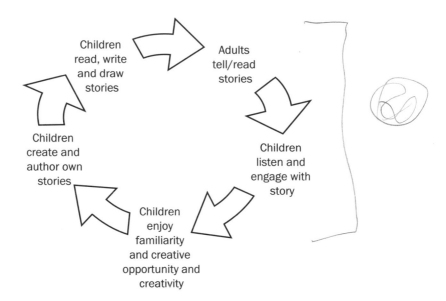

Figure 9.6 Cycle of storytelling/reading, adapted from Cliatt and Shaw (1988).

It is possible that by focusing on a story in this formative and progressive way children feel less threatened by the writing. In this way writing stories can enable a child to feel empowered to control the direction of the story, making the work more meaningful and a natural evolution of the cycle.

Of course the storyteller does not always have to be the adult, and a project called 'Storytelling Schools', which encourages children to tell each other stories, has been shown to help children with their speaking, listening, memory, confidence, empathy, ideas, sequences and plots (Rooke, 2015). This report suggests that 84 per cent of the children surveyed thought that storytelling improved their ability to write, and this was particularly so of children with English as a second language.

Stories through the media

Books and stories for both children and adults are adapted for the media every day with dramatic presentations of both classic (Dickens' *Christmas Carol*, Lewis Carroll's *Alice in Wonderland*) and modern literature (Michael Bond's *Paddington Bear*). The presentation of books and stories on the television, radio and film could be seen as an extension of written language, spoken aloud. Young children can see and hear the magic of books come to life in a visual medium. This could potentially help the child to focus on the essential features of the story, understanding the plots, structures and language, thereby entering into the experience more fully without entirely dispensing with the book, but adding a further dramatic dimension. However, when watching a film or listening to a recording it is not possible to engage with the text in the same way as when reading a book or listening to a skilled storyteller. For one thing it is not possible to pace and control the material, and it could be argued that this restricts the imagination and independence of thought. How many of you have read and enjoyed a book, then watched the film only to be disappointed that the characters do not add up to the vision that you have of them, either physically or in their response to the plot?

The media presentation of a book somehow alters that intimate triangular relationship between the author, the reader and the story because it introduces another element to the liaison, that of the director and their interpretation of that book. This becomes a four sided and far more complex relationship. What the child then sees is what was in the imagination of the director, thereby requiring very little effort on their part to visualise, create and construct.

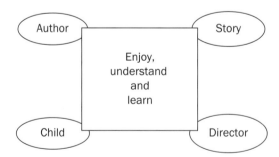

Figure 9.7 *Influence of a director on the child's relationship with a book.*

However, it could equally be argued that there are techniques available to the media that are not available to the author, and the use of practices such as signature tunes, sound effects, zoom-ins, slow motion and special effects could help to capture the child's attention and direct it to the salient aspects of the story, and these can later be reinforced and extended by the book. Children who would not otherwise read a particular text could be introduced to an author, or encouraged to read a book which they would not have considered doing in the past. I am sure that there are many adults and children alike who have read Tolkien's *Lord of the Rings* trilogy, as a direct result of viewing the epic films. This may well have made this complex text accessible to them, in a way that it would not have been before the films.

Scheme books

I could not close this chapter without some mention of reading scheme books, which are used extensively in most primary schools in England and Wales. Scheme books are ones that publishers spend years developing and attempt to apply modern science and research to their construction and content. They usually start with high frequency decodable words that gradually become more difficult in small, generally achievable, steps. Despite this, it is interesting that children (Levy, 2011) see them in a completely different light from other types of books. Children, and sometimes adults, often believe that scheme books *teach* reading and decoding, and are not seen as 'real' books at all. However, reading a scheme book often demands different skills; usually it is read aloud and every word on the page needs to be 'read'. Levy (2011) showed that if children were asked to teach a toy or doll to 'read', they consistently reached for a scheme book over a 'real' book. Levy (2011) even suggests that reading scheme books *discourages* the reading process, because working through a scheme, at differing levels of competence, can dishearten children if they see others 'progressing' through the scheme faster because their aim is to complete the scheme and get to the authentic reading. This can lead to a complete disinclination to want to read, from those who see the scheme as a mountain to climb.

Proficiency in reading is often assessed by the grade of the scheme book, if not by the teacher, then by parents and other children. Levy (2011) showed that children were not inclined to attempt books of the 'wrong' grade or colour. A struggle to progress through the scheme can result in feelings of failure and a negative attitude to reading in general. Of course in contrast, those who progress well through the scheme see themselves as successful, and therefore capable of moving to non-scheme books. Levy (2011) suggests that this demonstrates that scheme books do not require a meaningful engagement with text, but do shape children's perceptions of themselves as readers.

Chapter reflections

Research into story reading and telling has repeatedly found (Wells, 2009) that of all the activities occurring in a family environment, sharing stories and access to a wide range of stories and story material was the most important to language acquisition. Through stories children gain sustained and concentrated experience of the organisation of both written and oral language, with characteristic rhythms, intonation and structures as well as linguistic conventions such as alliteration, repetition, metaphor, onomatopoeia, irony, exaggeration and anecdotes. Through stories children learn not only how books 'work', but also how all expressive language works.

Learning to read begins the first time an infant is held and read a story…Children who never have a story read to them, who never hear words that rhyme, who never imagine fighting with dragons or marrying a prince, have the odds overwhelmingly against them.

(Wolf, 2008, p 20)

As you approach the last chapter of this book I attempt to draw together the underlying themes of the previous chapters. I hope to demonstrate how an understanding of the holistic child, and their ability to acquire a skill which is not innate, but influences every corner of their lives, is caused by the human brain's amazing ability to make connections and learn language in all its forms.

DEVELOPING CRITICAL THINKING

'*There are three kinds of lies: lies, damned lies, and statistics.*'

This is a famous quotation often ascribed to Disraeli or even Mark Twain, but it is not really certain to whom it can be attributed; however, you have probably heard it many times before along with '*you cannot trust statistics*' or '*statistics can be made to say whatever you want them to*'.

I can already feel that some of you are tuning out at the very mention of numbers, but if you are to think critically and analytically it is important that you can at least interpret some simple statistical analysis, which you may come across in your reading. When interpreting research results you will need to be certain that you are not accepting of a statement involving numbers that you do not question. Only then can you assess the reliability and validity of the research. In other words if the research were to be done again in the same way, with the same or similar sample, would it come to the same conclusions, and does it measure what it says it does?

This does not require you to do complex calculations but to understand basic terms such as:

Mean

Mode

Median

Percentage

Standard deviation

Basic frequency distribution

Ability to read a graph displaying numerical information.

This book is not the one to offer you the know-how of this information, but most books on research methods will have chapters related to these, simply explained, in a non-intimidating manner.

Statistics can be used to study trends over time, or to make comparisons between groups, and can help you to understand large and complex data sets. Statistics are used in many differing aspects of your everyday life, as can be seen in Figure 9.8, but they can also be used to provide background to a study or to support research findings.

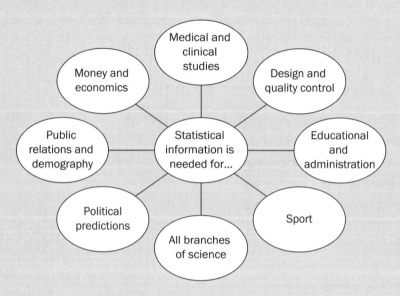

Figure 9.8 *Everyday uses for statistical information.*

Critical thinking activity

» *Can you think of any statistics which have significantly affected educational issues?*

» *Can you think of any other uses for statistics in everyday life? Complete the following chart.*

Statistics used in	How can it be useful?
Weather prediction	
Predicting the likelihood of a major emergency	
Insurance	
Occurrence of disease	

Further reading

Mellon, N (2000) *Storytelling with Children.* Stroud: Hawthorne Press.

For those of you who are aspiring storytellers this is a 'must have' read. This is an emotionally charged and passionate book which examines the skill of sharing stories with children. Nancy Mellon offers practical advice, for those who have already tried storytelling, to help improve your technique. She also offers guidance and courage to empower those who have not tried this before, allowing you to trust your imagination, creativity and inventiveness. This is not a book of theory, rather a hands-on guide to enjoying the art of storytelling.

Children's literature referred to in this chapter

Ahlberg, A and Ahlberg, J (1999) *The Jolly Postman.* London: Puffin.

Bond, M (1988) *Paddington.* New York: Harper Collins.

Bruna, D (2006) *Miffy and the Gallery*. Haydock: Ted Smart.

Campbell, R (1985) *Dear Zoo.* London: Puffin.

Carle, E (2002) *The Very Hungry Caterpillar.* London: Puffin.

Carroll, Lewis (2013) (originally published 1871) *Alice in Wonderland.* USA: Create Space Publishing Platform.

Dahl, R (1964) *Charlie and the Chocolate Factory.* London: Puffin.

Dahl, R (1978) *The Enormous Crocodile.* London: Puffin.

Daynes, K and Allen, P (2008) *See Inside Planet Earth.* London: Usbourne.

Donaldson, J and Scheffler, A (1999) *The Gruffalo.* London: Macmillan Children's Books.

Dr Seuss (1962) *Green Eggs and Ham.* London: Harper Collins.

Dr Seuss (1979) *I Can Read with My Eyes Shut!* London: Harper Collins.

Gray, N and Cabban, V (2000) *Little Bears Grandad.* London: Little Tiger Press.

Hutchins, P (1968) *Rosie's Walk.* London: Read Fox Books.

Kitamura, S (2008) *Stone Age Boy.* London: Walker.

Runton, A (2004) *Owl: The Way Home and the Bitter Sweet Summer.* London: Marietta.

Scieszka, J and Smith, L (1993) *The Stinky Cheese Man and Other Fairly Stupid Tales.* London: Puffin.

Sendak, M (1963) *Where the Wild Things Are.* New York: Harper and Row.

Tolkien, J R R (1954) *Lord of the Rings.* London: George Allen and Unwin.

References

Browne, A (2009) *Developing Language and Literacy 3–8.* London: Sage.

Chartered Institute of Public Finance and Accountancy (CIPFA) (2013) *UK Annual Library Survey.* London: CIPFA.

Clark, C and Hawkins, L (2011) *Public Libraries and Literacy: Young People's Reading Habits and Attitudes to Public Libraries, and an Exploration of the Relationship between Public Library Use and School Attainment.* London: National Literacy Trust.

Clark, C and Rumbold, K (2006) *Reading for Pleasure: A Research Overview*. London: National Literacy Trust.

Cliatt, M and Shaw, J (1988) The Story Time Exchange: Ways to Enhance It. Childhood *Education*, 64 (5): 293–298.

Cooter, R B (1991) Storytelling in the Language Arts Classroom. *Reading Research and Instruction*, 30 (2): 71–76 [EJ 424 278].

Dahl, R (1964) *Charlie and the Chocolate Factory.* London: Puffin.

Dickinson, B (2015) *Free the Word–and Your Child.* Telegraph Weekend Section: Saturday 13 June 2015.

Ellis, R (1997) *Second Language Acquisition*. Oxford: Oxford University Press.

Isbell, R, Sobol, J, Lindauer, L and Lowrance, A (2004) The Effects of Storytelling and Story Reading on Oral Language Complexity and Story Comprehension of Young Children. *Early Childhood Education Journal*, 32 (3) (December): 2004.

Kloet, C (2015) *Writing and the Children's Book Market.* www.writersandartists.co.uk (accessed 02.07.15).

Lamb, C (1880) *Essays of Elia*. New York: Putnam and Sons.

Levy, R (2011) *Young Children Reading: At Home and at School*. London: Sage.

McDonald, R (2014) Picture Books. In Bower, B, *Developing Early Literacy 0–8*. London: Sage.

Meek, M (1982) *Learning to Read*. London: Bodley Head.

Mellon, N (2000) *Storytelling with Children.* Stroud: Hawthorne Press.

Programme of International Student Assessment (PISA) (2009) *PISA 2009 Assessment Framework: Key Competencies in Reading, Mathematics and Science*. Paris: OECD.

Rooke, J (2015) *The Impact of Storytelling Schools on Children's Writing in Tower Hamlets Primary Schools: Evaluation of Roll-Out Phase 1: 2013–14.* University of Winchester, www.storytelling-schools.com/wp-content/uploads/2015/04/4315-STS-Evaluation-Report-Jonathan-Rooke.pdf (accessed 03.07.15).

Save the Children (2014) *Read on, Get on.* London: Save the Children Fund.

Tancock, C (2014) Tales and the Oral Tradition. In Bower, V, *Developing Early Literacy 0–8*. London: Sage.

Wells, G (2009) *The Meaning Makers: Children Learning Language and Using Language to Learn* (2nd ed). Bristol: Multilingual Matters.

Whitehead, M (2010) *Language and Literacy in the Early Years 0–7* (4th ed). London: Sage.

Wolf, M (2008) *Proust and the Squid: The Story and the Science of the Reading Brain.* Cambridge: Icon Books.

Wray, D and Medwell, J (1991) *Literacy and Language in the Primary Years*. London: Routledge.

10 The holistic child: a whole brain approach to language acquisition

The child
is made of one hundred.
The child has
a hundred languages
a hundred hands
a hundred thoughts
a hundred ways of thinking
of playing, of speaking.

A hundred always a hundred
ways of listening
of marvelling, of loving
a hundred joys
for singing and understanding
a hundred worlds
to discover
a hundred worlds
to invent

a hundred worlds
to dream.

The child has
a hundred languages
(and a hundred hundred
hundred more)
but they steal ninety-nine.
The school and the culture
separate the head from the body.

They tell the child:
to think without hands
to do without head
to listen and not to speak
to understand without joy
to love and to marvel
only at Easter and at Christmas.

They tell the child:
to discover the world already there
and of the hundred
they steal ninety-nine.

They tell the child:
that work and play
reality and fantasy
science and imagination
sky and earth
reason and dream
are things
that do not belong together.

And thus they tell the child
that the hundred is not there.
The child says:
No way. The hundred is there.

Loris Malaguzzi (translated by Lella Gandini)
founder of the Reggio Emilia Approach in
Edwards et al (1998, p 3).

Introduction

The final chapter of this book attempts to bring together all the component parts that have been considered thus far and acknowledges that although each part is important in its own right it will not produce the language literate adult that the government and society demands. Instead each part forms part of a complex jigsaw that eventually makes the well-rounded citizen, with a global perspective to life.

For children to thrive and grow they need support which is multidimensional, and such support requires a sound understanding not only of the holistic development of the child but also government policy in health and education, ensuring provision for maternal and infant care, integrated services and environmental awareness.

A holistic approach

A holistic approach to language development is threefold in nature: first, it means not dividing language up into segments, under titles of skills to be achieved, but seeing language as a whole, each element impinging upon and influencing the other. Second, it is about focusing upon the whole child and the development of the person within. Third, it is being aware of the circumstances, environment and regime under which the child lives. Clearly this approach will be challenging, but it formulates a learning journey for the child, allowing them to discover active relationships between the various aspects of their education, at all levels. This encompasses an understanding that learning language, whether spoken, written or read, goes far beyond a classroom or a nursery, but allows the child to engage with the world and culture that they inhabit. Because a holistic approach to language learning encompasses the child's whole development, it can empower the child with confidence so that they can examine the context in which they live, question, challenge and reflect upon the views and values of that society.

A holistic approach to learning language is not a linear process in the way in which this book, and others like it, might suggest. Rather it is an ongoing, expanding and distributive process in which you learn different aspects of language in an ever extending spiral, which continues throughout life (see Figure 10.1). Even as an adult you learn more about language every day, whether it is new words that you hear in the media, new structures or meanings read in the newspaper, a special and developing love of literature or new opportunities to write and communicate ideas. Each aspect feeds into the other, and in this way your knowledge and understanding of language matures and evolves.

Wray and Medwell (1991) suggested that the process of learning the differing elements of language (reading, writing, speaking and listening) has so many similarities that they need to be considered as a whole. They talk of an active process, involving the children constructing their own insights into language, which comes at the very heart of all learning, as a shared consciousness with others:

A language with which to discuss language.

(Wray and Medwell, 1991, p 226)

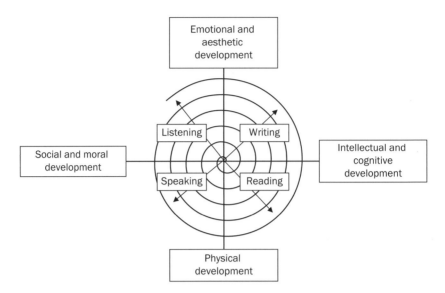

Figure 10.1 *A spiral of holistic language learning.*

Interdependence of language development

The concept of a holistic approach to language development is that it channels everything that we do as humans. The unique individual remains at the centre and becomes the foundation of learning, requiring an integration of understanding about ourselves, our culture and society. Language is an essential aspect of ourselves as Homo sapiens and provokes the mind into thinking and knowledge, allowing reflection upon the self. It is therefore the fundamental element of the process of self-construction, offering personal discovery by introducing alternative constructs to select from.

Holistic language development assumes an interdependency of all areas of the child's development and all aspects of a child's life. These areas are so connected that progress, or lack of progress, in one area has an influential effect on all other regions. This is reminiscent of the analogy of the butterfly fluttering its wings in the jungle and creating a hurricane several weeks later in another part of the globe, as the movement of the air creates a ripple effect (Chaos Theory – attributed to Edward Lorenz, a microbiologist in the 1960s). So this involves addressing the needs of a child's cognitive, social, emotional and physical domains, as well as their sensory, aesthetic and moral development, their health, nutrition and living environment. As each child in your care is unique and living in a distinctive environment, this can be achieved only through close and regular observation, to monitor progression and development, allowing the child to function as a whole and singular individual. However, if it is to be successful, it is imperative that this holistic approach is extended to include parents/carers, other family members and local and national communities.

Influential, analytical, critical

Wolf (2008) likened language development to Darwin's theory of evolution. Darwin saw how genes evolved, adapted and altered to form an almost infinite number of creatures, plants and beings; so language allows humans to create infinite numbers of thoughts, and it has changed the lives of everyone on the earth.

> *Thousands of lives have been altered or lost, depending upon whether a sacred text like the bible is read in a concrete, literal way or in a generative, interpretive way.*
> (Wolf, 2008, p 17)

Language allows us to go beyond ideas, to become increasingly autonomous, transforming our lives to meet with our historical and cultural times. You must remember that however you learn language (and this is still a scientific mystery), it is probably not a completely natural phenomenon, as thus far science has not found genes or brain structures *exclusively* devoted to language. This probably indicates that humans are not 'designed' to use language, and in evolutionary terms it is a relatively modern achievement. Certainly the more complex refinements of language, such as reading and writing, are only a few hundred years old. It is currently not possible to pinpoint when the various aspects of language first emerged, but it is unlikely to have been an instantaneous happening, rather a gradual development of the human brain, probably combined with and responding to cultural and environmental changes.

It is also unlikely that language occurred in one place, but at several sites across the globe as Homo sapiens emerged and spread their influence. The brain adapted and developed structures to respond to the cultural and environmental conditions in a Darwinian, evolutionary fashion.

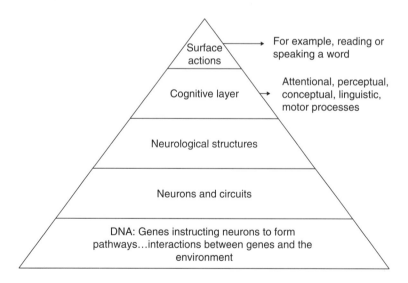

Figure 10.2 *A pyramid of language, adapted from Wolf (2008, p 11).*

Policy and politics

Politics and government in the United Kingdom are involved with the production of policy on a number of different levels.

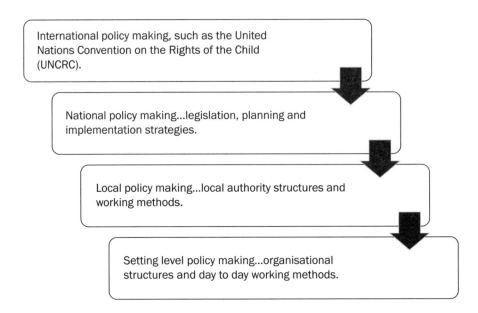

Figure 10.3 *Political policy production levels.*

Very superficially these areas of governance are controlled by elected or appointed representatives of the communities with left or right wing views (and all in between). On the left of government are those who believe in equality and idealism, where we pay and distribute taxation to ensure equality of wealth and opportunity. On the right are those who believe that market forces should prevail, and will ensure that those who work hardest will earn most and be allowed to keep what they earn. Clearly this is a very brief and even stereotypical snapshot of politics in Britain today.

Critical questions

» *List any evidence that you can find to indicate policy changes in care and education, according to political persuasions. One has been suggested for you:*

1. *Segregated education: grammar schools versus comprehensives.*

2.

3.

» *Choose one of these, and with a colleague, discuss their implications for children and society. Try to consider all sides of the argument and to offer evidence for your views.*

» *Write down the essential elements of the views discussed, and try to divide these into opinion and well-evidenced debate.*

The politics of language learning

If I were to ask you what has the greatest influence on a child's life and life chances, it is possible that you would say something like 'love' or 'families'. If I were to suggest that politics probably has the greatest influence, you may at first reject that idea. However, the extent to which the political climate influences children's development is immense and some historical examples might be as follows.

- In 1972, the Secretary of State for Education and Science commissioned the Bullock Report (A Language for Life), to report on English language development in schools.

- Prime Minister Tony Blair's New Labour campaign in 1996, which hinged on his mantra of '*education, education, education*'.

- The rapid expansion of nurseries to accommodate working parents, when Chancellor Gordon Brown wanted to increase taxation revenues by encouraging more people into work.

- The standards debates which have accompanied the increase in testing and assessment of even our very youngest children.

- The production of the Statutory Framework for the Early Years Foundation Stage (DfE, 2014) and the Early Years Foundation Phase in Wales (Yr Adran Plant, Addysg, Dysgu Gydol Oes a Sgiliau, 2008).

However you examine the issues, children's language development is being directly affected by legislation and advisory frameworks which are politically motivated, and on occasions could be described as party political points scoring. Reflect for a moment on the parliamentary debates regarding the way that we teach children to read: synthetic phonics, analytical phonics, whole word, real books etc.

In 1996 under the Conservative administration and Prime Minister John Major, the Desirable Outcomes for Children's Learning was introduced with common outcomes for language and literacy. This, of necessity, influenced practitioners' attitudes to children learning language, as it now became a judgement criteria for inspections, which could potentially affect their employment and funding in early years. Political changes to the National Curriculum, Key Stage 1, have also placed a downward pressure upon how we develop children's language to meet the needs of the curriculum and politically set standards. In the late 1990s came the National Literacy Strategy, with a Literacy Hour implemented in all state funded English schools, and this brought very specific requirements of content and pedagogy. The following quotation by Whitehead (1999) demonstrates the feeling of some working in early years at the time:

> The language of military expeditions, of the violent overthrow of a state, of compulsion and intolerance, may make politicians and civil servants appear fashionably 'tough' but very young children, who are just starting to read and write, or who have problems with literacy are not criminals and do not deserve to be terrorized – nor can they be coerced into literacy.
>
> (Whitehead, 1999, p 108)

Clearly this does not sit well with the concept of language developing at the child's own pace, naturally and calmly, the picture that I have created previously in this book. It is also a long way from the holistic strategy which puts the child at the centre of learning language.

Political overview

The expansion of nursery provision between 1990 and 2000 was immense and according to Ball and Vincent (2005) the number of nursery places quadrupled in that time. Since the New Labour Government in 1997, the policy change and development for early years has been rapid and increasingly centralised to government.

Table 10.1 Historical overview of political interventions in early years.

Date	Policy change	Comment
1998	The responsibility for managing nursery provision transferred from the Department for Health to the Department for Education and Employment.	A Comprehensive Spending Review took place.
1998	Department for Education and Employment National Childcare Strategy.	The government took greater responsibility for the care of children and families.
1999	Sure Start programme begins in areas of disadvantage.	The aim was to eradicate child poverty by 2020.
2000	Desirable Outcomes for Children's Learning expanded into the Curriculum Guidance for the Foundation Stage.	Overseen by the Department for Education and Employment.
2002	Childcare Review led by Baroness Ashton, Minister for Sure Start, Early Years and Childcare.	To assess the future demand for childcare.
2002	Childcare Strategy. Recognised the need to increase the number of qualified childcarers.	Updating the UK National Childcare Strategy 1998.
2002	Introduction of the Nursery Education Grant.	For all four year-olds.
2003	Every Child Matters (Green Paper for consultation).	Report by Lord Laming following the death of Victoria Climbié.
2003	Introduction of Birth to Three Matters.	Framework of practice to raise the status of those working with very young children.
2004	Children Act 2004.	Amended the Children Act 1989.
2004	First Children's Commissioner for England appointed.	Professor Al Aynsley-Green

Table 10.1 (*cont.*)

Date	Policy change	Comment
2004	Ten-year Childcare Strategy.	On the basis of the recommendations of the Effective Provision of Pre-school Education (EPPE) report (Sylva et al, 2004). Recommended Children's Centres in every local community.
2005	Children's Workforce Strategy: a strategy to build a world class workforce for children and young people.	Increasing skills for practitioners.
2005	Children's Workforce Development Council (CWDC) established.	Supporting the implementation of Every Child Matters.
2006	Childcare Act 2006. (The first Childcare Act in the history of Britain.)	Aimed to help local authorities to implement better safeguarding services. Legislated many aspects of the ten-year strategy.
2007	UNICEF report placed United Kingdom at the bottom of league table of 21 industrialised nations.	An overview of children's well-being.
2007	Department for Children, Schools and Families (DCSF) established.	Previously DfES (Department for Education and Skills). Attempted to bring children and family services under one umbrella, as was happening in many other nations across the world.
2007	Children's Plan released.	Building Brighter Futures.
2007	Introduction of the Early Years Foundation Stage.	For all children from 0 to end of Reception year, in all forms of provision.
2008	Introduction of Early Years Foundation Phase in Wales.	Welsh Assembly. For all children in Wales three–seven years.
2008	Budget paper to end child poverty and increase social mobility.	Ending Child Poverty: everybody's business.
2010	The Foundation Years: preventing poor children becoming poor adults.	MP Frank Field's Report.
2011	Early Intervention: the next steps.	Graham Allen Report.
2012	Early Years Foundation Stage and Development Requirements.	Amendment order 2012.

Table 10.1 (*cont.*)

Date	Policy change	Comment
2012	Foundations for Quality: independent review of early education and childcare qualifications.	Cathy Nutbrown review of childcare and education qualifications.
2013	Local Authority (Duty to Secure Early Years Provision Free of Charge) Regulations.	Local authorities have a *duty* to secure sufficient childcare for working parents.
2013	Introduction of the Early Years Teacher Status.	Building upon the foundations of the Early Years Professional Status.
2014	Statutory Framework for Early Years Foundation Stage (DfE).	Updated framework.
2014	Children and Families Act.	Giving greater protection to vulnerable children.
2015	Free funding for some two year-olds to attend nursery.	Local authority discretions apply.

The changing nature of childhood

There is no doubt that the politics of society and the community have significantly affected the lives of young children. Kellet (2010) talks about the decline of local shopping, theme parks replacing community leisure spaces and patterns of working which have resulted in fewer social experiences and less one-to-one contact time between parents and their children, resulting in fewer opportunities to practise language. Kellet (2010) also points out that in a highly litigious culture, where we are becoming more risk averse, it restricts children's social spaces and chances to play with peers in an 'adult free' zone. Instead it is being replaced by solitary, virtual environments with very few language experiences or opportunities for social engagement.

> Cyberspace is radically changing the nature of children's social interaction and friendships. In the UK the private nature of family life is giving way to an ever more public regime of scrutiny and regulation.
>
> (Kellet, 2010, p 6)

Kellet (2010) claims that this is radically changing the entire nature of childhood. Of course you could reply to Kellet that the nature of childhood (whatever that means to you) has always been a changing and evolving concept. To look back to the Victorian concept of childhood, the child was 'seen and not heard', and childhood was short, as children were expected to work and contribute to the family. At that time children were seen more as a commodity than a precious flower to be cosseted and nurtured.

Certainly it may be shocking for you to consider that places involving care and education, such as schools and nurseries, are some of the most controlled and measured environments outside of prisons and secure institutions. They are heavily regulated by central government and frequently overseen by adults appointed by, what some would call, 'bureaucratic institutions' of the state. Some would even argue that they then develop policy according to partisan dogma and one-sided leanings. From this you can see that policy development is hard to separate from *party* politics or perhaps the cynics would say, vote winning politics!

Policy implementation

You have already seen that differing layers of governance affect policy, from central government to local councils, often with differing political persuasions competing against each other, which can inevitably result in tensions and inconsistencies. According to Action for Children (2008), a person turning 21 years of age in 2016 will have been subject to and affected by over 400 different major governmental announcements, that is, Acts of Parliament, funding streams, policy strategies etc. They claim that on average each new initiative lasts a little over two years, before being repealed or changes made. Statistically this makes the chances of getting it 'wrong' very high, potentially making a huge difference to the way that practitioners and teachers work with children.

A further complexity to consider is that, although the elected UK government has direct responsibility for care and educational policy formation in England, because of devolved powers of governance to the various areas of the United Kingdom, policies in Wales, Scotland and Northern Ireland may be directly opposed to the organisational arrangements in England. One example of this is the Welsh Language Act (1993) which safeguards the status of Welsh in all schools in Wales, ensuring that Welsh is taught in every school in Wales and has parity with English.

According to Siencyn and Thomas (2007), in 2007 approximately 35 per cent of three-year-olds in Wales were in Welsh medium settings (where the entire curriculum is taught through the medium of Welsh), and in some areas this number was up to 90 per cent. In Wales the Welsh Assembly Government (WAG) has taken a very different stance to early years, with the Early Years Foundation Phase established for children aged 3–7 years. This offers a much greater significance for play and the holistic nature of learning. With strong links to personal and social development the opportunities for interaction and communication are potentially greater than for children in formal education in England. The Welsh language is prominent and there is concern that formal reading and writing are introduced too soon in England. The assessment of children in schools in Wales also differs from England, with an emphasis upon teacher assessment, no publication of league tables and the abolition of tests for seven year-olds.

These are only some of the differences of policy, but they reflect the differing experiences that children in one part of the United Kingdom will have compared to another, due to what could be described as political manoeuvring.

CASE STUDY

Government changes

The year 1999 saw the establishment of the Sure Start Initiative under the New Labour Government of Prime Minister Tony Blair, which was further promoted under the Gordon Brown Government in 2007. However, by 2010, with the election of the Coalition Government, under the leadership of Prime Minister David Cameron for the Conservatives and Nick Clegg for the Liberal Democrat Party, the emphasis on early years was less, and the policy of Sure Start was slowly diminished. The Coalition Government oversaw the closure of the Children's Workforce Development Council (CWDC) and demonstrated a greater commitment to the role of the health visitor and to the care of children in their own home, rather than a group setting.

This demonstrates how policy development can change rapidly with the political whim. However, practitioners need to understand that they have the right to question this, and believe that they can influence policy developments.

Critical questions

» *What role should government intervention play in the pedagogy of early years settings?*

» *What role has the state to play in early years care and education?*

» *Should government support widespread maternal employment?*

The broader agenda

Policy development is often part of a much broader agenda, and policies relating to improving language and literacy development in young children could be seen as part of a much wider government strategy. Certainly a case could be made for the following advances, if the language skills in our children and adults were to be improved:

*   a reduction in poverty;
*   increasing employment potential;
*   growing tax raising potential for the treasury;
*   improving social control;
*   reducing anti-social behaviour;
*   reducing burdens on the judicial system;
*   improving health, mental health and welfare;
*   reducing the burden of benefit payments;
*   reducing costs to the National Health Service.

Cost savings from such a list would clearly be very attractive to any incumbent government and the prevailing political agenda. The emphasis in the Early Years Foundation Stage (DfE, 2014) on communication and language as a Prime Area, highlighting improving listening, attention, understanding and speaking, can be explained when you consider the previous list. However, the other Prime Areas of physical development and personal, social and emotional development demonstrate the government's commitment to a holistic approach to early years.

> *Early years policies cannot be viewed in isolation from the wider political agendas which shape them. A change in government not only produces new policies but also new policy goals and underlying principles, depending on these agendas.*
> (Baldock, Fitzgerald and Kay, 2013, p 34)

Training

For many children their school or nursery becomes the dominant institution in their life. The school starting age in England and Wales is the term following their fifth birthday, yet the majority of four year-olds attend formal mainstream classes in schools. This is different to almost all other European countries where formal schooling does not begin until six or even seven years of age. If learning language is truly a holistic experience, engaging all areas of development, it is vital that all those working with young children have well-grounded and up-to-date knowledge and understanding of child development. Page et al (2013) point out that the content of teacher training programmes for those trainee teachers wishing to work within early years neglects child development training, and a high proportion of teachers working in early years are not trained to work with such young children. This could potentially jeopardise the children's experience of learning language as a whole supporting package, integrated into all areas of their development, and therefore providing a rich language background, supporting and supplementing the home learning environment. Ensuring that teachers have a good understanding of child development will enable them to see the world from the perspective of the very young children in their care and ensure that they are adopting developmentally appropriate practices. Interestingly universities offering the new Early Years Teacher Status, established by the government in 2013, are keen to recruit those who are already well versed in child development and observational techniques.

Critical questions

» *Find out which department in your local authority is responsible for early years policy development.*

» *Find out who is responsible for early years in your local authority.*

» *How is early years funded in your local authority?*

» *What are the policy goals for early years in your local authority?*

» *Look on your local authority website for details of policy implementation plans and for opportunities for debate and consultation. Try to get involved with those discussions.*

A holistic approach to development

Most people who have been trained to Level 3 in childcare and education will be familiar with acronyms for the all-round development of the child or holistic development, such as PIES, PILES, SPLICE, PILESS etc. Such acronyms help you to recognise the importance of different areas of a child's learning providing a framework to organise observations, planning and reflection. However, you also need to recognise the interdisciplinary aspect of development, and that each of these areas develops alongside, dependent upon and interdependent with, each other. Bruce and Meggitt (2012) suggest that if each of these areas of development is separated out into distinct strands, then you will see the child as a '*collection of bits and pieces*' (p 218) instead of a well-rounded individual. They talk about a 'web' of child development, which is a useful analogy.

However, in order to think about development in a truly holistic manner, I believe that you need to consider the child within a much wider perspective. The acronyms above have been around for a very long time, and have helped childcare and education practitioners across the English speaking world to consider the whole child. For this reason I do not propose to abandon them, but rather to extend and enhance the analogy, to see development and context in a parallel fashion. Therefore I propose the following acronym (PILES), to help you to study language development and to understand that you cannot separate language from any one of the following and really gain a meaningful understanding of that developmental area.

P hysical	**P** olitics and economics
I ntellectual	**I** nheritance (what you are born with)
L anguage	**L** ifestyle (the views, opinions and values of the family you are born into)
E motional	**E** nvironment (the physical conditions or surroundings in which you live)
S ocial	**S** ociety (the people who share our planet and their interactions with you)

As each child is a unique individual so is each practitioner; you each have your own life experiences and philosophies, influencing your practice, your ideals, aims and expectations. Frameworks and acronyms, although useful, need to be set within that context and background and intelligently applied to your analysis of any particular child or circumstance.

Chapter reflections

So how can practitioners, parents and carers positively influence a child's opportunities to develop language and communication skills? This chapter has emphasised that the approach needs to be a holistic one that encompasses all areas of development, without prioritising one over another or attempting to segment speaking and listening from reading and writing, as each flows into and facilitates the other, building brick upon brick, each creating connections between each other and spreading outwards delivering depth and breadth to the learning. The cement between the bricks of a house consists of complex chemical reactions to establish adhesion and cohesion; in the same way cognitive activity builds a complex mesh of neural connections to enable learning.

Effective language learning is fundamental to the quality and quantity of our modern lives. This can happen only if there are opportunities for children to enhance and develop their skills by repetition in a risk free environment, with adults who show a genuine interest in them. Adults need to learn to listen to, as well as talk with, the children and to have the patience to wait and allow a conversation to flow at the pace of the child. This is a partnership approach between the child, family, practitioners and the community – the shopkeepers, police, waiters and waitresses and anyone with whom the child comes into communication or contact. The implication here is that the whole of society is responsible for children learning language; in line with the old African proverb 'it takes a village to raise a child', teaching language needs to be a communal effort.

Political parties also need to play their part and be prepared to investigate interventions, to support families with adequate parenting programmes, improvements to home learning environments, reducing poverty, improving nutrition, healthcare etc.

> *We know that 10 million children are dying each year due to preventable causes. But far less well known is that 200 million children under 5 in the developing world, over one third of all children, are not fulfilling their potential for development. Because of poverty, under nutrition, micronutrient deficiencies, and learning environments that do not provide enough responsive stimulation, children are developing more slowly or failing to develop critical thinking and learning skills. This could affect their entry into school, their performance and persistence through school and their eventual success in life.*

(UNICEF, 2006, p 1)

Final thoughts

This book has attempted to provide an insight into language development in the early years, and explain how language has developed from a pre-language society to the present day. It has emphasised the importance of children learning language in a holistic and integrated manner, and has also shown the complexity of the area, so inevitably much has been left unexplained or is lacking in depth. In truth this lack of depth can, in many instances, be due to man's general lack of knowledge and understanding of the workings of the brain, and of how learning really takes place. Clearly much more research needs to be undertaken, but any research relating to humans presents huge ethical and moral difficulties, particularly when researching something as complex and unseen as human brain activity. It could be argued, as Tomasello (2003) does, that language development is the most important and distinctive skill that humans achieve, and therefore should have top priority for research funding and academic understanding. However, the pace of understanding of how children learn language has progressed disappointingly slowly in recent times.

I would suggest that there are certain areas for research which should receive top priority, but you may be able to think of others.

- Investigation into very early brain development and differentiation, and its influence upon a child's ability to learn language.

- Research to date appears to indicate that the way that reading is taught in schools has the potential to deter children from reading for pleasure. An investigation into teaching methods which promote reading as exciting and achievable, thereby turning the child who can read into a 'reader'.

- An investigation into the very early detection of potential reading differences, such as dyslexia, to ensure that appropriate support is available to the child *before* reading and language failure becomes an issue.

- With the explosion of online reading media we need to better understand the differences between digital and hard copy reading processes. At present these are seen in teaching pedagogy as the same, but much more research needs to be undertaken to verify or reject this premise.

You have seen that different organisations of the brain are possible and the variously 'wired' brains of those with dyslexia are, according to Wolf (2008),

> the most visible evidence that the brain was never wired to read. (p 215)

However, such variations may in an evolutionary sense be more suited to new technology and means of communication which have not yet been invented or even conceived of.

As a nation we need to consider language development in the twenty-first century and what we really want for our children, whether functional literacy (as described by Collins and O'Brien, 2003), as the minimum needed to meet personal and social needs in general education), is enough for children to operate within society, in employment and recreation. Perhaps we need to aim for something more, and for our children to become critically literate, able to engage with and enjoy text, to understand the implications of language at a higher level of thinking.

> the more children are spoken to, the more they will understand oral language. The more children are read to, the more they understand all the language around them, and the more developed their vocabulary becomes.
>
> (Wolf, 2008, p 84)

DEVELOPING CRITICAL THINKING

Melanie had to write a 5000 word assignment for her degree course; she worked so hard on the preparation, gathering the information and then writing a critically appropriate text. When she thought that she had written all that she could, she put a big full stop at the end and breathed a sigh of relief. Does this sound like you when writing your assignments?

The problem was that Melanie had written 5000 words without considering leaving wordage for a conclusion. Imagine for a moment that you read a really good novel from the library, but when you get towards the end you realise that the last chapter has been ripped out, or that you watch an exciting television programme and just as it approaches the end you have a power cut, and cannot see the conclusion. How disappointed would you be? All that, and you do not get to see who was the murderer in the murder mystery or who fell in love with whom in the romance. That is a little like the assignment with no conclusion.

It is important that when planning your work you consider the word allocation for each part of your assignment (see Chapter 5) and that the conclusion is seen as a vital part of the assignment. After all everything that you have written thus far is working towards this conclusion. Throughout this book I have talked of the importance of creating arguments and of questioning what you read. The conclusion is the place to draw together the threads of those arguments and to thoughtfully consider the weight of evidence for your supposition. Remember that this is the last opportunity that you have to convince your reader of what you have written by reflecting on your findings while acknowledging that there may be other views. This is the last thing that your reader will remember about your work, and they need to see deep understanding of your subject.

This is not the time to be apologetic about your work; saying that *you* think that the work is 'rubbish' is unlikely to endear your work to an assessor. However, there may be some limitations to your work, which you need to let the marker know that you are aware of, for example a small sample or limited time schedule for a longitudinal study. This may be the place to suggest further research, more in-depth study or recommendations for the future.

There should be no new material in your conclusion, but neither do you want to make it a tired repetition of what has already been said. There will be many aspects to your assignment, but your conclusion should concentrate on the major themes. Always start your conclusion by returning to the original title of the assignment brief and ensure that you have addressed the original question and that you leave your reader with a vivid impression of your thoughts and ideas.

Critical thinking activity

Read and critique the following conclusion written by a student on an early childhood studies degree course.

> *This essay has provided evidence that supports planning and assessment and how it is a vital part of education and understanding children's development. Parents, practitioners, health visitors, teachers, speech therapists and other professionals involved in a child's life and development have the legal and professional obligations to the child to ensure that they are thriving and that they have opportunities to achieve and progress. The first few years of a child's life are very important to their speech and language development,*

they learn and progress so much in a short span of time. Whichever side of the nature/nurture debate that you stand it is undeniable that assessing and planning for children's speech and language development is beneficial. All the theories provided support a different, yet equally important view of how and why children develop their speech and language ability. All theorists have their own strategies and ideas to promote communication and language development. Although, in my personal opinion, I feel that children's communication is nature, for example babies crying at loud noises. It is unlikely anyone would role model this fear to them; instead it is a reflex from instinct, whereas I feel that language is something that is role modelled to a child. An example of this is seen in the Romanian orphanages, where the children who were at the back of the room had less language than those close to the front. If language was something that they learned for themselves, why was there this discrepancy? Why when role modelled effectively does language learning progress?

» *Has the author acknowledged that there may be other possible conclusions from the evidence?*

» *Does the writer suggest further realistic research or recommendations?*

» *List the good features of this conclusion.*

» *What do you feel needs to be improved?*

» *Does this conclusion offer a sense of completion?*

» *Does the conclusion indicate the main issues of the assignment that the writer wants to emphasise?*

Further reading

Baldock, P, Fitzgerald, D and Kay, J (2013) *Understanding Early Years Policy* (3rd ed). London: Sage.

This text looks at the range of policymaking in early years, from an international perspective to national policymaking, local policymaking and setting policymaking. The authors examine the nature of policymaking, its importance and relevance to the early years practitioner. This is one of the few books that look at dimensions of policymaking in the devolved areas of the United Kingdom, and how differing structures of governance affect children, families, practitioners and settings.

References

Action for Children (2008) *As Long as It Takes: A New Politics for Children*. London: www.actionfor children.org (accessed 29.06.15).

Baldock, P, Fitzgerald, D and Kay, J (2013) *Understanding Early Years Policy* (3rd ed). London: Sage.

Ball, S J and Vincent, C (2005) The 'Childcare Champion'? New Labour, Social Justice and the Childcare Market. *British Educational Research Journal*, 31 (5): 557–570.

Bruce, T and Meggitt, C (2012) *Child Care and Education* (4th ed). Oxford: Hodder and Arnold.

Collins, J and O'Brien, N (2003) *The Greenwood Dictionary of Education*. Westport, CT: Greenwood.

Department for Education (DfE) (2014) *Statutory Framework for the Early Years Foundation Stage*. Nottingham: DfE Publications.

Kellet, M (2010) *Rethinking Children and Research*. London: Continuum International.

Kurzweil, R (2006) *The Singular Is Near*. New York: Penguin.

Malaguzzi, L (1996) The Hundred Languages of Children (translated by Lella Gandini). In Edwards, C, Gandini, L and Forman, G (eds) *The Hundred Languages of Children: The Reggio Emilia Approach – Advanced Reflections.* London: Ablex.

Page, J, Clare, A and Nutbrown, C (2013) *Working with Babies and Young Children* (2nd ed). London: Sage.

School Curriculum and Assessment Authority (1996) *Desirable Outcomes for Children's Learning: On Entering Compulsory Education*. London: Department for Education and Employment.

Siencyn, S W and Thomas, S (2007) Wales. In Clark, M and Waller, T (eds) *Early Childhood Education and Care: Policy and Practice*. London: Sage.

Sylva, K, Melhuish, E, Sammons, P, Siraj-Blatchford, I and Taggart, B (2004) *The Effective Provision of Pre-school Education (EPPE) Project: Findings from Preschool to End of Key Stage 1*. London: DfES/Institute of Education, University of London.

Tomasello, M (2003) *Constructing a Language*. Cambridge, MA: Harvard University Press.

UNICEF (2006) *Programming Experiences in Early Child Development.* New York: Early Child Development Unit.

Whitehead, M (1999) *Supporting Language and Literacy Development in the Early Years*. Buckingham: Open University Press.

Wolf, M (2008) *Proust and the Squid: The Story and Science of the Reading Brain*. Cambridge: ICON Books.

Wray, D and Medwell, J (1991) *Literature and Language in the Primary Years*. London: Routledge.

Yr Adran Plant, Addysg, Dysgu Gydol Oes a Sgiliau (Department for Children, Education, Lifelong Learning Skills) (2008) *Framework for Children's Learning for 3–7 Year Olds in Wales*. Cardiff: Llywodraeth Cynulliad Cymru (Welsh Assembly Government).

Glossary

Aetiology: the causes behind a condition being present.

Aphasia: a condition of the brain which leads to problems using language. This may result in a difficulty understanding words, and mistakes when selecting appropriate words.

Arcuate fasciculus: nerve fibres connecting the Broca's area of the brain with the Wernicke's area.

Central coherence: an ability to 'see the big picture' when in context. Weak central coherence is often associated with children on the autistic spectrum.

Ciliogenesis: the process by which super slim growths, called Cilia, form on a cell's surface. These beat to move fluids such as mucus over the cells.

Co-morbidity: when two or more conditions co-occur together.

Damaged disposition hypothesis: forcing children into formal conventions of learning for mathematics and language too soon can damage their willingness to engage with that learning.

Echolalia: unnecessary repetition of speech, such as is seen in a child learning to talk.

Ectopic cells: cells not in their usual place or position.

Electroencephalography (EEG): the measuring of electrical activity in different parts of the brain

Generativity: the ability to generate a supposedly infinite number of ideas and propositions by using words and sentences; even understanding words that we have not heard before if they are in appropriate context.

Glottographic:	this is a set of graphic signs that correspond to sounds and phonemes, based on the sounds of speech.
Grammaticalisation:	changing a content word into a functional word. This is a historical process whereby over time words acquire new status and become incorporated into the grammar of a language. This is a cognitive linguistic approach to language change, for example, *going to gonna*
Graphophonic:	letter–sound, or sound–symbol relationships.
Iconicity:	the similarity between a written symbol and its meaning, eg a circle for the word 'moon'.
Infant directed speech (Motherese: Parentese):	speech often used by adults when talking to babies and young children, usually high pitch, simple words and sentences with repetition.
Intermodal perception:	the ability to integrate information from two or more senses, eg sight and hearing.
Language acquisition device (LAD):	first proposed by Noam Chomsky in the 1960s. This is the theory that there is an inbuilt human brain capacity, to acquire and produce language.
Lexicalisation:	converting thoughts into recognisable words from an appropriate language.
Lexicon:	a person's vocabulary or inner dictionary.
Linearity:	one dimensional, in a line.
Magnetoencephalography:	neuroimaging technique for measuring magnetic fields within the brain.
Magnocells:	large cells or neurons, which form part of the visual perception system. Also called M-cells, they lie in the magnocellular layer of the brain.
Monogenesis:	something that originates from a single source.
Morpheme:	the smallest meaningful, grammatical unit of language, which cannot be sub-divided, that is, cat (one morpheme) or unlike (two morphemes: un/like)
Mother tongue:	the familial language.

Neuronal migration: the way that neurons travel from their origins to their required position in the brain.

Neuroprosthetics: controlling movement in prosthetic limbs with brain activity.

Onset: beginning or initial sound of a word.

Ontogenetic: the development of an individual from conception to adulthood.

Oronyms: a phrase that sounds the same but is spelt differently...The stuffy nose/The stuff he knows...grey tape/great ape.

Orthographic knowledge: the understanding of spelling and how letters form together to make meaningful words.

Overgeneralisation: sometimes referred to as 'over-extensions' or 'virtuous errors'. Extending one word's meaning to include objects that are not related to it...a child calls all men 'da da'.

Perceptual constancy: the ability to recognise that something remains the same even when other stimuli are different. For example, you recognise a school friend many years later, despite the ageing process changing their appearance.

Phoneme: the smallest unit of sound in language that changes the meaning of a word...Cat and Bat.

Phylogenetic: the evolutionary relationships of a species.

Polygenesis: something that originates from a number of independent sources.

Recursion: the ability to tack clauses onto clauses...'The house that Jack built'...the malt, the rat, the cat etc.

Rime: the final phoneme of the word.

Self-fulfilling prophecy: positive or negative expectations of a person (whether correct or not) that affect a person's actual behaviour or outcome.

Syntactic planning: arranging words in the right order.

Syntax: the grammatical arrangement of words into sentences.

Telegraphic speech: two or three word combinations to communicate...'da da go'.

Traditional orthography: conventional spelling and letters of a language; an alphabet based system.

Universal Grammar: a theory proposed by Noam Chomsky in the 1960s that the ability to learn the grammar of language is hardwired into the human brain.

Visual acuity: this is your ability to detect visual detail and shape, and is a measure of your central vision.

Visuospatial function: this is your ability to see and understand an object in space and time. It is about having a visual map in your memory, and understanding that an object does not actually get smaller the further you are away from it, even though it would appear to do so to the eye.

Zone of Proximal Development (ZPD):   relates to a theory proposed by Lev Vygotsky in the 1970s, that there is a difference between what a child can learn independently, and what they will learn with adult assistance.

Index